Professional Writing

Palgrave Study Guides

Authoring a PhD
Career Skills
Critical Thinking Skills
e-Learning Skills
Effective Communication for
  Arts and Humanities Students
Effective Communication for
  Science and Technology
The Exam Skills Handbook
The Foundations of Research
The Good Supervisor
How to Manage your Arts, Humanities and
  Social Science Degree
How to Manage your Distance and
  Open Learning Course
How to Manage your Postgraduate Course
How to Manage your Science and
  Technology Degree
How to Study Foreign Languages
How to Write Better Essays
IT Skills for Successful Study
Making Sense of Statistics
The Mature Student's Guide to Writing (2nd edn)
The Palgrave Student Planner
The Personal Tutor's Handbook
The Postgraduate Research Handbook

Presentation Skills for Students
The Principles of Writing in Psychology
Professional Writing (2nd edn)
Research Using IT
Skills for Success
The Student Life Handbook
The Student's Guide to Writing (2nd edn)
The Study Skills Handbook (2nd edn)
Study Skills for Speakers of English as
  a Second Language
Studying the Built Environment
Studying Business at MBA and Masters Level
Studying Economics
Studying History (3rd edn)
Studying Law
Studying Mathematics and its Applications
Studying Modern Drama (2nd edn)
Studying Physics
Studying Programming
Studying Psychology (2nd edn)
Teaching Study Skills and Supporting Learning
Work Placements – a Survival Guide for Students
Write it Right
Writing for Engineers (3rd edn)
Writing for Nursing and Midwifery Students

Palgrave Study Guides: Literature
General Editors: John Peck and Martin Coyle

How to Begin Studying English Literature
  (3rd edn)
How to Study a Jane Austen Novel (2nd edn)
How to Study a Charles Dickens Novel
How to Study Chaucer (2nd edn)
How to Study an E. M. Forster Novel
How to Study James Joyce
How to Study Linguistics (2nd edn)

How to Study Modern Poetry
How to Study a Novel (2nd edn)
How to Study a Poet
How to Study a Renaissance Play
How to Study Romantic Poetry (2nd edn)
How to Study a Shakespeare Play (2nd edn)
How to Study Television
Practical Criticism

Professional Writing
The Complete Guide for Business, Industry and IT

Second Edition

Sky Marsen

First published 2003
Second edition published 2007 by
PALGRAVE MACMILLAN
Houndmills, Basingstoke, Hampshire RG21 6XS and
175 Fifth Avenue, New York, N.Y. 10010
Companies and representatives throughout the world

PALGRAVE MACMILLAN is the global academic imprint of the Palgrave Macmillan division of St. Martin's Press, LLC and of Palgrave Macmillan Ltd. Macmillan® is a registered trademark in the United States, United Kingdom and other countries. Palgrave is a registered trademark in the European Union and other countries.

ISBN-13: 978-0-230-54298-3
ISBN-10: 0-230-54298-0

This book is printed on paper suitable for recycling and made from fully managed and sustained forest sources. Logging, pulping and manufacturing processes are expected to conform to the environmental regulations of the country of origin.

A catalogue record for this book is available from the British Library.

A catalog record for this book is available from the Library of Congress

10   9   8   7   6   5   4   3   2   1
16   15   14   13   12   11   10   09   08   07

Printed and bound in China

Contents

Figures and Tables

Figures

Tables

Acknowledgements

Various people have supported the writing of this second edition. In particular, I would like to thank Robert Biddle, at the Human-Oriented Laboratory, Carleton University, Canada, for his invaluable suggestions on Internet communications and digital writing. He has helped me keep the book reliably updated in this area of accelerated and unpredictable change. Also, I extend thanks to colleagues and students at the California Institute of Technology (Caltech), who have given me valuable feedback on teaching activities and the framing of communication tasks – especially Steven Youra, for our insightful exchanges on communicating technical concepts to non-specialists, and Ken Pickar's engineering teams for their input on teamwork and project management.

Preface

Under current trends, the twenty-first century will be characterised by an increasing diversification of the consumer market, global communications, and the collapse of traditional professional boundaries. In this climate, competence in transferring skills, addressing diverse audiences and understanding emerging needs becomes paramount for professional success. To a very large extent this competence is enhanced by the ability to understand, construct and manipulate written information in order to use it effectively in a variety of situations. Good business means good writing!

This book is a comprehensive introduction to major aspects of professional writing for different media. Its content is interdisciplinary, offering a rare opportunity to synthesise methods and ideas developed in text analysis, journalism and management. By combining conceptual aspects of written communication with practical applications, the goal of this book is to assist readers to express ideas effectively in different written formats, in a variety of professional contexts internationally.

● Distinctive features

In comparison with other texts on professional writing currently available, this guide differs in two main ways.

It is direct, concise and student-oriented. It has expressly avoided the density of many other books on writing, opting instead for a more hands-on approach, which student writers should find very accessible. The aim was to design an easily consultable text that includes brief and straightforward instructions on selected areas of interest, gives analysed examples that place the instructions into perspective, and provides the opportunity for practice with follow-up activities. By emphasising the big picture of professional writing tasks, it gives the readers an understanding of their strengths and weaknesses, allowing them to concentrate on some areas more than others, to pinpoint their areas of interest using accurate terminology, and to decide what extra resources they would need if they chose to pursue an area in more depth.

Its content is eclectic. It is not a book on grammar, or on report writing, or technology journalism as such. Rather, it is an analytic overview of all these different fields of professional communication. This eclectic quality is consistent with the current business scene, where corporate job descriptions are becoming more and more generalised to allow for changes in duty allocation within positions and for the emergence of new position titles. The way that guidelines are offered here assumes that readers want to gain an insight into the basic issues, terminology and skills that relate to each field, but may not wish, at this stage, to specialise in one particular field. For more focused practice, the book includes references to other sources that deal with specific topics in more detail.

Audience

The book was written primarily as a university text for one-semester undergraduate courses in professional writing. However, it is by no means limited to this audience. Because it gives useful tips and conceptual resources to overcome the most common trouble spots in professional writing, it will serve as a practical guide to anyone who wants to become more confident in choosing an appropriate style and layout to suit the occasion. Those who will benefit most from the guidelines offered here include:

- students in professional writing courses;
- new professionals with an educational background in information technology or science, who are thrust in to a professional situation that requires the production of formal written documents (such as consultancy reports, newsletter articles, or copy for a website) without prior training;
- scientists and technologists who want to inform management or the public of a new development, product or invention in their field, but lack the linguistic and/or communicative expertise to produce an effectively constructed written text.

Skills

By working through the book, readers will gain the skills to:

- understand and use essential terminology and key concepts in describing written communication;

- understand and use the requirements of writing investigative reports for clients and management, journalistic articles for the wider public, and digital texts;
- adapt written communication for a specific audience and purpose;
- perceive writing as a process involving planning, drafting, revising and editing, and become aware of their own procedures of writing;
- locate, manage and manipulate information using a variety of printed and electronic sources;
- understand the uses of writing in collaborative projects and in project management;
- produce sophisticated arguments, and be critical of arguments and statistics used in other documents, and in popular media.

Trajectory

The book consists of 10 main chapters and one reference chapter:

Chapter 1: The writing process

This chapter looks at the planning and thinking aspects of writing. It discusses ways to analyse audiences and to overcome writer's block. Here you will find guidelines on generating ideas to tackle a written task, and on making the most of drafting and revising techniques.

Chapter 2: Research and information management

This chapter looks at the role of investigating, reading and recording information in the preparation of professional documents. It explains the importance of summarising skills in recording and communicating information to third parties. Here you will find guidelines on research skills, preparing questionnaires for interviews, using the Internet to obtain data, and using the APA (American Psycological Association) style of referencing to document your sources.

Chapter 3: Style and effect

This chapter looks at elements of style and tone, and their effects on audience perception. It discusses such aspects of writing as appropriate length of sentences for different effects, word choice and sentence variety as a technique to maintain reader interest. Here you will find answers to questions relating to clarity, precision and conciseness and on the stylistic differences between professional and journalistic writing.

Chapter 4: Business and technology journalism

This chapter discusses document types used to inform the public of recent developments in technology, science and business, including feature articles and press releases. Here you will get some ideas on producing zesty and compelling articles, while still maintaining a high informative level.

Chapter 5: Writing for the digital media

This chapter takes the discussion from print to digital writing. It describes the use of writing in multimedia, and examines the differences between print and electronic writing. The chapter includes some tips on designing and evaluating the content, appeal and usability of websites, and on choosing appropriate fonts, colour and page design for digital documents.

Chapter 6: Reports and proposals

This chapter looks at two major professional documents, investigative reports and proposals. It puts these into perspective by examining the differences between essays, articles and reports (the main kinds of documents professionals produce), and explains their structure and components.

Chapter 7: Critical thinking

This chapter looks at aspects of reasoning and persuading in professional documents and mass media texts. It examines issues of faulty or manipulative reasoning, and overviews the uses and abuses of statistics in the popular media. This is where you will find guidelines on avoiding simplistic reasoning, on reading critically, and on enhancing your persuasive skills.

Chapter 8: Business document formats

This chapter discusses common documents produced in business contexts. These include everyday communication texts, such as agendas, minutes of meetings and letters, as well as the texts that accompany products, instructing users on how to use them, such as technical documentation.

Chapter 9: Working in teams

This chapter overviews the role of teamwork and collaboration in projects. It describes different role allocating models for team projects, and explains the stages of project management and the terms used to describe its elements.

Chapter 10: Job applications

This chapter looks at some important considerations in the job-hunting process. These include ideological and personal factors, such as assessing your values and professional aspirations, as well as practical techniques, such as writing your CV. Here you will find guidelines on job networking, self-promoting and applying for specific jobs.

Appendix: Writer's reference

This section looks at grammar, punctuation and sentence structure. It is a reference tool for all aspects of writing and can be used at any stage in a particular writing task, or be revisited at different times in the duration of a course.

● Second edition

In its second edition, the book has a clearer identity, and a stronger focus on communicating technical and specialist information to non-experts. It analyses in more depth two main document types, business reports and feature articles, especially in relation to selecting, organising and expressing concepts and ideas to those with less knowledge on the subject than the writer, such as managers and administrators, members of groups specialising in different fields, and the wider public.

The main model is that of the investigative report, a document written after research to advise management or a client about a problem, change or initiative, and to recommend action. This model document is chosen because it is arguably one of the most complex professional tasks, since it entails multiple procedures: finding information from different sources, selecting pertinent aspects for the particular occasion, synthesising main points for a third party, and presenting them in an accessible, effective and appealing way.

The changes made for this second edition include:

- all chapters have been revised and updated;
- all chapters have a different organisation, with a clearer layout of explanations, and activities placed at the end of the chapter;
- reports and proposals have a separate chapter and more information is included on their structure and components;
- a new chapter has been included on other business document formats, and this includes descriptive reports, such as agendas and minutes of meetings;
- a section has been added on writing technical documentation for users of equipment;
- a new chapter has been added on teamwork and project management;

- the chapter on writing magazine articles has been considerably expanded, and given a clearer focus on business and technology journalism – a growing area of communication for specialist professionals;
- the chapter on grammatical aspects of writing has been expanded and placed as a reference at the end of the book, from where it can be accessed and revisited at any stage to guide with sentence-writing issues

I hope this book makes your venture into the world of professional writing both enjoyable and stimulating!

1 The Writing Process

Focus on:

▶ Writing as a process that involves planning, drafting and revising
▶ Audience, purpose and format analysis
▶ Generating ideas

Writing is a skill that is acquired through conscious and persistent effort: it is not an instinctive skill that we are born with. There are several reasons why writing is more complex than speaking. One reason is that it is separate from any form of physical interaction: the writing stage can take place at a totally different time and place from the reading stage. This is why writers must try to perceive their text from the readers' point of view and write in a way that is clear and relevant to their audience. Another reason is that writing is thought-active. The simple fact that you want to write about a topic triggers thought processes that give this topic a particular shape out of a range of alternatives. To use a computing metaphor, your mind reconfigures the topic in a way that allows it to be downloaded in a written form. This then influences the direction your text will take. If this direction is unsatisfactory, you have to think about the topic differently, reshaping it and reorienting it. The changes that take place from thinking to writing explain why many novice writers complain that their final result is not what they initially wanted to express, or that what they mean comes out differently on the written page.

Because of the complexity of written communication, a successful written text does not emerge spontaneously, but requires considerable preparation and revision. Even a brief memorandum may require more than one draft. And although much business and technical writing follows standard formats and phrases, each task presents a new problem to solve with a unique audience and situation. This chapter looks at some major, tested, techniques for creating written documents quickly and efficiently, from concept to delivery copy. We focus on the idea-generating aspects of writing through to the organisational and analytical skills that develop through careful revision and editing.

The techniques discussed here are not the only way to write; there are almost as many variations of the writing process as there are writers. If you already have a successful practice for writing that produces first-class results, you have no reason to vary it. However, if you often get stuck when attempting written tasks, or fail to communicate effectively what you intend, the guidelines offered here will prove very valuable.

In order to proceed confidently with written tasks, think of writing as consisting of three stages: the planning or conceptualising stage, the drafting stage and the revising stage. In contrast to what is commonly believed, it is the first and third stages that require the most time and attention. You will find that by having a clear vision of what you want to accomplish (stage one), and giving yourself adequate time to rephrase, delete, rearrange information and add information to sections (stage three), you are creating your work. In fact, many professionals who make their living from writing state that planning and revising takes about 85 per cent of the time assigned to a task. The drafting stage is just a bridge between careful planning, and structuring information. All well-prepared professional documents require this process of writing, although how long each stage takes varies depending on the length and significance of the document.

● Audience, purpose and format

The first thing to do when planning a written task is to make sure you understand what the task requires. Ask yourself what the purpose of the document and your intended result are. All reading changes in some way the reader, so in what ways do you want to change your readers? This will determine how ready you are to write (how much planning and research you need to do), and, if the task does not specify, what document format would be most appropriate. Would a memo be suitable or would you need to produce a full investigative report? Would it be better to send a letter or write an email message? Having a clear idea of the *audience*, *purpose*, and *format* of your document is a vital step in producing successful written communication. In particular, ask yourself the following questions:

- What do your intended readers already know about the topic? In what areas are they likely to be specialised (so that you may form analogies between your topic and those areas)?
- Why will they read this document?
- What do they need to know? What do they *not* need to know?
- How much detail do they need? How much of the big picture do they need?
- What purpose(s) does the document serve? For example, does the document inform? Analyse? Clarify? Persuade? Will it be used as the basis for a decision?

- What is the standard format for presenting the information your audience requires? Are they expecting to read a report or an article? Is there reason to vary this format?

Audience Analysis

Every act of writing takes place in a new context, with a unique time, place or reader to take into account. **Audience adaptation** refers to the skill of arranging words, organising your thoughts, and formatting your document to best achieve your desired effect on your target audience. **Audience dynamics** refers to the relationship that writers form with their readers through their style, and through the amount and structure of information they provide. The audience dynamics are effective when the readers get a sense of satisfaction that the questions raised in the text were relevant to their interests, and the answers or solutions provided were convincing. In contrast, audience dynamics are ineffective when the readers feel frustrated or offended because the writer's tone is condescending, the answers or solutions provided are simplistic in relation to the complexity of the questions, or the argument is emotive and based on generalisation. To maximise your ability to achieve effective audience dynamics, assess the readers' needs, knowledge and interest by conducting an audience analysis before writing. Audience analysis is part of your research, and will be discussed more in Chapter 2. Here we look at how this research relates to the planning stage of a writing project.

Marketing executives and consumer researchers, who have a strong interest in understanding market responses, and who, therefore, conduct extensive research in mass perceptions, take into account five factors of audience analysis:

- Technical background
- Status
- Attitude
- Demographics
- Psychographics.

Technical background refers to the readers' knowledge (or lack of knowledge) in the topic that you are writing about. How much technical terminology should you use to avoid sounding either too condescending or too obscure? Should you begin with the big picture to put the reader into perspective, or go straight to the details that you want to focus on? Are you writing to people of the same educational background as yours (i.e. your peers), or to those of different training?

Status refers to the writer's degree of authority and/or power relative to the reader. Are you writing to your boss, to a group of peers, or to someone who is junior to you? Is your reader a client with whom you intend to continue doing business, or the general public that you can only see from a bird's eye view? Are you an expert presenting information to a non-specialist audience, or a novice showing to an authority how much you know about a subject?

Attitude refers to the state of mind you expect the readers to be in when they read your document. Will your message find them hostile, neutral or positive? How motivated are they to read your document? Are you proposing revolutionary changes to a situation you think your readers will resist changing? Are you informing them of a breakthrough that will undoubtedly improve the quality of their lifestyle, and that they will be happy to know about?

Demographic analysis works on the principle that the population can be grouped, and that each group shows a tendency to think or behave in broadly similar ways. Demographic characteristics include the following:

- Gender
- Occupation
- Social class (i.e. income level)
- Age
- Location/nationality (i.e. international or local audience).

From a person's demographic profile, certain inferences can be made about their degree of knowledge, expectations and aspirations, though they are not always foolproof. For example, in most Western societies a middle-class white woman is probably educated to upper secondary school or tertiary level – but not necessarily. Also, teenagers are not likely to be classical music fans, but, again, this may not always be so. Demographic research is based on the lowest common denominator of prevailing social trends and, therefore, operates mostly on stereotype.

Psychographics refers to the lifestyle, values, leisure activities and social self-image that the readers are likely to have. Marketing research shows that people react favourably towards products and services that they see as representative of themselves. Similarly, your readers will respond differently to your message according to their values. What are their interests, opinions and hobbies? In the rapidly changing and diversifying contemporary world, interests and values are less and less tied to demographic issues. For example, when computer games first started to develop, they were associated with a target market of young males in the 15 to 25 age group. As this form of entertainment evolved, the target market changed, and there are now computer games that attract females, older males, and other demographic groups. An analysis of the computer game market, therefore, is more likely to benefit from a psychographic examination that would see the computer game market as a special interest group, rather than a demographic.

Demographic and psychographic analyses are especially relevant in journalistic and public relations writing, where you address a wider public.

Your audience analysis will determine your choice of *content* -what and how much information you need to give – and *style* – how you will present this information. Style will be examined in more detail in Chapter 3. Here it suffices to say that it refers to the emphasis you put on certain ideas and the tone that you adopt in relation to the information you present: your overall attitude and approach as this manifests in the language you use. Your style is formed through your word choice and sentence structure. So, following the results of your audience analysis, you may decide to show a lighthearted approach through your writing – or maybe an evaluative, serious, pompous or respectful approach.

In all, for a text to be successful, there must be **writer-reader complicity**. In other words, the readers must feel that the writer is on their side, supporting their interests and respecting their needs. If readers feel that a writer treats them as an example of a general category, rather than as specific individuals or a specific company, they are more likely to resist accepting the information given.

For example, the following text comes from a government information leaflet telling employers about laws governing sexual discrimination and equal opportunity. It is tactless and creates ineffective audience dynamics because, by grouping all employers into one category, it implies that the readers may be practising gender discrimination. Also, it fails to bring in the main topic (Equal Opportunity Act) until the very end, when there is actually no space to give any information about it.

> Sexual discrimination is practised by various employers, in retail, small business, industry and corporate environments in a number of parts of the country; it is an important community problem and a direct cause of considerable personal distress.
>
> As an employer, as a Human Resources Officer, or as a business owner, it is important for you to know about the Equal Opportunity Act 1975.

Here is a revised version, which creates more complicity between the issuing authority and the readers by addressing the readers directly and showing them that the information given is for their benefit. Also, this version has improved presentation and appearance by including a title and bullet points, and by introducing the main topic earlier.

> ### Employers and the Equal Opportunity Act
>
> You can play an important part in preventing sexual discrimination if you are responsible for employing staff in
>
> ▶ retail
> ▶ small business
> ▶ industry
> ▶ corporations.
>
> The Equal Opportunity Act has been legally enforced since it was passed by Parliament in 1975. This Act makes it illegal for anyone to discriminate – to treat people unfairly because of their gender, race, colour, descent or ethnic origin.
>
> If you know of anyone in your business environment that rejects a suitable candidate for a position because of their gender, tell them about the Equal Opportunity Act. You can also ask the Commissioner for Community Relations for more information.

Audience levels

In addition to analysing your main, or *primary*, audience in relation to the five categories described above, you should also consider if you have *immediate* and *secondary* audiences. In many cases, the person who will first read the document is not the primary audience. It could be a manager or editor, an intermediary between the writer and the primary audience – this is the immediate audience. The immediate reader often acts as a form of filter or quality control agent of the information before it reaches the primary reader. Additionally, you could have a secondary audience of readers who are likely to read the document even if they are not the target group.

Consider an example. If you submit an article for publication to a specialist magazine, you are writing for a public that is interested in the topic of your article; they are your primary audience. However, before the article reaches this audience, it will be read by the magazine's editor, who will make the final decision about whether to publish the article or not. The editor is, then, the immediate audience (and maybe the only audience, if s/he rejects the article!). If published, the article may also be read by readers who are not primarily interested in the topic: they could be journalism students, for example, studying the article as an example of writing. They would be the secondary audience.

Matters get complicated when a document has different levels of audience – primary, immediate and secondary – who have different interests and/or subject knowledge. Such cases make it difficult to imagine who you are writing to. A solution to this problem is to include a section that gives background and definitions of terminology for novices, and/or to include an appendix with more technical details for experts. This way you would be distributing information in a clearly marked and accessible way to the different groups of readers. Returning to the example of the article to the editor, you should include a letter with your article explaining to the editor your goals in writing the article, and justifying your content and stylistic choices (indeed article submissions are generally accompanied by a proposal). This way you address the editor's concerns, and cater for your primary audience's anticipated questions.

These factors of audience analysis will become increasingly familiar and relevant as you progress through the book.

● Generating content

After analysing your audience and determining the purpose and format of your document, it is time to think about the content. This is where researching and thinking come in. Depending on the audience and purpose, different types of research would be relevant. For example, you may decide that interviewing would supply you with essential facts; or you may decide that doing a historical research on a topic would be more suitable; or perhaps a combination of methods would help (more on research in the next chapter).

Collecting facts, however, is not sufficient. You need to think about the significance of these facts and to interpret them. This is where your skills of analysing ideas (tracing their constituent elements) and synthesising them (evaluating their significance in a given context) come in. The process of generating ideas tests your capacity for critical and creative thinking: your ability to imagine all possible aspects or factors of a problem. Analytical thinkers do not simply arrive at the most obvious solution to a question; they test out a range of possible answers and keep an open mind. As happens with chaos theory, sometimes information that initially seemed irrelevant proves to be the key. To be able to trace analogies between seemingly disparate topics and to suggest innovative solutions are skills highly sought in corporate environments. In fact, at the cutting edge of many industries and business endeavours, you will find individuals who are not only highly motivated and organised, but also creative and versatile in their thinking.

The following are some ways to generate ideas. Try them and see which combination suits you.

Brainstorming

Having done some research, brainstorming lets you list all the ideas that come to your mind randomly about a particular topic. Brainstorm by writing single words, phrases, or full sentences – whatever comes to mind. Many writers find that brainstorming in groups is particularly productive.

Mind mapping

Mind mapping is similar to brainstorming but more visual and less linear. Create mind maps by:

- Starting with a word or image central to your topic.
- Placing it in the middle of a big sheet of paper and drawing a line radiating out from it to a major subdivision of the topic.
- Circling that subdivision, and drawing a line radiating out from it to a more specific subdivision.
- Continuing the process until you run out of ideas.

Mind mapping is especially useful to those who find it easier to assimilate and understand schematic information than linear or sentence-based reasoning. See Figure 1 for an example of a mind map based on a report on DVD piracy.

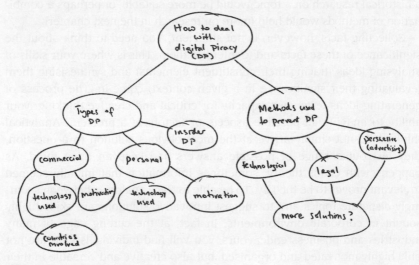

Figure 1   Mind map

Asking journalists' questions

Journalists' questions begin with what is known as the '5W's and 1H' inter-rogatives:

Who?
What?
Where?
Why?
When?
How?

You can approach your task by listing as many journalists' questions about your topic as you can. Questioning encourages you to look at a topic from many different perspectives, and may help you to narrow the issue that you are investigating. Journalists' questions are especially useful when your task involves much factual information, because they actually force you to answer them by providing specifics rather than open-ended or ambiguous statements.

Bouncing ideas

Bouncing ideas means talking about your project to someone. The aim here is to listen to yourself talk about your task, so it is not important if your inter-locutor is versed in your topic or not. In fact, some writers find that talking about their topic to someone who is a total outsider helps them to clarify issues.

If you are having trouble solving a particular problem, talk about why you are having trouble. Variations on this method include talking to yourself or talking into a tape recorder, which has the advantage of capturing your thoughts exactly. Some people are most productive in generating and developing ideas when they can move around and create kinetic energy.

Writing scientific categories

If your topic involves interpreting a scientific development or process to a non-specialist audience, simplify and analyse the topic in your own mind by brainstorming as many statements as possible under these categories:

Existence: How can the existence of X be shown?
Quantity: How large/small is X? How fast?
Comparison: Is X greater/less than Y? In what ways is X different from Y?
Correlation: Does the speed of X vary with its weight?
Causality: If X occurs, will Y also occur? How do we know?

Outlining

With outlining you first come up with section topics, then a summary of the document, and then gradually expand your ideas to create the final document. After some brainstorming, extract the key themes that you identified and give them headings. Under each heading, brainstorm some more points that are related to the heading's theme. Having 'filled' the headings, you will have chunks of information on each theme, which make up a summary of your final document. You can then decide what sequence would be most appropriate, and reorder your section headings in that sequence. Outlining is effective for 'top-down' writers, those who begin with a big picture plan of the whole document, and then build up the details as they go. When writing a report, the outline acts as a first draft that can be submitted to a manager or client to show the progress of a project.

Storyboarding

This is a spatial type of outlining used in film and multimedia projects. Small screens are drawn on a page depicting the main visual elements of major scenes in a project. Under each screen is some script describing the main action and indicating any areas that need to be developed for the particular scene. In the case of writing, the screen can be replaced with a descriptive

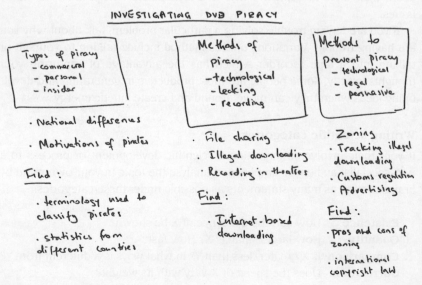

Figure 2   Storyboard

heading. Spatial experimentation can help you find a logical order in which to present your ideas. For both outlining and storyboarding, do not delete documents or files until the project is finished, because you may find that information you thought was redundant becomes relevant again at a later stage.

Figure 2 is a storyboard of a report on DVD piracy. The outline distributes section headings without, at this stage, considering the final sequence.

● Drafting

When you brainstorm and use the other techniques for generating content described above, you are basically drafting. The drafting stage proper comes when you feel you have gathered enough information and have a clear idea where you are heading, so it is now time to expand confidently. When drafting, you will often find that much of your planning will change. Drafting is when you put into practice the ideas you generated in the previous stage and see how they work in expanded form. Make yourself receptive to influences that can provide direction and inspiration: keep your topic in the back of your mind in your everyday activities. Read, watch, listen critically, and seize all that is productive for your purposes. Also, be open to serendipity – inspiration through sudden, previously unrecognised connections. Many great scientific and technical discoveries were made accidentally, by sudden awareness of previously unseen analogies.

If you get stuck when drafting, do not attempt to complete the draft in one go. Instead, let it incubate by putting it on the 'back burner' of your mind and coming back to it later. The time lapse between giving up on a draft and coming back to it could be a few minutes, hours, overnight, or more – depending on project deadlines, of course! In the meantime, you can do something else that, even though it may seem irrelevant, allows your thoughts to gestate. In fact, in professional contexts more often than not you work on many projects simultaneously, so time management – and letting go of one project to move to another – become significant skills.

Table 1 gives a definition of major conceptual actions that you perform when drafting a document. These are common to both academic and professional situations.

Overcoming writer's block

If you find that it is difficult to generate ideas about a specific topic, leading to annoying and costly delay, try one or a combination of these 'unblocking' techniques.

Account for	Give reasons; explain why something has occurred.
Analyse	Take apart an idea, concept or statement in order to evaluate it. This type of answer should be methodical and logically organised.
Argue	Systematically support or reject a viewpoint by offering justification and evidence for your position while acknowledging the opposite point of view.
Assess	Judge the worth or value of something critically.
Comment on	Discuss, explain and give your opinion on the ideas presented.
Compare	Set items side by side, show their similarities and differences, and provide a balanced description.
Criticise (or Critique)	Point out strengths and weaknesses of the subject; support your judgement with evidence.
Define	Explain the precise meaning of a concept. A definition answer often follows the DEMF model: Definition, Examples, Main theorist(s) and Further information.
Discuss	Explain an item or concept, and then give details about it with supportive material, examples, points for and against, and explanations for the points you put forward.
Evaluate	Discuss the material, and reach a conclusion either for or against the concept being discussed and evaluated.

Table 1 Writing actions

Freewriting offers one method of clearing and opening your mind. You can freewrite by writing non-stop, on any topic, for a specific length of time. Do not stop to edit or evaluate what you are writing, and, if you cannot think of anything, keep repeating your last word or phrase until you get going again. The point of freewriting is to unblock your thought processes, and put you in the mood to express ideas in writing. The topic or relevance of what you are writing is, at this stage, put aside. Many writers find that freewriting allows them to approach their task in an uninhibited way.

Writing to the resistance means writing about why you are having trouble

Examine	Analyse the topic, give pros (points for) and cons (points against), or offer a critical judgement about it.
Explain	Offer a detailed and exact explanation of an idea, principle or set of reasons for a situation or an attitude.
Generate	Propose new ideas or new interpretations of available subjects.
Hypothesise	Propose a statement or set of statements that can be used as the basis for testing conclusions.
Illustrate	Provide examples to demonstrate, explain, clarify or prove the subject of the question.
Integrate	In a logically related way, draw together two or more subjects not previously connected.
Interpret	Explain the meaning of something, make it clear and explicit, and evaluate it in terms of your own knowledge.
Justify	Give reasons supporting a particular position on the subject. This could be a positive or a negative position.
List	Present issues or subjects in an itemised series. In many cases, listing can be done in point form.
Outline	Give an organised ordering of information, stating the main points or ideas and omitting details.
Review	Examine, analyse and comment briefly on the main points of an issue.

Table 1 – cont.

tackling a task, or why you are being frustrated in your investigations. This process may help you break through a puzzle, or identify more clearly what it is about the forms of evidence you are dealing with that makes them difficult. Writing to the resistance works especially well in cases when you feel so perplexed or overwhelmed by a topic that you find it difficult to write about in a systematically logical way. It may help you to trace a rational pattern in chaotic thinking.

Responding and mirroring should help you get in the mood for writing, by engaging with other texts. Read a text of the format in which you are writing (for example, if you are writing a report, choose a report, if a magazine article, choose a magazine article) and write an informal critique of it. If you could ask the writer questions about it, what would you ask? What do you think could have been done better in the document? Rewrite a section to improve it. What is particularly effective in the document, and why? If the document asks a question, answer it. By responding this way to the text, you are building motivation and direction to work on yours. This technique is also called 'mirroring', a term from the world of acting. Trainee actors learn to perform by reflecting in their behaviour what they observe in a partner – responding to a smile with a smile, to a frown with a frown, etc. This is based on the idea that any form of action is also, by extension, a form of communication, that is, it is meaningful in relation to a context and a set of participants. Clearly, then, this is relevant to writing too, and can fruitfully be exploited as a 'warm-up' or 'unblocking' technique.

'Blind' writing is a solution for compulsive editors. If you feel critical about every word you produce and constantly delete and rewrite the same sentence, it may be better not to see what you write. Try typing with a dark screen to help you achieve momentum and mass before crafting your output.

● Revising and editing

Revising is arguably the most important stage of the writing process. Many inexperienced writers jump straight from writing to proofreading without going through the revising process, often with unfortunate results.

In longer projects, it is important to take a break between writing and revising. By this stage of the writing process, you are likely to be tired of the project. To revise, you should be able to see the text again anew (which is, in fact, the literal meaning of 'revise'). Proper revision is not simply correcting errors in spelling and grammar – the task of proofreading. Rather, you must decide, honestly, whether the writing is really effective in relation to audience and purpose. If it is not, it takes creativity and vision to figure out what needs to be changed and how. Revising can also be brutal; sometimes the best way forward is to delete material that may have taken hours or days to draft.

An important part of revision is making sure you have a sustained focus and purpose throughout the document. Focusing encourages you to establish what the main point of your document will be. Every document, from the shortest memo to the most intricate report, must contain one overriding point – the main message of the text. Make sure this point stands out, by stating it in a complete sentence at several different stages of the writing process.

Ask yourself: **What is the focal point?**
And: **What is its significance in the given context?**

Revising involves a series of steps, each asking the writer to consider a series of questions moving from general to specific concerns. When you have a complete document, start revising with the conceptual content: have you included all necessary information? Did you answer the question that you set out to answer? Did you test the hypothesis? Will readers understand the main points and their pertinence? Is the overall 'look' of the document attractive and compelling?

After this, check the organization of the document: is this the most appropriate ordering of information, or should you reorganize paragraphs? Remember that, in addition to a 'logical' sequencing of information, there is also a 'conventional' sequencing that depends on the type of document you are writing. Journalist writing, for example, would begin with the most important information first, and would have a catchy lead instead of a formal introduction (more on this in Chapter 4).

At this stage, also rethink the audience: is the style appropriate? Do you need to define terms or give more information? Have you given too many details on a subject your audience is expected to be fluent in? Look at examples and explanations: are they specific, clear and interesting, and not exaggerated, vague, repetitive or contradictory?

Then move to paragraphs and check for unity and cohesion: is each paragraph about one main point? Is all information included in the paragraph

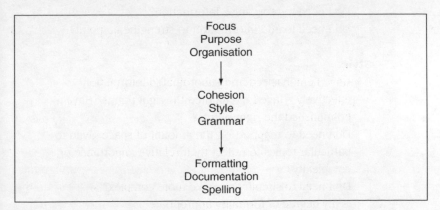

Focus
Purpose
Organisation

↓

Cohesion
Style
Grammar

↓

Formatting
Documentation
Spelling

Figure 3   The revising process

relevant to this main point? Does each paragraph flow from the previous one, so that the reader can understand the transition between one point and another?

Finally, proofread and edit the text for grammar, word choice, punctuation and spelling: do your sentences and words provide the appropriate 'rhythm' for the type of document and audience? Are all sentences grammatically correct, clear and concise? Have you avoided unnecessary repetition or wordiness?

Figure 3 shows the stages in the revision process.

Here is a revision chart to guide you in asking the right questions that will lead to the delivery of a polished and professional document. These questions will become clearer as you work your way through the book.

Revision Chart

Context
- [ ] Am I writing to the right person?
- [ ] Have I learnt as much as I can about my readers?
- [ ] Will there be immediate and secondary audiences?

Content
- [ ] Is all the information I intended to convey there?
- [ ] Do I need to reformulate my argument or main message?
- [ ] Do I need to deepen or extend my analysis?
- [ ] Do I have irrelevant information? Should I narrow the scope in terms of range, time, place or action?
- [ ] Do I need to reorganise information?
- [ ] Do I need to add information to strengthen a point?

Style
- [ ] Have I emphasised and subordinated information effectively? Have I highlighted the right points? Have I diminished the right points?
- [ ] Do I need to reapportion the amount of space given to particular topics to reflect their relative importance or complexity?
- [ ] Do I need to simplify or make more complex?
- [ ] Is my degree of formality appropriate?

- [ ] Is my tone acceptable for the purpose and content?
- [ ] Are my sentences active and concise?
- [ ] Have I used informative headings that reflect the content of the sections?
- [ ] Have I used sectioning and point-listing so as to highlight important points?

Structure

- [ ] Have I used enough sentence variety to make the writing less monotonous and more compelling?
- [ ] Have I used enough flow and transitions to make the writing coherent?
- [ ] Have I used punctuation correctly?
- [ ] Are subjects, verbs and pronouns consistent?
- [ ] Are sentences, points and headings parallel?
- [ ] Is my spelling consistent and have I checked problematic words that are not picked up by the spellchecker?
- [ ] Have I checked the structural/grammatical areas that I know I am weak in?

Layout

- [ ] Have I formatted paragraphs correctly and consistently?
- [ ] Do I need to add, delete or adjust graphics (tables, graphs, charts, drawings, photos)?
- [ ] Do I need to adjust the visual aspects (font size, style and consistency, white space, formatting)?

● Tips for successful writers

As a conclusion to this chapter, here are some guidelines for effective writing on which many successful writers agree. Whether you want to write creative texts, professional documents, scientific reports or promotional articles, these are some rules that writers worldwide have found valid and practical.

1. *Do not wait for inspiration.* Writing creates itself rather like eating is said to arouse the appetite. Most professional writers write on a schedule to meet publishing deadlines, whether they initially feel

like it or not. So start writing before you have thought out completely what you want to say. It does not matter if you start by writing nonsense, repetitions, fragments or mind maps. You will discover what you want to write by writing and not just by thinking. Your document will eventually write itself.

2.   *Revise as you write.*   Most professional writers do at least two, and sometimes many more, drafts of anything they write. To be a successful writer, you should see yourself both as innovator (coming up with new ideas and new connections between ideas) and editor (re-arranging and cutting out parts of your text).

3.   *Be observant.*   All kinds of writing emerge from experience, so the more experience you get in your chosen field the better a writer you will become. Also, being a good writer means being good at dealing with people. Writing always has readers and the more you understand people's behaviour and reactions the better a writer you will be.

4.   *Record different types of material.*   Professional writers keep a record of ideas, objects or events that catch their eye, even if these may not seem relevant to what they are writing at the moment. Writers carry a notebook and pen everywhere and many carry a small tape recorder to record their thoughts and observations immediately as they come. Some day what you recorded will find its way into your writing.

5.   *Use physical details of writing consistently.*   Most writers have their preferred tools and stick to them. This could mean using the same desk, which is located in a special place in your study, using a specific type of pen or computer, using a type of font, or keeping your writing in special files and folders.

6.   *Get feedback.*   In contrast to what some people wrongly believe, writing is not a solitary activity. A written text is meant to be read, so discuss your projects with friends and colleagues, and distribute your drafts for comments when possible. Other people may be able to give you valuable insights on your work that you would have missed if you worked in isolation.

7.   *Learn the rules of your language.*   Successful writers know standard English very well. Although writing is based to a large extent on skill, imagination and knowledge, it is still a technical medium dependent on grammatical rules. Even if you want to break those rules, as many writers in fact do, you first need to know what they are.

Activity

Here is the profile of a founder and Chief Executive Officer (CEO) of a software development company, Andrew Bates. It is written by a Project Manager, who reports directly to the CEO. Read the profile and discuss how Bates as an audience would influence your writing decisions. How would you present documents to him? What would you make sure that you do and do not do? After discussing this, write a profile of an audience (individual or group) to whom you write extensively. See if it shows you some aspects of communication that you previously ignored, and note how this profile will affect your future writing to this audience.

Profile of a CEO

Andrew Bates is in his mid forties and is an aggressive creative leader. He is competitive, driven by the desire to encourage the growth of the firm that he leads. He works long hours and he demands that his employees do the same. Bates wants his people to be smart and imaginative and he listens to what they have to say. He wants graphs and charts in documents, and is not swayed as much by arguments and reasons as by facts and figures. He is a secretive man, and wants to keep his family life out of his public career. Although he has been married for about ten years, he is rarely seen with his wife at public events, where he chooses to participate alone. He has no children. He has an international orientation and has worked and studied in many countries. He is well qualified, with a PhD in Computer Science from the University of London and an MBA from Harvard University. Although originally from a Scottish background he has no close community ties with his native country; he prefers to be considered a 'universal citizen'. Bates's leisure-time activities include sailing and reading science fiction.

2 Research and Information Management

Focus on:

► Types of research
► Types of sources
► Legal and ethical issues in using sources
► Use of sources: summarising and synthesising

In many cases, creating professional documents means finding information, assessing its relevance for your purpose, and integrating it in your text. Analysing the information you find not only provides you with facts and usable data, but also makes you aware of the effects of different styles and writing strategies on audiences. As all good writers are by definition also good readers, text analysis skills are essential in highlighting the structures and methods of organisation in which a writer presents ideas. Being able to understand facts, issues and arguments is fundamental for successful participation in any kind of professional activity. Correlatively, being able to critically analyse the shortcomings and ambiguities of a document assists in avoiding such problems in your own writing.

This chapter considers the role of research in writing, and describes how information can be analysed and recorded. It begins with a description of types of research, goes on to explain how sources may be evaluated, continues with an overview of legal and ethical concerns in using sources, and ends with instructions on summarising and synthesising information. The last section provides an outline of APA (American Psychological Association) referencing style.

● Types of research

The research process

Regardless of the type of information you require to tackle your project, five steps are essential in the data-gathering process:

1. Identify the information that you require.
2. Identify potential sources of information.
3. Decide upon appropriate search strategies.
4. Evaluate the source and content of the information that you find.
5. Use the information.

Primary and secondary research

Research is divided into *primary* and *secondary*. Primary research includes direct observation, preparing questionnaires and interviewing, undertaking fieldwork, and conducting experiments. Secondary research includes the consultation of printed and electronically transmitted material. Primary research leads to the presentation of empirical data, has a more applied focus, and is, therefore, generally written in an analytical and descriptive fashion. Secondary research searches for historical backgrounds, different points of view on an issue, recorded precedents of a situation and theoretical perspectives. As a result, it generally lends itself to techniques of synthesis, interpretation and evaluation.

Primary research: focus groups, interviews, user observation and surveys

Primary research consists of the knowledge you have obtained through first-hand experience. It includes research associated with laboratory experiments, marketing research carried out with focus groups, and statistical evaluations based on responses to set questions. Here we focus on some points to consider when collecting primary data by conducting interviews.

Because your work in professional contexts often means developing products and services for the market, or dealing directly with the public, the ability to detect client needs and responses is very important. An effective way to monitor client reactions to a decision or product is by means of controlled interviews. In fact, many corporations have the interviewing process built into their marketing and public relations procedures through **focus groups**. These tend to be organised at transitional periods of a product or project's development (known as the life cycle of product development), and involve inviting a selected sample of the target audience, and discussing with them specific problems, needs and expectations. Focus groups have a facilitator, who asks questions and generally leads and monitors the discussion and responses.

Focus groups place facilitator and group in a face-to-face situation that allows for more negotiation of questions and enables members of the target group to interact and respond to each other's comments. The company thus receives feedback on the value and usability of a product, on ways that would make the product more appealing and competitive, and on common complaints regarding the product's design. They can subsequently make alterations that would make the product more functional and/or more attractive, and thereby increase their customer numbers. Famous examples of product change as a result of focus group feedback abound: one of these is the development of the now widespread flip top for toothpaste tubes to replace the previously common screw top, which, as focus groups revealed, used to annoy consumers.

The physical proximity that characterises the focus group situation brings into play non-verbal communication, such as body language, and conversational aspects such as intonation, turn-taking and silence gaps, all of which contribute to the feedback received during the interaction. However, the success of the discussion depends to a large extent on the quality of the questions asked. Whether in person-to-person communication or in surveys, make the most of questions by taking the following points into account:

- Research your target audience following the guidelines given in the previous chapter. You should have a clear idea of who you are communicating to before deciding on questionnaires and methods of interviewing.
- Decide whether it is appropriate to administer the questionnaire one-to-one, in a focus group, by mail or by email.
- Decide how you are going to approach the respondents to obtain consent.
- Decide if the information will be confidential or not, and make sure respondents know too. Usually, the researchers do not include the name of respondents in any published findings; however, if they do, they may need formal consent, as in a signed release.
- Decide whether the information you seek is best obtained by open or closed questions, or a mixture of both. Open questions start with the 5Ws and 1H (*What? Why? Where? Who? When? How?*), and require the respondent to create a response. Closed questions give only a set number of options; the respondent ticks boxes or ranks items on a scale.
- Make sure that your questions are not ambiguous. Will your respondent understand what you are asking for?
- Make sure that each question asks for one piece of information only.
- Make the questionnaire attractive and easy to use by including headings, a clear layout and an effective sequencing of questions to enable a linear progression and prevent returning to previous questions in zigzag.
- Keep questions short.
- Try your questions out on someone first.

When conducting interviews face-to-face, or focus groups, keep the following factors in mind:

- Allow the interviewee time to respond. Do not be afraid of silence.
- Maintain eye contact, be professional and impartial. Do not antag-onise your interviewee or make personally intrusive remarks.
- Avoid leading questions (questions that presume an answer in advance, such as 'Don't you think it's true that ...' and 'wouldn't you say that ...?').
- Ask easy questions first to build rapport, trust and connection between yourself and the interviewee. Ask short, impersonal and general questions first. Leave difficult or sensitive questions for the latter part of the interview.

If you are dealing with people or animals, do not launch into your research without considering the ethical consequences of your action. Will you be harming your subjects? Engaging in illegal activities? Dealing with confidential information? In many cases, you may need to submit your proposal to an ethics committee for approval before conducting primary research. In other cases, you may need to obtain releases of information, or sign confidentiality agreements.

In cases where the feedback that you wish to obtain is related to usability of equipment or tools, **user observation** is a popular method of primary research. This involves inviting a sample group of target users of the product to try out the product by following the documentation provided. Engineers, designers and communication specialists observe the users, and note points of misunderstanding and glitches, as well as the areas where the product was used effectively without problems. They then decide if problematic areas are in the design or in the documentation (or a combination), and make a plan to amend and revise the product and its documentation.

If the information you require involves a large number of respondents and statistical data, **surveys** are a useful method. Table 2 shows the question categories of surveys, with examples of each category.

Secondary research: print and electronic sources

Secondary research refers to the activity of obtaining information from published sources, including books, journal articles, newspaper and magazine articles, government publications, corporate publications and online journals. Different sources are valid for different subjects, and professionals know what these are by being immersed in their fields, and through experience. Strategies to help you keep up to date with current developments in your field include networking with relevant groups, and joining professional associations. In addition, many organisations and professional bodies

1. *An open-ended question*. This allows respondents to supply their own answer with little guidance:

    Who would you like to see as the corporation's Chief Executive Officer?

2. *A closed-ended question with unordered answer categories*. This provides several possible answers and asks respondents to select one:

    Who would you like to see as the corporation's Chief Executive Officer?
    1. A
    2. B
    3. C
    4. D
    5. E

3. *A closed-ended question with ordered answer categories*. This provides several possible answers and asks respondents to rate each according to degrees of intensity:

    For each of these candidates, please indicate how much you would like that individual to be the corporation's Chief Executive Officer.

	Strongly favour	Somewhat favour	Somewhat oppose	Strongly oppose
a. A	1	2	3	4
b. B	1	2	3	4
c. C	1	2	3	4
d. D	1	2	3	4
e. E	1	2	3	4

4. *A partially closed-ended question*. This provides several possible answers, but also allows respondents to select a different answer if required:

    Who would you like to see as the corporation's Chief Executive Officer?

    1. A
    2. B
    3. C
    4. D
    5. E
    6. Other (specify)

Table 2 Survey questions

5. *Ladder-scale question*. This provides a scale on which respondents can rate the performance or degree of probability:

On a scale from 0 to 10, where 0 means you rate the job the CEO is doing as extremely poor and 10 means you rate the job the CEO is doing as extremely good, how would you rate the job CEO X is doing?

Extremely poor   Extremely good

0   1   2   3   4   5   6   7   8   9   10

6. *Lickert-scale question*. This asks respondents to evaluate the likelihood of particular actions:

How likely do you think you will be to support the election of X as the corporation's new Chief Executive Officer?

1. Very likely
2. Somewhat likely
3. Neither likely nor unlikely
4. Somewhat unlikely
5. Very unlikely

7. *Semantic differential question*. This asks respondents to give impressionistic answers to a particular object by selecting specific positions in relation to at least nine pairs of bipolar adjectives on a scale of one to seven. The aim is to locate the meaning of the object in three dimensions: evaluation (e.g. good–bad), potency (e.g. strong–weak) and activity (e.g. active–passive). This method is useful in studying emotional reactions and attitudes and gauging the differences in outlook between cultural groups.

How would you characterise X as the corporation's CEO?

Good _ Bad
Strong _ Weak
Decisive _ Indecisive
Moral _ Immoral
Intelligent _ Stupid

Table 2 – *cont.*   Adapted from Marsen (2006, pp. 122–3).

require their members to regularly update their knowledge and qualifications through professional development training.

Besides the expertise you acquire though experience and association, work projects will require you to investigate specific topics and problems. We now look at some strategies to help you access sources of information, and at different types of sources. Before identifying potential sources or starting any form of research, you should have a clear idea of your objectives. This comes with audience, purpose and format analysis, as described in the previous chapter. Once this is done, and you have some idea of what you are looking for, adapt the following procedure according to the requirements of your topic:

- Search for journals in your topic. For example, if your research is on surveillance technologies, check journals on video and photographic equipment, on new media technologies, and on privacy issues. Many of these have online access, and most allow you to search inside the publications to see if they have published articles in your topic of interest.
- Do a Google Scholar search using keywords associated with the topic. Google Scholar is much more likely to direct you to trustworthy, expert work, as opposed to Google standard, which will give you too many hits, most of which are not likely to be of the quality you require. When searching, use a variety of keywords associated with the topic. For example, if you are researching 'smoking', look for 'tobacco', 'nicotine', 'lung diseases', 'cigarettes', etc.
- Search reference material, such as dictionaries, thesauri, encyclopaedias. A considerable number of these can be found online. However, if your work consists to a large extent of writing, you will find that building a library of reference material will prove very useful for your tasks. The market abounds in dictionaries of various sorts – quotations, humour, famous speeches, clichés, etc. – and a good collection of these will often prove instrumental in helping you come up with the right idea. Reference material will also point you in the right direction even when it does not itself offer the answer to your question. The online encyclopaedia *Wikipedia* (www.wikipedia.org), for example, provides information of varying quality and depth; it can, however, direct you to the sources that may be more suited to your requirements.
- Do a library search: many organisations are affiliated with research institutions and universities that have substantial libraries. Others subscribe to online database services, such as the Online Computer Library Center (OCLC), the Research Libraries Information Network

(RLIN) and DIALOG, which cover a wide range of subjects and can be searched by keywords. Search library catalogues for names of experts in your topic; search databases for keywords of the topic. Databases such as ProQuest will give you a range of sources, while LexisNexis will point you to popular sources, such as newspaper articles.

- Get company annual reports, government reports, newsletters and information material from institutions and corporations that are related to your topic. These are often available online, although you may need to subscribe. Even if these documents defend the interests of the issuing organisations, they can still offer valuable factual information.

- Follow up articles and books that are included in the references and bibliography sections of published material.

- For current information and recent developments, search press releases and news sections of corporate and governmental websites. Almost all organisations contain a page on their websites where they publicise their breaking news. This is usually called 'For Journalists' or 'Press Room', and it is where you can get press releases and information on new products. If you work in the fields of science and technology, a central source of press releases is www.eurekalert.org

- Contact professionals for advice on major publications and journal titles in specific fields. These professionals include academic staff in university departments, editors of key journals in your specialty and public relations representatives of relevant companies.

- Browse library bookshelves with the call number related to your topic. You may well serendipitously come across useful material that you would not have otherwise planned to get. Also, browse the catalogues of publishers that deal with your topic for recent publications.

Clearly, sources abound. In most instances, there is a higher risk that you will suffer from information overload than from a shortage of data. The problem now becomes which sources to use and which to avoid – the topic of the next section.

● Evaluating sources

In truth, there is no totally foolproof way to establish the credibility of a text: new data constantly emerge that destroy previously accepted 'truths'; bias is insidious; and mistakes are made. One safeguard for credibility is to ensure that the text has been accepted by the community in which it belongs, as happens, for example, with peer-reviewed material. Peer-reviewed articles have been read and approved by experts in the field prior to publication. The peer review process takes place in these stages. First, a writer submits his or her text to the editor of a journal or a publishing company. The editor, in turn, sends it to reviewers who are familiar with the knowledge in the field. If the information provided in the text is acceptable, the reviewers recommend that the article proceed to publication. The reviewers could also recommend revisions and amendments to the text, and they could also advise that the text is not worthy of publication.

This method, however, is also inconclusive. Both Galileo's and Einstein's theories, for example, were rejected by the scientific community when they were first formulated. The opposite situation also happens: a theory may be accepted when it is actually nonsense. In a well-known recent example, Alan D. Sokal, a professor in physics, wrote a believable but actually totally made-up account of post-modernism in physics. Sokal decorated the article with difficult technical terms, which looked impressive but really did not mean much at all. He sent it to a prestigious, peer-reviewed journal specialising in cultural analysis, called *Social Text* (issue 46–47, 1996). After the article was published, Sokal revealed the deception, which has become known as the 'Sokal Hoax'.

In still other cases, one discourse community, or group of specialists, may find fault with a text where another will not. This is a symptom of the diversification of knowledge and the multiplication of specialties, even within one discipline. An author may send an article to a journal, for instance, and have it criticised and rejected by reviewers. S/he may then send the same article to another journal, where it is accepted without hesitation. This shows that knowledge is regulated according to the cultural values of specific groups, who set the criteria for its assessment. Attaining expertise in a professional or scholarly field, therefore, in many ways means being accepted by the community that is formed around this field. It also means that, as a writer, you should not be discouraged by an initial cold reception to your work, but continue looking for your 'niche'; and, as a researcher, you should be aware that publications reflect certain perspectives, and follow a particular tradition of thought.

Keeping all this in mind, when deciding whether an information source is likely to be accurate and reliable, consider the following factors:

- Has the information been peer-reviewed? This will show you at least if a community of specialists have accepted it as 'true'.

- How prestigious or credible is the information source? Publications with a reputation for impartiality and rigour would be more selective of their material.
- Does the writer give references for information cited? Are these references accurate? An article that is based on personal opinion only may make a good editorial, but it would not provide a solid basis for an objective and comprehensive assessment of an issue.
- Has the writer considered a range of information sources, or relied on just a small number of sources? Are the information sources themselves reliable? Writers should not only show rigour in their own thinking, but also enure that the sources they rely on have done the same.
- What organisation does the writer belong to? What is the reputation of this organisation? Non-profit organisations may have ideological biases just as 'big business' may have financial biases, and the possibility of these should be taken into account when assessing the information.
- What organisation funded the research? Many funding organisations have vested or political interests in assisting certain forms of research, as opposed to others, to come to light. Learn as much as you can about the values and political structure of research funding agencies.
- Did the writer conduct primary research? If so, does the writer state what kind of research was conducted, how it was conducted, and what the sample size was? Is the sample population typical or exceptional in some way? If a questionnaire was used, was it anonymous? Was the interview conducted face to face, by mail, or by email? Are copies of the questionnaire included? The results of primary research depend strictly on the methods used.

Types of sources

Following the above discussion, and keeping in mind that the boundaries between types are not always clear-cut, I propose the following typology of sources, going from most to least authoritative. This typology complements the typology of style described in Chapter 3.

(a) Scholarly

Scholarly sources include academic or research-based journals, research monographs, university textbooks, and anthologies of essays on academic disciplines. Most scholarly journals are published by universities or professional bodies, and scholarly books are published by publishers specialising in 'serious' work. These sources are written in language specific to their discipline (insider language, or jargon), and always cite their own sources. Writers of such sources make a conscious effort to make their assumptions explicit and to persuade the readers with logical and systematic reasoning rather than emotive appeals or generalisations. The audience for such documents is peers, and students being initiated into the conventions and language expectations of the discipline. Consequently, the style and terminology of these sources is not 'easy' or obvious for outsiders.

Scholarly sources are the most authoritative because their authors, in most cases, have a professional commitment to keeping debates open, while acknowledging and building on previously received knowledge.

(b)   Specialist

Specialist sources include magazines on science, technology and social topics, and serious non-fiction, such as popular science. The aim of such documents is usually to inform a non-specialist public of technical topics in an accessible way, and thereby to publicise or popularise otherwise daunting or overly complex concepts. The intended audience of this type of source would be an educated and informed reader with no or little expertise on the topic presented, but with a commitment to gaining new knowledge, and, consequently, with a longer attention span than a reader of lower-level documents (see below).

Authors of specialist documents attempt to entertain as well as inform, and therefore tend to rely more strongly on analogy, metaphor and dramatisation than authors of scholarly documents. They do, however, cite sources, although the technique of integrating these in the text is often different from that in scholarly documents, which use formal referencing styles. Serious non-fiction often uses similar techniques of referencing as scholarly work. Specialist magazine articles, in contrast, name researchers and their professional positions in the body of the articles, rather than in endnotes or end-of-text references. In addition, in magazines of this type, the role of visuals becomes important, with attention paid to aesthetics of layout and design.

Specialist documents are an excellent source of information on a rather superficial level. If more depth or analysis is needed, such documents can refer you to the original, more formal sources.

(c)   Public

These sources include governmental, corporate and legal documents, such as public statements issued by government agencies, and corporate information, such as can be found on organisational websites and in public relations material. As these documents are generally addressed to the general public, the language is clear and unambiguous, and concepts are made as simple as possible. This is especially so with government and business documents since the establishment of the Plain English campaign, which emphasised reader-based aspects of communication and propounded a direct and informal approach to public writing.

Documents belonging to this category tend to assume a low attention span, and do not expand on a topic more than is necessary to get their point across. Many have a promotional edge, and, even when they are not selling a product, they support the issuing organisation's interests – as happens with press releases, for example. Public documents are usually a good source of facts (often the only source of facts about a corporation or government policy), but should always be read critically, and interpreted according to the requirements of a specific project.

This category includes (non-tabloid) local newspapers and non-specialised, general interest magazines, as they too address the general public, aiming to appeal to the low common denominator of a community's interests and sensibilities.

(d) Sensationalist

Sensationalist sources base their information on rumour, fabrication or exaggeration, rather than on any form of empirical or interpretative research, and are, therefore, the least credible type. In fact, they do not merit to be classified as sources of research at all, unless you use them as examples of the distortion of information in the popularization of knowledge. Many popular magazines and newspapers fall into this category, especially the ones that appeal to thrill and sensation as opposed to any form of truth or reflection. These sources appeal to the gullible and escapist tendencies of their readership.

The Internet

Today information on any subject can be retrieved in a wide variety of formats and through a range of channels, and the plethora of information can make it difficult for researchers or investigators to decide on which sources to use. The temptation for many is to automatically search the Internet. Although this can be productive, you need to be cautious to avoid potential problems.

It is difficult to estimate how much information and how many documents are available through the Internet at any one time. Whatever number people might estimate, one minute after the estimation there will be more. The size of the Internet in terms of the amount of information contained is one of the factors that, while making it a strong support for learning, can also limit its potential. Sometimes there is just too much information to be found, which makes assessing the credibility of information difficult, and which can also be extremely time consuming.

For example, those who received primary and secondary education before the 1990s are accustomed to consulting (and trusting) textbooks and encyclopaedias for facts about specific events. This attitude is now being seriously challenged by the quantity and quality of information on the Internet. If you do an Internet search for the answers to seemingly straightforward factual questions such as 'Who invented the microscope?' and 'In what year was the telescope invented?' you may come up with some surprises. You will probably find a range of names and dates offered as the right answer, depending on such factors as different definitions, different methodologies of research, different interpretations of events – even personal preference! This suggests that, because of its lack of control over what is published, the Internet is not always a reliable source of information – but it can certainly give you alternative views and different sides to an issue that you may wish to investigate further.

One way to avoid such problems is by recognising that the Internet, besides being a source, is, in fact, a medium. This means that although sources of information may be transmitted through the Internet, they can still be evaluated with reference to the typology proposed earlier, like print sources. The presence of 'walled gardens' on the Internet is a case in point. For example, many sites are encrypted, and require a special password to access the information they contain. A seminal instance of this is digital libraries, which require subscription for access. In fact, many digital libraries from scholarly institutions or reputable publishers have valuable resources online, but limit their access to subscribers or members.

Many scholarly and specialist journals offer the option to access materials both online in Hypertext Markup Language (HTML), or Portable Document Format (PDF), and in print. This is the case, for instance, with popular science publications *New Scientist* (www.newscientist.com) and *Scientific American* (www.sciam.com), and the techno-savvy magazine *Wired* (www.wired.com), which have both online and print versions. An interesting additional element to using the Internet as a medium in such cases is the option to open articles to discussion and comment. In fact, often writers of articles enter the interactive discussion to offer clarifications on points they have made in their articles, and to respond to reader feedback.

Similarly, broadcast companies transmit news stories online as well as through the older media of radio and television (see, for example, www.bbc.co.uk and www.cnn.com). Finally, government agencies and corporations publish information on their policies and products online, and these can be very useful when you search for facts and figures, and for contacts from whom to obtain more details.

Other Internet sources include:

- *Blogs and wikis.* These are popular online forums for discussion and collaboration. Easily designed with authoring tools that can be downloaded from sites such as www.blogger.com, blogs enable users to interact in real time to exchange ideas and opinions, or to produce collaborative documents where all writers contribute and can edit each other's work. Blogs can be very productive in their interactive and collaborative function. However, they should not be used as the sole or main source of information because their informality and experimental nature generally does not lead to definite information but, rather, to work in progress, or to directions that need more exploring through other means.

  Blogs (originally weblogs) are authored by individuals or groups, and have a serial nature, offering commentary on a particular topic. The credibility of this commentary, as in other media, depends on the reputation and expertise of the blogger. In contrast, wikis are not serial, but are based on an evolving taxonomy structure. Some wikis are open and some are closed. However, wikis generally allow the community to add, edit and restructure contents. High-quality wikis have communities of volunteers who continually check and edit content to ensure credibility. They generally also attribute edits and changes to particular individuals, and may also include a change history with comments and discussion showing the rationale of the changes. *Wikipedia* is an example of such wikis. In all, wikis reflect the interests and knowledge of the participants.

- *Discussion groups.* You can find discussion groups on practically any topic imaginable. These can be useful for exchanging information with similar-interest peers, who may direct you to the information you need for a project. At the same time, remember that, however insightful the information you obtain may be, it does not represent all the input the topic can generate, and requires careful scrutiny and balance with material from other sources. For straightforward topics, discussion groups can be useful in encouraging and documenting questions and answers. Also, to find the answer to a query about a narrow topic, discussion groups may be the best resource.

- *Personal websites.* These are the least credible of Internet sources, and could, in fact, be placed in the sensationalist category. The Internet's decentralised and open structure allows anyone with server space and minimal technical knowledge to set up a site and post whatever they want on it, so the best advice is to avoid personal websites altogether for research purposes (unless personal websites are the topic of your research).

Table 3 lists some questions to ask when deciding if an Internet source is credible.

Internet evaluation checklist

☐ Is the information presented on the site comprehensive and unbiased? Does it describe clearly where the information came from and what its purpose is? Sites that present opinions based on personal experience or belief should be avoided when credible data are required.

☐ What is the style and quality of writing of the site? No organisation that takes itself seriously would condone sloppy or ungrammatical writing, so if you find this in the site, be careful. As with other types of written communication, the text of a site should use the terminology and style that are recognised and used by its target audience.

☐ Does the site clearly state its purpose? Sites whose purpose is ambiguous or hard to find, may be of dubious value.

☐ Does the site include the author's name and affiliation? Does the author have credentials in the field that he/she is writing? Suspect anonymous sites (unless they are sponsored by a well-known organisation).

☐ Does the site include a date of updating? As with all publications, the date that the information was last reviewed is vital in assessing its reliability.

☐ Does the site include contact details? The purpose of the Internet is to be interactive, so a site that does not allow you to contact the author is suspect. Ideally, the site should have contacts for both designer and writer.

☐ Does the site have links to other sites and/or references to other sources? What is the value and reputation of these other sources? Links function like references in printed texts, allowing the reader to obtain further information or different points of view on a topic. A site that is self-sufficient is more likely to be based on personal, unsupported, opinion.

Table 3 Checklist for evaluating internet sources

Searching the Internet

Currently, there are more than 100 search engines that can be used to locate information on the Internet. The search engines differ in:

- the number of records in their databases
- the search options they provide
- the way they abstract information
- the way they index information
- the way they present information
- the frequency with which they update their databases.

An important feature of search engines is their increasingly commercial nature. For example, many engines will place prominently paid advertisements related to a search according to criteria set by advertisers. Advertisements should be distinguished from search results, and some engines make this difficult. Also, some engines are suspected of reducing or eliminating search results for products or services that compete with those owned by the search engine company. Finally, some search engines censor results to appease political authorities in some countries.

Another important issue is that many websites actually exist for the sole purpose of being found in search results. These often have many words that people might search for, and contain advertisements or links to other sites. Some of these sites promise their content only to those who register with an email address, which then leads to spam advertising messages.

Therefore, choosing the right search engine can mean the difference between finding a lot of useful information and a lot of useless information. Users should have some awareness of the qualities of the different engines so that they can choose the one that best meets their needs.

There are four main types of search engines: *Index/Database*, *Spider/Robot*, *Retrieval* and *Meta-Search*:

Index/Database engines use databases of Uniform Resource Locators (URLs – website addresses) together with abstracts of their contents. A search involves scanning the information in the database and returning URLs that match the search conditions. This form of search engine consists of URLs that have been collected and indexed manually.

Spider/Robot engines use a database that has been created by a program that continually and automatically scans the Internet and collects and indexes URLs. *Retrieval* engines take the request from the user and scan the Internet for

URLs that match. There is no database involved and each request involves a new Internet search.

Meta-Search engines use several different engines at the same time when searching and constitute a very advanced form of Internet searching.

Searching tips

The following tips are generally valid for many search engines and searching activities on the Internet.

1. *Use multiple words.* You will get more refined results from several words than from a single word. For example, 'Detective Sherlock Holmes' will yield more relevant results than "Sherlock Holmes" or 'detectives'.
2. *Use similar words.* The more similar words you use in a search, the more results you will get back; for example, 'restaurant, cafe, bistro'.
3. *Capitalise when appropriate.* Capitalise proper nouns. Capitalised names that are adjacent are generally treated as a single name and not as two separate words.
4. *Use quotation marks to set off phrases.* Use quotation marks to find words that are part of a set phrase; for example, 'deep blue sea'. Otherwise, you may get pages that include the word 'deep', the word 'blue', and the word 'sea'.

● Managing information: avoiding plagiarism

The general context

Plagiarism means copying or in some way reproducing someone else's work without giving them credit or acknowledgement. In many ways, it is a form of stealing – consistent with the etymological root of 'plagiarism', which in Latin means 'kidnapping'. In our era of collaborative writing and digital re-mix, however, things are not as simple as they sound. It is sometimes unclear where the boundaries between one's own and someone else's work lie. This section attempts to shed light on some pertinent issues.

Using another's work without permission and/or credit signals one of three different situations: *copyright breach*, *plagiarism* or *invasion of privacy* (Branscum, 1991; Howard, 2003; Leval, 1990).

Copyright is a legal issue. If you use without permission work that has been published in a tangible medium or patented, you breach copyright and are liable to (often very costly) lawsuits. Any item that has been published is protected by copyright law, and this includes Internet sources. Copyright law originated in England to protect the printing trade. Since then, it has become part of a set of laws, together with patent law and trademark law, that regulate intellectual property. Copyright expires after a certain amount of time, when the work becomes part of the public domain. As copyright laws tend to change regularly, it is always advisable to check the copyright status of an item you want to use. At the time of publication of this book, for works created after 1977, the term of copyright protection is the life of the author with 70 additional years for individuals and 95 years for corporate authors (Karjala, 1999).

Copyright law was designed to protect the rights of producers of literary and artistic artefacts. After all, these individuals make a living from their products, and these should be protected to encourage their producers to continue creating. However, public access to such artefacts also needs legal protection, so the *doctrine of fair use* was created as an amendment to copyright law. Fair use entails using a part of a work for purposes that benefit the public good, such as for education. According to fair use, you may use another's work without permission if:

- you are using only a fraction and not the complete item
- you give credit to the original source
- the item has been published and is, therefore, not private
- the purpose is educational
- your use of the material will not affect the market value of the original.

Government documents are considered public property (government employees are paid from taxes), and are not copyrighted. This does not mean to say, however, that you can copy material from them without citing the source – this would be plagiarism.

If you reproduce a work or part of a work without acknowledging the original creator, and present it as being your own, you are plagiarising, even in cases where the work is not copyrighted. For example, Shakespeare's work is now in the public domain; however, if you copy a part of it and present it as your own, you are plagiarising the work, even if you are not liable to legal action for doing so. With plagiarism we leave the domain of law and enter the domain of ethics.

Copyright protects only the tangible expression of an idea – not the idea itself. Plagiarism regulations cover the unacknowledged reproduction of the idea itself. Knowledge and ideas are academic currency: through the exchange of ideas, the academic community sustains itself and contributes to the well-being of society as a whole. Individual scholars produce and publish ideas for their livelihood, and any unacknowledged use of their hard work is both injury and insult. This accounts for the heavy penalties universities impose on students convicted of plagiarism; although legal sanctions do not apply in such cases, the ethical violation carries an equally serious consequence – exclusion (temporary or permanent) from the community.

Plagiarism can be avoided by:

- *summarising*: expressing in your own words the gist of a document, and citing the source
- *paraphrasing*: expressing in your own words the gist of a part of an idea, and citing the source
- *quoting*: copying the exact words of a section of the original document, putting them in quotation marks to set them off from your own words, and citing the source.

All ideas that you take from other texts need referencing. The only exception is **common knowledge** – the equivalent of the public domain in copyright law. Common knowledge consists of propositions and statements that did not originate with the writer (or speaker), but that are accepted facts in the wider community. Examples include such propositions as 'Rome is the capital of Italy', 'The Sun is a star' and 'Two plus two equals four'. This, however, is not always so straightforward because knowledge, in many cases, is dependent on the community in which it is used. A proposition that may be considered common knowledge among quantum physicists, for example, may not be so among another group. This is why, as with other aspects of writing, analysing your audience and purpose will point you in the right direction on ways to integrate knowledge in your document.

Finally, when using another's work you may also be invading their privacy – a legally sanctioned offence. This generally occurs when you publicise information that the originator kept personal or private. If you publish your roommate's journal on the Internet, for example, you are infringing on their privacy. If you publish the journal and present it as your own, you are also plagiarising! In professional contexts, privacy issues often arise with email and Internet use. It is contestable if a manager has the right to 'spy' on employees' email exchanges and the sites they visit on the Internet. For some, the manager does have this right, since the employees are using computers, Internet provision and time supplied by the company. For others, email is private if it is not exchanged for professional purposes, and should not be accessed by employers, even if the employee exchanges it during work hours.

The professional context

As the last example shows, the professional world presents a challenge to conventions regarding plagiarism and privacy. Instances exist in business and industry where presenting another's work as your own is accepted practice. Examples include **boilerplate text** and **public relations documents**.

Boilerplate is standardised text that can be reproduced verbatim, or with minor alterations, for different audiences and documents. For instance, letters sent to clients to inform them of company developments or changes work on the boilerplate model – all recipients get basically the same letter, with only the opening address differing. Similarly, a lab whose members often apply for funding may have a set description of the lab and its operations, which individual members may use, unchanged, in their proposals. In such cases, the individual whose name appears on the document is not the same as the one who wrote a section of the document.

Public relations documents are also often anonymous, attributed to anyone who may be a PR officer at a particular time, or written by someone other than the one whose name appears on the document. For instance, corporate websites and promotional material, such as brochures, often contain segments written by different individuals, and they can be updated by rewriting some sections, reorganising information by cutting and pasting from different sections, etc. – all without acknowledging the original source. Press releases contain the name of a media relations officer from whom the press can obtain more information, but this does not mean the release was written by that person. Furthermore, speeches and articles of Chief Executive Officers (CEOs), and other senior personnel, are more often than not written by the company's professional writers, but presented as the CEO's own words. The original writer in these cases has nothing to show but financial remuneration and secret pride!

These cases are more variants than aberrations of the plagiarism conventions discussed in the previous section. In the corporate world, the company takes precedent over the individual in matters of production. In many cases, new staff are asked to sign agreements stating that their work belongs to the company; producing material that the company can use is part of their job description. This is publicly known and acknowledged as business convention; therefore the CEO who puts his name on an article written by his writers is not morally or legally reprehensible. In such instances, the corporation is seen as a body ('body' being, in fact, the etymology of 'corporation'), and acting as an individual. Stepping outside the boundaries of a company, however, would transgress this convention. If a writer of X company, for example, used material that a writer of Y company wrote, s/he would no doubt be plagiarising, not to mention breaching copyright if the work was published.

Ongoing writing projects in business contexts are generally open to rewrite, and, therefore, have many writers, who most often remain anonymous, or are given a group or position title. These projects include public relations documents and style manuals, which are regularly updated and changed. Other documents, especially those that involve major finalisable projects, follow rules akin to those of academic contexts. For example, proposals to management for funding and/or approval of a project always include writers' names, and so do reports describing the results of an investigation. Also, in such reports, the writers are expected to cite their sources of information, and to quote, summarise and paraphrase as appropriate.

Besides giving credit where it is due, citing sources, in both professional and academic contexts, enhances a writer's accountability. As a researcher and problem solver, refer to sources to:

- show you have consulted relevant material and can advise authoritatively
- support your findings and recommendations by linking them with independent data
- enable readers to follow up material for more information.

● Managing information: summarising

In professional contexts, it is highly unlikely that you will read things for pleasure only. Your reading will involve some form of action that you need to take in relation to the information you have read. For this reason, it is vital not only that you understand accurately the meaning of the text, but also that you can place the information within the overall context to which it relates. In addition to critical thinking skills, this entails the cognitive abilities of deduction and classification. Both abilities are put into practice in the technique of summarising. By summarising information, you are rendering it into usable form, and you are also checking your understanding of it.

Purposes of summarising

If you ever have the feeling of being overwhelmed by information overload, you will find the art of summarising a tool for survival. By summarising, you can condense large chunks of information into small, workable bits without losing the essential points. Unlike a paraphrase, a summary may include some of the same wording as the original. Summaries are normally about 10 per cent of the original, and may go up to 30 per cent, in certain circumstances. Summaries serve the following purposes:

- *Recording information*. A summarised document is much easier to file and classify than a long one. Keeping a summary of a document on file gives you fast access to the information contained in the document, and helps you decide if this document is useful and if you want to retrieve it.
- *Communicating information*. It is easy to communicate information from a document to a third party if it has been reduced to its basics. Summarised information can be integrated in your own text, both written and oral. Also, by summarising your own documents, you can give your target audience an overview of your message and help them decide whether your document is suitable for their needs. When writing to a publisher, or submitting a paper to a conference, for example, you would be required to send in a summarised version – an abstract – first. When submitting a report, the executive summary will be the section which will be read first.
- *Understanding information*. Even in cases where you do not need to record or communicate a message, you may find that summarising a long and/or complex document puts it in perspective and helps you understand it better. Also, summarising your own document should show you if your writing is coherent and clear. If you find that you have difficulty in summarising your work (in other words, answering the question, 'What is this about?'), chances are you need more revision.

Writing summaries

Professional contexts present two main types of writing that lead to tasks of summarising: factual information and persuasion. Although these types often seem to overlap in a document, there is still a fundamental difference in the main purpose of the writer: the intention of a specifications manual is not the same as the intention of a proposal, even if both aim in some way to direct the reader's actions. When attempting to summarise a document, begin by distinguishing whether the main focus is explanatory or persuasive.

If the document is explanatory, decide which information should be included in the summary to maintain the original meaning; you do not need to change the order in which the information is presented, unless a different sequencing would make the document more reader-friendly. If the document is persuasive, on the other hand, an effective method of beginning your summary is with a statement of the writer's argument or claim, even if this is not clearly stated in the original, or if it comes towards the end. For example, you could begin your summary with the phrase, 'This article argues that . . .', or, 'In his article, "title", X, a cognitive scientist, claims/proposes/suggests that . . .' The remainder of your summary would be a selection of supporting sentences that exemplify, explain or substantiate the writer's claim. This satisfies the summary's purpose of clarifying meaning and facilitating recording and retrieval.

Prepare to write a summary by following these steps:

1.   Read through the text and make sure you understand its main focus and purpose. Do not attempt to summarise while you are reading the text for the first time. This will confuse you and make you lose sight of the main message. Make sure you understand whether the message is persuasive or explanatory.

2.   Go back and divide the text into chunks of information (you may find that each paragraph contains a major point or idea, or that information is distributed in sections – a lot depends on the length of the document).

3.   Write one or two sentences on each of the main ideas of the text. Then, restructure them in a coherent paragraph, paraphrasing some material and adding and extracting words where necessary.

4.   Check your summary against the original. Ask yourself if it captures the message of the text and if it makes sense on its own. Make any final amendments if required.

A summary should be:

- *Comprehensive*: select as many important facts and concepts as the length of the summary will allow
- *Accurate*: make sure you do not distort the writer's stance
- *Neutral*: you should act as the writer's representative, not critic. If you include an evaluation or critique of the writer's ideas, you should distinguish these from the summary itself
- *Independent*: the reader should make sense of the summary and understand the main message of the writer without having to read the original text.

● Documenting sources: APA format

In the course of their academic training and professional careers, writers need to learn several different styles of documenting their research in texts. We end this chapter with an overview of one of the most common formats, the APA (American Psychological Association) style. The APA style is often chosen because of its simplicity: there is no need to reorder and renumber references, as happens with other styles.

The APA method of presenting articles, books and websites is shown below. Consult the *Publication Manual of the American Psychological Association* for more details. Also, consider using a referencing software program, such as *EndNote*, which will automatically create in-text and end-of-text references for your document, using whatever style you choose.

In-text referencing – print

The APA style does not use footnotes. Instead, note the author's last name, the date of publication, and (if relevant) the page number in the body of your text. The reader will look to the list of references at the end of your text for full bibliographical details. For example:

> See Bazerman (1998) for further information.
>
> 'Typography is the art and style of printing' (Bowden, 1997, p. 136).
>
> Bruce (as cited in Bazerman 1998, p. 10) lists seven advantages of information literacy.

If there is no date, use n.d. (no date). If there is no page (as in many electronic sources), give as much information as possible on the actual positioning of the data to which you refer. The preferred method is to note the paragraph number (for example, para. 5). If the document contains section headings, include also the section heading).

In-text referencing – electronic

For in-text documentation of electronic sources, use author–date for sources where the author is known, and URL for sources that involve a whole site.

> 'As Brandt (2000) points out, language is theatrical.'
>
> 'IBM recruits new employees through its web site (www.ibm.com).'
>
> 'The *Journal of Evolution and Technology* publishes articles on possibilities of human enhancement through technological means' (http://jetpress.org)

End-of-text referencing

Books

A book with one author
> Johnson, B. E. (1998). *Stirring up thinking.* Boston: Houghton Mifflin.

A book with two authors
> Morgan, G. and Banks, A. (1999). *Getting that job: How to establish and manage your career into the new millennium.* Sydney: HarperCollins.

A book with three (or more) authors
> Akmajian, A., Demers, R. A., Farmer, A. K. & Harnish, R. M. (2001). *Linguistics: An introduction to language and communication.* Cambridge, MA: The MIT Press.

An edited book
> Bazerman, C. & Paradis, J. (Eds). (1991). *Textual dynamics of the professions.* Madison: University of Wisconsin Press.

A second or later edition of a book
> Bordwell, D. & Thompson, K. (2005). *Film art: An introduction.* 7th ed. New York: McGraw Hill.

A book without an author (listed alphabetically by first main word in title)
> *Microsoft Project 4 for Windows Step by Step.* (1994). Redmont, WA: Microsoft Press.

Note: Titles of books are italicised. Titles of articles and other documents are neither italicised nor put in quotation marks.

Articles, encyclopaedia entries, and chapters

A chapter in an edited book
> Herndl, C. G., Fennell, B. A. & Miller, C. R. (1991). Understanding failures in organizational discourse. In C. Bazerman & J. Paradis (Eds). *Textual dynamics of the professions.* Madison: University of Wisconsin Press.

An encyclopaedia entry
> Bergmann, P. G. (1993). Relativity. In *The new encyclopedia Britannica* (Vol. 26, pp. 501–508). Chicago: Encyclopedia Britannica.

A journal article
  Bekerian, D. A. (1993). In search of the typical eyewitness. *American Psychologist, 48,* 574–576.

A weekly magazine article
  Sayle, M. (1995, July 31). Did the bomb end the war? *The New Yorker,* 40–64.

A monthly magazine article
  McClelland, D. (1998, October). Digital cameras: photo finish. *Macworld,* 48–51.

Review in magazine or journal
  Gleick, E. (2000, December 14). The burdens of genius [Review of the book *The Last Samourai*]. *Time 156,* 171.

Note: For a film review, write [Review of the motion picture].

Other sources

Government document
  U.S. Census Bureau. (2000). *Statistical abstract of the United States.* Washington, DC: U.S. Government Printing Office.

Corporate or government report without an author
  American Psychiatric Association. (2000). *Practice guidelines for the treatment of patients with eating disorders* (2nd ed.). Washington, DC: Author.

Electronic sources

An electronic publication, author known
  Heuer, J. (1999). Keeping an open mind. In *Psychology of intelligence analysis* (chap. 6). Retrieved 20 July 2007, from www.cia.gov/csi/books/19104/art9.html

A web-site, corporate author
  IBM. Home-Page. Retrieved 20 August 2007 from http://www.ibm.com

An article from an online journal
  Myers, T. (2001). Modernity, postmodernity and the future perfect. *New Literary History 32.1.* [Electronic version]. Retrieved 3 August 2007 from http://muse.jhu.edu/journals/new_literary_history/toc/nlh32.1html

Note: Include [electronic version] only if the journal appears also in print format.

Films

Use director's name instead of author's, and production company or distributor instead of publisher:

> Proyas, A. (Director). (1998). *Dark City* [Motion Picture]. United States: New Line Cinema.

Activities

1. Watch or listen to a television or radio interview, and notice how it was conducted. How did the interview compare with the guidelines given in this chapter? How would a different approach have produced other results?

2. Discuss the ways that you could use the following sources of information in a written document. Decide what other sources you would need to consult to complement these.

   ● A university textbook on software engineering.

   ● A report on smoking published by an anti-smoking organisation.

   ● A *Discovery Channel* documentary.

   ● An article on cosmetic surgery published in *Vogue*.

   ● Information on cosmetic surgery published on a plastic surgeon's website.

   ● An article on globalisation written by a left-wing radical.

   ● Data published on an academic's personal web page in a university's website.

   ● A website set up by a special-interest community group emphasising the dangers of genetically modified foods.

   ● A press release published on a major corporation's website.

   ● An interview with a scientist published in *Nature*.

3 Style and Effect

Focus on:

▶ Style and format
▶ Writing clearly, accurately and concisely
▶ Style aesthetics
▶ Cohesion

Even if you have all the conceptual aspects of a written project thought out, and have a plan of the information that you want to communicate, you may find that you get stuck in some other areas. For example, you may find that you have difficulty in putting ideas into words, cannot think how to begin, or how to end, a sentence, or find that your sentences are invariably too short, or too long. Furthermore, since style differs quite drastically from spoken to written form, attempting to write as you speak can only lead to ineffective communication (unless, of course, you are writing dialogue). As the poet T. S. Eliot famously once said, if we spoke as we write, we would find nobody to listen, and if we wrote as we speak, we would find nobody to read. This chapter will give you insights into recognising and choosing appropriate style and expression for particular documents, and in constructing your sentences in an effective and clear manner.

The chapter looks at considerations of word choice, and at the arrangements of words that emphasise different elements and produce varying degrees of objectivity and subjectivity. These are the components of style: the effect produced by combinations of balance, emphasis and tone. Just as the clothes you wear, your hairstyle and the way you move give away much about your status, personality and cultural affiliations, your choice of style and grammar tells your readers whether what you say concerns them, and whether they should read it as serious, humorous, urgent, and so on. Stylistic choices 'colour' writing, making the first and longest lasting impression.

● Audience considerations

The most important considerations in choosing your style are audience and purpose. If writing for complete outsiders or novices, for example, you may find that to be clear you have to use definitions and explanations that lengthen the text. If that is what would ensure reader understanding, then so be it – you cannot be as concise and direct in this situation as would be appropriate in a different situation. Also, when writing about a delicate or controversial topic, you will need to take care to avoid using phrases that are loaded with offensive connotations, especially if the audience is the general public. Phrases with offensive connotations would be suitable, however, if your purpose was to provoke! Similarly, it is sometimes impossible to be precise when quantifying a situation. In that case you could give a range, average, or approximation. In all cases, choose a style that supports your message and is aligned to the situation in which your writing takes place.

In all, clarity and writer–reader complicity should guide your stylistic choices. When reading others' writing, use the guidelines given in this chapter to analyse and understand what flatters you, offends you, leaves you indifferent, angers you, enlightens you or seduces you. Then use the insights you gain to control your own writing.

Finally, a word on formatting documents addressed to the general public. In addition to the style of writing, the visual aspect of a document is very important, especially in public or mass media documents where the aim is to draw attention, or to catch the reader's eye as they are skimming through a magazine or newsletter, or scanning through a brochure. Research on audience response has indicated that people are more likely to tackle a document that does not look cluttered. It is therefore advisable to leave as much white space as practicable in public documents.

In addition, similar research has found that we live in a screen-based culture with television acting as the basic text standard. In contrast to the pre-television era, when people approached a text from a left-to-right and top-to-bottom orientation (as in reading), the general public would now be expected to approach a text from the centre. For this reason, advertising space in newspapers tends to be more expensive at the centre than at the sides. This is a useful tip for when you are formatting and ordering a document aimed at the wider public, such as an information brochure. It is not as prominent in formal business writing, such as reports, where the attention of the audience is more reliably secured.

⬤ A typology of style

Classifications and typologies impose sometimes artificial boundaries between elements that are often as inclusive as they are exclusive. They can be useful, however, in highlighting similarities and differences in the composition of these elements. The following typology of style is not intended as representing distinct and unchanging wholes. Rather, it suggests some criteria that could be used to discern and understand stylistic choices that produce different effects, and that are conventionally expected in different contexts of communication. Just as it is inappropriate to attend an executive board meeting in your pyjamas, so it would be inappropriate to adopt an informal style for a formal occasion and vice versa.

In many cases, written material can be classified as a certain document format. As a simple illustration of this point, think about how a shopping list looks when compared with a car manual, or a letter compared with a script for a play. Knowing what type of text we are reading helps to clue us into what sort of language we might expect the writers to use, how they will organise their material, whether they are likely to include graphs and other illustrative material, and so on.

Traditionally, text types have been classified under genres, with such titles as expository, persuasive, narrative, etc. However, this classification can be misleading as many texts are actually multi-generic (i.e. they contain more than one type of mode of expression). For this reason, when analysing a piece of writing it is more useful to focus on style than text format. This classification recognises that one text format, say a report, can contain sections composed in a different genre and style.

This book looks at two main types of style, which we can call **specialist** and **journalistic**. The basic distinguishing criterion between them is audience dynamics. Specialist style addresses a specific audience who may have insider knowledge of the subject, or at least a vested interest in it. Journalistic style addresses the general public and is the preferred choice when the writer wants to increase the popularity of a topic, or publicise a product. Note that this distinction is based on stylistic choices of words and sentence structures and not on the truth value of the content – for example, science fiction texts are written extensively in specialist style even though their content is based primarily on imagination.

Specialist style

Specialist style is suitable for an audience with a specific interest in the topic, because they may be managers, administering the business aspects of your professional field (as in reports to management or to team members), or have a practical interest in accessing the knowledge offered, often because they want expert advice on how to solve a problem (as in reports to clients). Characteristics of this style are:

- Strong use of quantitative or quantifiable information: where possible give numbers, facts and measurable data – but make sure you explain them.
- Factual tone produced by minimal use of evaluative adjectives: avoid words that show personal preference, such as 'wonderful', 'horrendous', 'delightful', 'heartbreaking', etc.

- Use of abstract entities as agents of actions rather than people: where possible, use words that refer to things as agents in a sentence. For example, it would be better to say, 'The project is developing on time' instead of 'I am developing the project on time', and 'Data suggest ...' instead of 'I think ...'.
- Focus on the topic rather than on readers' anticipated response towards it: avoid using direct questions, such as, 'Don't you think that . . . ?', or 'Wouldn't you . . . ?' and expressions that attempt to tangle the reader in appeals to common sense, such as, 'We all feel that . . .', 'Of course, everybody knows . . .'.
- Description and analysis of topic, presented with critical distance: describe a situation objectively, even if you have strong feelings about it.
- Use of listing and points: include some bullet points or numbered lists to highlight, detail or prioritise information.
- Use of complete words. Avoid the use of contractions ('it's for it is', 'haven't for have not', etc.), as they give writing a 'spoken language' or 'chatty' tone.

Here are extracts from the introduction and conclusion of a report written by the IT manager of an insurance company to department managers, on the dangers of new computer viruses for the functioning of the company's network. Notice the direct approach that tackles the main topic immediately, the use of specifics, such as names and dates, and the impersonal presentation of facts.

> This report examines the type of computer viruses that are currently circulating and that constitute the greatest threat to the company's network system during 2007. The viruses discussed are Sircam, Love Bug and Code Red. These are especially destructive and attack the Windows operating system, especially through Outlook and MP3, which form the backbone of the company's network.
>
> Given the insidious nature of these viruses, prevention is very important. All employees should follow these precautions:
>
> - Make sure the anti-virus software installed on all computers is functioning and updated. Check the bottom right corner of screens for an icon of a sealed computer monitor. If this is not there, contact the System Support section immediately.

- Do not open any suspicious email attachments. Open only those attachments that you are expecting or that are clearly justified.
- Make sure all important files are backed up so that information can be retrieved even if a virus attacks or deletes files.

Journalistic style

Because it addresses a very wide audience, and comes in a variety of formats, journalistic style is more complex and harder to define. The main purposes of documents written in this style are to inform the public of a development or event, to entertain them by presenting a personal commentary on an issue that is of collective concern, or to influence and motivate them to adopt a certain attitude towards an issue. In this respect, anything that popularises a subject would use journalistic techniques to an extent. Popular science, for instance, is written in this style. In fact, even some academic or professional textbooks, including this one, are written in journalistic style, as they too aim to present specialist information in a readily accessible manner that can be understood by non-specialists.

Journalistic writing can vary from factual (such as reporting news stories), to informative (such as the scripting of scientific documentaries), to promotional (such as marketing products in business publications), and to polemic (such as the opinionated and biased style of editorials). The next chapter is devoted to an analysis of journalistic writing. As regards style, the general characteristics of journalistic writing are:

- Chatty tone produced by colloquial words and phrases, question–answer format and sentence fragments
- Appeal to emotion and common sense
- Consistent use of generalities and exaggeration
- Consistent use of imperatives (sentences that begin with command words) and exclamations
- Direct address to the reader: 'you' and 'we'
- Dramatisation of events through use of colourful metaphors and visual language

Here is an extract from a journalistic piece written by the same IT manager that wrote the specialist example of the previous section. This time the manager is writing for the IT column of a local newspaper, and dealing with the same topic as his report – computer viruses. Notice the chatty tone, the direct address to the reader and the use of exaggeration:

Be prepared for Armageddon. Just as you are farewelling last year's unprecedented cataclysm of computer viruses, a whole new army – better, smarter and stronger- is marching in.

What can you do? Sit tight. If you don't already own anti-virus software, invest in some. If somebody sends you a love email, resist the temptation – don't open it. Love Bug is rampant. In case the worst happens, copy your files on memory sticks and CDs. Remember, do something before a virus attacks: better safe than sorry!

● Writing clearly, accurately and concisely

The above section describes the differences between specialist and journalist styles. There are also, however, some similarities. Both types compose documents that describe, inform and explain more than theorise, speculate or elaborate, as is the case with academic documents, for instance. Therefore, both specialist and journalist writing is more effective when it is clear, accurate and concise.

Writers spend a lot of time researching and thinking about the best words and sentence structures to create the desired effect on target audiences. To be successful as a writer, and especially one with a serious public responsibility, you must have an eye for detail. As Stephen King advises, to create compelling writing that impacts on readers' perceptions, 'you must take your objective one bloody word at a time' (King, 2000: 136). Here we look at some tips to help you write effectively.

Clarity

Clarity encompasses precision and conciseness. In most cases, the more precise and concise your writing is, the clearer it is. Obscure expression and verbosity are not, generally, conducive to clarity. Clarity should be assessed from the point of view of the reader, so attempt to take the reader's perspective when composing a document. Although in the planning stage you are writing for yourself, when revising adopt the reader's point of view in order to clarify your ideas and give direction to your writing.

One way to assist clarity is to be as specific as possible. This is achieved by knowing exactly what you want to communicate and to whom, and by choosing relevant information to convey your message. Make sure each piece, section or chapter is about one topic only and that all information you give relates to that topic. Avoid changing the topic or including irrelevant information. Also, avoid writing in a way that forces the reader to waste time by rereading the document to decipher 'hidden meaning'. For example, the following announcement would have been very clear to those who wrote it or 'insiders', but very confusing for passers-by and visitors:

> Due to renovations, the first floor will be on the second floor, half the third floor will be on the second floor and half will remain on the third. Second floor will move to the third.

In addition to having a clear focus, follow a logical pattern of organisation that will be easy for the reader to understand. Usually, this means going from the more general to the more specific, from assumed shared knowledge to new knowledge, from 'big picture' to details, or from definition of a problem to its analysis and then to its proposed solution. When revising the document, keep in mind that the reader should not have to go backwards or forwards to understand your message but can continue reading in a linear order.

One test of the quality of professional writing is the ease with which it can be summarised. If you find a document is hard to summarise, chances are that it needs revising to refine it of digressions, ambiguities or inconsistencies. Use this test on both yours and other people's writing.

At the sentence level, clarity is often achieved in these ways:

1. Favour topic–action structures.   This means focusing your intended meaning on the central parts of the sentence, the subject, verb and object. Begin by naming the agent or main topic and proceed by specifying the action, what the agent does. For example, the following sentence, on the costumes of players in a game, has 'the first player' as the subject of the first part of the sentence and 'the keeper' as the subject of the second. This is misleading, however, because the intended subject is actually each player's costume and not the players themselves.

Confusing: The first player wears a special leather suit that is designed for fast movement and the ability to slip through the opponent's clutches, while the keeper wears a heavily padded costume to protect him from aggressive attacks.

Revised: The first player's special leather costume is designed for fast movement and slipping through the opponent's clutches, while the keeper's costume is heavily padded to protect him from aggressive attacks.

Also, the following sentence includes the redundant and confusing ideas of 'design' and 'ability' when the aim is to describe what a prototype does:

Confusing: The prototype is designed to ensure that it would be able to maintain consistency among all products of the same series.

Revised: The prototype ensures consistency among all products of the same series.

2. Avoid more than two nouns in a row.

Sometimes writers try to make their writing more concise and technical by eliminating prepositions (in, of, etc.), and linking nouns in a chain. Unfortunately, this is often done at the expense of clarity and accuracy. Make sure that elegant style and clarity win over brevity and the tendency to repeat jargon indiscriminately.

Confusing: He designed a new graphics construction language.

Revised: He designed a new language for constructing graphics.

Confusing: The project includes a long-term failure prevention program.

Revised: The project includes a long-term program to prevent failure; or The project includes a program to prevent long-term failure.

3. Break up long sentences,

especially if they contain more than one piece of information. Usually, sentences that contain one piece of information, even if this includes details on that item – are clearer to grasp in one reading.

Confusing: Although this methodology has been tested worldwide on different formats and has been hailed as the most effective currently available, we have decided not to use it in this experiment because the present situation requires more rigorous techniques of controlling testing procedure.

Revised: This methodology has been tested worldwide on different formats and has been hailed as the most effective currently available. However, the present situation requires more rigorous techniques of controlling testing procedure. Consequently, in this experiment, we have decided not to use it.

Confusing: This is a science fiction action film set in the year 2025 about a self-centred superstar of a world sport phenomenon called Destruktion, which has eclipsed the popularity of all sports, who is targeted by a terrorist group.

Revised: This is a science fiction action film, set in the year 2025, when a world sport phenomenon called Destruktion has eclipsed the popularity of all other sports. The film is about a self-centred superstar of this sport, who is targeted by a terrorist group.

4. Position phrases correctly. When you order words and phrases in a sentence, make sure that nouns agree with all their subject positions. It can be especially misleading when the noun immediately following an opening phrase cannot be identified with the noun of the phrase. This has the effect of confusing agents and actions and potentially leading to incorrect attribution of responsibility.

Confusing: As an experienced manager, my boss gives me little supervision.

Revised: Because I am an experienced manager, my boss gives me little supervision.

5. Position information effectively. If you do not intend emphasis, position the main or most important information (the result of the action) at the end of the sentence. However, if you do intend emphasis then position the item that you want emphasised in a prominent position, usually at the beginning of the sentence.

Emphatic: The end of a sentence is the place where important information should appear.

Non-emphatic: The place in a sentence where important information should appear is at the end.

Accuracy

To make your writing more accurate, follow these guidelines:

1. Favour quantification. If you can give measurements and numbers, instead of ambiguous words, then do so.

Vague: This policy has been effective for several years.

Revised: This policy has been effective since 1995.

Vague: Many people attended the event.

Revised: About 200 people attended the event; *or* Attendance for the event this year was 20 per cent higher than last year.

2. Avoid words with many meanings. Think of a word that is specific to the meaning you intend in the sentence. For example, a commonly used word with many meanings is *over*:

During	The experiment must take place over the winter
Onto	The fertilizer was spread over the field
More than	This disease affects over 10 per cent of the population
From	We collected data over three locations
Of	Apply two replications over six dilutions
To	Statistical sampling was applied over the data
Across	Sampling was stratified over taxonomic groups
Through	Dust accumulates over time
With	The company policies changed over time

Consider some examples with the word *wrong*:

Vague:	The decision was wrong.
Revised:	The decision was financially costly for the company.
Vague:	This number is wrong.
Revised:	This number is incorrect.
Vague:	Cheating is wrong.
Revised:	Cheating is unethical.
Vague:	He was wearing the wrong clothes.
Revised:	He was dressed inappropriately.

Words that have many meanings also include evaluative adjectives whose meaning is relative to the speaker's judgement such as 'nice', 'terrible', 'good', 'big', etc.:

Vague:	This team contains good members.
Revised:	This team contains conscientious and hard-working members.
Vague:	The manager's decision was terrible.
Revised:	The manager's decision was irresponsible; or
	The manager's decision was based on short-term profit only.

3. Define terms and favour specific words instead of phrases, where possible. This sharpens your writing, making it more direct. However, be careful not to offend readers by putting them in categories and labelling them. Discretion is advised.

Vague:	Clear documentation pleases people and may increase the people who buy our software.
Revised:	Clear documentation pleases users and may increase our clients.

Vague: Strict regulations are in place to protect against people who break into computers and steal information.

Revised: Strict regulations are in place to protect against hackers.

Conciseness

The above sections show that, to be clear and accurate, you sometimes need to expand on a point, and use more words. This does not condone verbosity or 'babbling', however. Being direct is important in professional writing if for no other reason than because, in many cases, 'time is money', and readers want to know if a document answers their question or addresses their need without having to analyse it in detail. Some writers believe that by including as many details as possible and repeating information they become clearer. Trying to 'drill in' information, however, may draw attention away from the main message and confuse the reader. In most cases, by stating clearly and directly your point at strategic points in the document you have a better chance of getting your intended meaning across.

You can make your writing concise by avoiding long, crowded and wordy sentences, especially if they are in succession. If you write one or two long sentences, make sure the next sentence is short to break the density. Also, following these tips will help:

1. Favour the active voice where possible. Passive sentences are wordier, and can also be confusing if they do not reveal the agent of an action.

Wordy: The work was finished by the engineers before the deadline was reached.

Revised: The engineers finished the work before the deadline.

Wordy: The policy decision was met with disapproval by the public.

Revised: The public disapproved of the policy decision.

2. Avoid 'there is/are' at the beginning of sentences.   In many cases, we overuse these words, even when they are not necessary.

Wordy: There are several conclusions that we can draw from these results.

Revised: We can draw several conclusions from these results; *or* From these results, we conclude . . .

Wordy: There are several organisations that belong to the union.

Revised: Several (*give number*) organisations belong to the union.

3. Use modals (may, might, could, should, must) where possible. Some harbour suspicion that modals are informal; however, this is not true. Modals modify verbs and have a clear place in language.

Wordy: It is possible that the project will be funded.
Revised: The project may be funded.
Wordy: It is imperative that all options be considered before making a decision.
Revised: All options must be considered before deciding.

4. Use verbs where possible instead of nouns. Besides making sentences concise, verbs are action-oriented and give your writing a more direct tone.

Wordy: The experiments are not a demonstration of myogenesis.
Revised: The experiments do not demonstrate myogenesis.
Wordy: A vacuum chamber is not a requirement for this procedure.
Revised: This procedure does not require a vacuum chamber.

5. Avoid weak verbs.   Some verbs, instead of signalling action, depend on a noun to support them. In many cases, such verbs can be replaced by other verbs that do not require a noun such as 'take', 'make', 'do', 'give', etc.

Wordy: Researchers conducted an investigation of myogenesis.
Revised: Researchers investigated myogenesis.
Wordy: This study serves to show the results of the experiment.
Revised: This study shows the results of the experiment.

6. Use punctuation strategically.   If you find that your paragraph is getting cluttered with too many wordy or long sentences, it is often possible to use punctuation to cut down on words. This is especially effective when announcing or introducing a list of items.

Wordy: There are many reasons for climatic change, which include toxic pollution, deforestation and volcanic activity.
Revised: There are many reasons for climatic change: toxic pollution, deforestation and volcanic activity.
Wordy: Most professional writing can be divided into three categories. These categories are essays, reports and articles.
Revised: Most professional writing can be divided into three categories – essays, reports and articles.

7. Avoid wordy clichés. Some phrases are so commonly used in spoken language that they have become almost unconscious. Writing, nevertheless, gives you the opportunity to become more conscious of how you use language and allows for elimination of repetitive material. Here is a list of such clichés.

COMMON WORDY CLICHÉS

Wordy	Concise
a majority of	many (or number)
a number of	some (or number)
subsequent to	after
due to the fact that	because
for the purpose of	to
have the capability to	can
in the event that	if
so as to	to
in order to	to
with regard to	about
has the ability to	can
give a summary of	summarise
make an assumption about	assume
come to the conclusion that	conclude
take action	act
make a decision	decide
make a proposal about	propose
basic essentials	essentials
end result	result
cancel out	cancel
enter into	enter
completely eliminate	eliminate
at this point in time	now
there can be little doubt	definitely, certainly
in the absence of	without
higher in comparison with	higher than
may be the mechanism responsible for	may be why

● Aesthetics of style

Like other media, professional writing does not aim only to inform but also to please. Correct grammar, precision and conciseness are, therefore, not the only criteria by which to judge a written text. The text should also be diplomatic, elegant and sophisticated, and should give readers the feeling of being respected at the same time as being informed or motivated.

The best way to achieve this aim is by knowing the values, knowledge and interests of your audience. This will determine your choice of being formal, impersonal, chatty, hip, 'cool', or whatever other tone you think will be most appropriate. Keep in mind that style and content are two different things; your style will have a strong effect on how the reader accepts or understands your content but will not determine what this content actually is. For example, all these sentences contain the same information, but each construction combines different degrees of balance, emphasis and tone. Notice how each has a different nuance and reader effect:

(a)   Seen leaving the bank were two masked men with guns.

(b)   Two masked men were seen leaving the bank carrying guns.

(c)   Two masked men went out of the bank, and they were holding guns.

(d)   Holding their guns, the two robbers walked out of the bank.

(e)   It was as they were leaving the bank that the two armed thieves were seen.

(f)   What people saw was the shining steel of the guns that the two robbers carried as they left the bank.

The versions could be multiplied, but what this experiment shows is that you can draw attention to different parts of a topic by re-ordering parts of a sentence and, similarly, of a larger text. The changes in style in the above sentences are also a change in focus. Look more closely at some of these sentences.

Sentence (a) focuses on the event from an external perspective, with the 'seer' being an impersonal entity that watches from a bird's-eye point of view, from above. Therefore, this 'seer' is likely to be identified with the general public, and it is no surprise that this sentence would be the one most associated with newspaper headlines. Sentence (b) is similar in that it too is constructed in the passive, but the focus here is on the men rather than on the event, making the 'seer' more local and less public.

Sentence (d) is the one most closely constructed from the robbers' point of view, because it omits an external 'seer', and instead gives both verbs ('hold', 'walk') the same subject ('robbers'). Therefore, this sentence would go well in the robbers' story. Sentence (f) begins with the emphatic 'what' and then focuses on the guns, drawing attention to an object of fear. A common strategy in terror tactics, this stylistic device makes sentence (f) the most sensationalist in the list.

This brief analysis shows how written language creates images by orchestrating its units (words, sentences and paragraphs) in different combinations. Assume control over this stylistic manipulation by becoming aware of it in what you write and read.

Sentences and phrases

The first stage where you begin your crafting of style is the sentence. Therefore, the more practice you give yourself in constructing different types of sentences and observing their effects the better. This section gives the grammatical terminology of sentence categories.

The minimal definition of a sentence is a word group that contains a *subject* (someone or something that carries out an action) and a *verb* (the action carried out). This minimal word group is called a *clause*. Many sentences also contain an *object* (the recipient of the action, or the thing or person acted upon).

The report	recommended	changes
Subject	Verb	Object

If the word group has no subject or no verb, but still makes some basic sense by evoking an image, it is a *phrase*. This is not a complete sentence; it is a fragment. Fragments do have their place in writing: they create colourful and imagistic effects. However, although their use is justified and often even expected in creative writing and many kinds of journalism, fragments are basically ungrammatical and should be avoided in formal or specialist style.

Phrase: Trying to come to a decision
Sentence: Trying to come to a decision, the project members considered all options

To write complete sentences, make sure you have these qualities:

1. *A verb that shows time.*   Something happens or is described in the past, present or future. If the word group has no verb at all, it is a fragment, because nothing happens. Also, make sure your verb has a tense (time element). Even if a word group contains a verb, it fails as a complete sentence if the verb has no tense. Remember that gerunds (-ing words) and infinitives (-to do words) are not tensed verbs and can function as nouns or participles.

> *Fragment*:   The committee considering the proposal
>   ↓
> *Sentence*:   The committee considered the proposal
> *Sentence*:   The committee considers the proposal
> *Sentence*:   The committee will consider the proposal

2. *The absence of a subordinating word.*   A word group ceases to be a complete sentence if one of the following words or phrases is placed in front of it:

after	if	until
although	in case	when
as	provided that	whenever
as if	since	whereas
as though	so that	whether
because	that	which
before	unless	while

Consider, for example, this:

> While common law has long implied that there is a requirement for mutual respect and fair dealings in the employment relationship.

The 'while' at the beginning of the sentence implies that there is a second part to this sentence, which contrasts with the information given in the first. Without this second part, the sentence is not complete. To correct this problem, either put a comma after 'relationship' and add another clause, or take away 'while'.

Types of sentences

Sentences are classified into four categories:

- *Simple sentences* contain one main clause:

The report recommended changes.

- *Compound sentences* contain two or more main clauses connected with conjunctions:

  The report recommended changes, and established deadlines.

- *Complex sentences* contain one main clause and one or more subordinate clauses (clauses that would be fragments if disconnected from the main clause):

  (a) The report, which will form the basis of our decision, recommended changes.

  (b) The report recommended changes because these are the only way to solve the problem.

- *Compound-complex sentences* contain two or more main clauses and one or more subordinate clauses:

  The report recommended changes and established deadlines, because that is the only way to solve the problem.

Note that sentence types are more about the prioritisation of information than about length. In fact, a simple sentence can be much longer than a complex one, as seen in these examples:

Complex sentence:	The key that opens the door is small.
Simple sentence:	Early in the morning, in the dusky summer sunlight, the tall, blond man and his dog came out of the building from the back door, slowly and surreptitiously.

Sentences and style

Following the above guidelines, here are some tips on choosing your style:

Include variety. No document is justifiably boring, so make sure you introduce rhythm by alternating long and short sentences, using some active and some passive voice, and beginning some sentences with phrases rather than with subject-verb construction. For example, this extract from a report is concise, grammatically correct and precise. However, stylistically it is displeasing to the reader and monotonous, because of its succession of simple, short sentences and lack of linking words between sentences:

> Emailing is the most common Internet activity. Some of the infor-
> mation on emails is of sensitive nature. A technically savvy person
> can intercept emails. This person then has access to the informa-
> tion. In fact, there is little awareness of email's lack of security
> among general users.

In constructing your document, use a variety of simple and complex
sentences, with short, simple sentences for information you wish to emphasise. Because they condense meaning in a few words, short, simple
sentences have the greatest impact on the reader. The more you expand a
sentence, the more dissipated the meaning becomes. For example:

> The project team sent the data to the laboratory for testing. They
> expect the results back within two hours of dispatch. *It's not always
> so.* Sometimes they have to wait for hours, which means their
> whole project could be jeopardised. *It's a risky business.*

Notice how the two italicised sentences carry a lot of weight in this passage
because they comment on the rest of the information. They are also the
shortest of the five sentences.

Use subordination carefully.   Information in a sentence can either come
in the main clause or in a subordinate clause. The main clause foregrounds
information; the subordinate clause diminishes information. For example,
consider this sentence:

> The proposal, which was approved by the Board, will be imple-
> mented immediately.

The most important information here is in the main clause: 'The proposal
will be implemented immediately'. The subordinate clause, 'which was
approved by the Board yesterday', gives secondary information, or information that is assumed to be known by the audience and therefore back-
grounded. When using complex sentences with one or a number of
subordinate clauses, think carefully about whether what you subordinate
should not be given more importance by coming in a separate sentence as a
main clause. Remember that what you subordinate is received by your
reader, consciously or unconsciously, as secondary in relation to what you
give as main information. So, consider the rewrite of the above sentence:

> The proposal was approved by the Board. It will be implemented
> immediately.

Here the two items of information are balanced by being placed in two separate sentences – neither item is subordinated.

When writing complex sentences with more than one subordinate clause, be aware that the ways you combine main with subordinate clauses creates different effects. The different combinations are called loose structure, centred structure, and periodic structure. Here are the effects of each:

Loose: Sharks can be very dangerous when they smell blood, although they may not always be hungry.

Loose structures begin with the main clause and add subordinate clauses at the end. They project a relaxed, informal style imitating a conversation.

Centred: When they smell blood, sharks can be very dangerous, although they may not always be hungry.

Centred structures begin with a subordinate clause, then give the main clause, and end with another subordinate clause. They project a tighter and more formal sentence that gives the impression you are dealing with a complicated or serious matter.

Periodic: Although they may not be hungry, when they smell blood, sharks can be very dangerous.

Periodic structures begin with the subordinate clause(s) and lead to the main clause. They suggest that the information in the main clause is conditional on other factors, or that you concede a point to an opponent before asserting your opinion. Use this structure carefully, because, although it may increase the importance of the main clause, it delays it and could annoy the reader. Think about whether leading to a statement with a degree of suspense would be appropriate for the audience and purpose. This structure is more common in texts intended for oral speech, such as documentaries, than in formal report writing.

Use first and second person pronouns (I, my, you, we, our) differently in journalistic and specialist documents.   These pronouns refer to the writer and to the reader and are important in establishing a communicative link between the two parties. Overuse of 'I' constructions, however, can give your document a simplistic or, otherwise, arrogant appearance.

Similarly 'you' constructions can be inappropriately didactic or accusative, if used in cases where a more impersonal phrasing would be more appropriate. In many cases, as in formal reports for example, you are expected to focus on aspects of a situation and not on the reader's response to this situation. To decide on the best of use of pronouns, assess the nature and degree of audience complicity that you need to create.

For example, this extract is adapted from an editorial in *New Scientist* (30 June 2001). The uses it makes of personal pronouns is typical of journalistic editorials, but it would be highly inappropriate to choose this style in business writing, say, in a formal report to a client:

> So, it turns out that poisonous polychlorinated biphenyls (PCB) are turning up in our food more often than we thought. Should we panic? PCBs are in everyday food in high concentrations and we aren't even monitoring them. It makes you wonder what else is out there.

● Cohesion and transition

Cohesion

Cohesion words and phrases (or 'linkers' and 'signpost' words, as they are often called) show the relationship between one sentence and the next. Your train of thought will usually seem so obvious to you as not to be worth stating. But if you do not make it clear, you will force your reader to laboriously 'reverse engineer' your writing to discover your meaning. In professional writing, your reader may not have the time or inclination to do that.

If, for instance, the sentence you are writing is meant to contradict the meaning of the previous sentence, it is not a good idea to leave the contradiction sitting there, looking like a mistake. Signal actively to the reader that you intend a contradiction, by using 'but', 'however', 'in spite of', or some similar linking word or phrase – and make sure you use the correct grammatical structure to accommodate the linker you have used. If one sentence contains the result or consequence of a previous sentence, again, do not leave the reader to infer that you are talking about a result or consequence. Signal it by using 'consequently', 'as a result', etc. Remember to use signpost words if the relation between ideas is not obvious. Overusing such words or phrases can be tiring for the reader and can at times produce a condescending or harsh effect that may be detrimental to the quality of your document.

Table 4 gives some cohesion words that provide cohesion, and the relationships they express.

In addition to such cohesion words, methods for achieving cohesion include the strategic use of **synonyms**, the use of **referential pronouns** and **parallel structures**.

Type	Function	Examples
Enumerative	Introduces order in which points will be made	First, second; one, two; a, b; next, then, subsequently, finally, in the end
Additive	Reinforces or confirms what was said	Again, then again, also, moreover, furthermore, in addition, what is more
	Highlights similarity	Equally, likewise, similarly, correspondingly, In the same way
Logical sequence	Summarises the preceding	So, so far, altogether, overall, then
	Shows results of the preceding	So, as a result, consequently, hence, now, therefore, thus
	Explains or reformulates	Namely, in other words, that is to say, better, rather
Explanatory	Introduces examples	For example, for instance
Illustrative	Notes alternative	Alternatively, or again, or rather, but then, on the other hand
Contrastive	Shows opposite	Conversely, instead, on the contrary, by contrast, on the other hand
	Concedes the unexpected in view of the preceding	However, nevertheless, notwithstanding, still, though, yet, despite that, all the same, at the same time
Qualifying	Evaluates or expresses an attitude towards a statement	Surprisingly, in the final analysis, paradoxically

Table 4   Discourse markers and the relationships they express

Synonyms

Synonyms are words of closely related meaning and provide an effective solution to the problem of excessive repetition. In the hands of a competent writer, cohesion consists of a blend of repetition and variation. If you said 'approach' in one sentence and had to repeat the idea, you might choose 'method' in the next sentence. If you said 'skill', you could then use 'ability', and so on. That would give your reader variety without changing the meaning.

When using synonyms, be careful not to overuse them. Overwhelming the reader with a big range of words for an object or concept can be confusing and detracts from the clarity of your document. In certain cases, especially with regard to technical terminology, it is better to repeat a term rather than replace it with a synonym. Discretion is advised in this case.

Referential pronouns

If two sentences begin with the same subject, it is sufficient to use a personal or referential pronoun in the second sentence instead of the word itself (I, he, she, it, we, you, they, this, that, these):

> The report claims that the new incentive to include all financial figures in Intranet documents has not led to an increased interest in the company's economic development. *It* adds that most stockholders do not know how to access Intranet information.

However, guard against ambiguity: sometimes the use of a pronoun instead of a noun can be confusing, especially if there are several nouns in the previous sentence to which the pronoun might refer. In this case, it is better to repeat the noun:

> *Incorrect:* The report claims that the new incentive to include all financial figures in Intranet documents has not led to an increased interest in the company's economic development. Although *they* (?) are now available, most stockholders do not know how to access Intranet information.
>
> *Revised:* The report claims that the new incentive to include all financial figures in Intranet documents has not led to an increased interest in the company's economic development. Although *these figures* are now available, most stockholders do not know how to access Intranet information.

Parallel structures

Parallelism adds clarity to your paragraph. Parallelism refers to the similar grammatical structure of headings and sentences within a paragraph. The more mathematically inclined will recognise the distributive law in mathematics as analogous to parallelism in language: $x(a + b) = xa + xb$. The common element must work grammatically with each of the parallel elements; the grammatically parallel elements could be substituted for each other without needing to change the rest of the sentence. Check for parallelism when you include items within one category, or balance items on one level of information.

Not parallel:	These books are not primarily for reading, but they are used for reference.
Parallel:	These books are not primarily for reading but for reference.
Not parallel:	Not only is he a conscientious worker, but also he is very competent
Parallel:	Not only is he conscientious but also competent.
Not parallel:	Don't underestimate the value of defining technical terms. Prior knowledge on behalf of the reader should not be assumed
Parallel:	Don't underestimate the value of defining technical terms. Don't assume prior knowledge on behalf of the reader.
Not parallel:	Possible solutions for dealing with at-risk youth include implementing programmes and support measures through parent and child education, housing and physical, social and economic conditions should be changed.
Parallel:	Possible solutions for dealing with at-risk youth include implementing programmes and support measures through parent and child education, improving housing and changing physical, social and economic conditions.

Parallelism is very important in instructions, point lists and headings. For example, here are four introductions to a printer user guide:

A. Setting up the printer, maintenance, and what to do if something goes wrong are easy with Apple's step-by-step user guide.

B. Setting up the printer, maintaining it and troubleshooting are easy with Apple's step-by-step user guide.

C. Printer set-up, maintenance, and troubleshooting are easy with Apple's step-by-step user guide.

D. Apple's step-by-step user guide will show you how to set up the printer, how to maintain it, and what to do if something goes wrong.

Version A is awkward because the three elements that it lists are not parallel. The other three correct this error. Notice also how although all three are grammatically correct, there are slight differences in nuance with each choice. C with its noun emphasis is the most formal version, while D, with its clause structure and second person pronoun, is the most informal.

Transition

Transitional words, phrases and sentences regulate the flow of paragraphs and sections. You can transit from one paragraph to another using the techniques described in the above section. You could also use transitional sentences and, in longer documents, even transitional paragraphs between one section and another. Two common forms of transition are:

(a) *Using a short sentence to state briefly what you intend to say in the next paragraph.* You might say, 'So far we have been discussing unemployment. Now we consider inflation.' This could come at the end of one paragraph or at the beginning of the next, depending on length of paragraphs and on desired effect: the new paragraph would begin more intensely if its topic had already been introduced in the previous paragraph.

(b) *Repeating a key word or phrase so as to echo the point made in a previous paragraph.* You can also use synonyms for this purpose. For example, notice how this technique is used in the following extract from an article on evolution. I italicise the transitional sentences and the cohesive devices within each paragraph:

> Understanding the shape of the tree of life and the details of its branches is more than a quaint sideline of biology, even though the science of this quest – known as systematics – has come to be regarded by many biologists as dowdy and old fashioned, little more than stamp collecting. *But* such an understanding is probably the best foundation for a larger appreciation of life, including evolution, ecology and behaviour. *As* Colin Patterson, a palaeontologist at the Natural History Museum of London,

says: 'To retrieve the history of life, to reconstruct the evolutionary tree, is still the aim of evolutionary biology.' *Getting it right is therefore important.*

Getting it right, however, is much harder than might be imagined. Inferring an evolutionary relationship from morphology rests on identifying anatomical features, or characters, that are shared by two species because of their common descent. *Such features* might include the shape of teeth, the form of a particular nerve canal, the number of certain flower parts, and so on. *Ironically*, the thing most likely to confound the well-intentioned systematist in identifying such characters is the power of natural selection itself. Many shared characteristics do not reflect a common ancestry, but instead are the result of distantly related species independently adapting their bodies to meet the demands of similar lifestyles. (Lewin, 1998, p. 37, *my emphasis*).

Activities

1. Analyse a business document with regard to the sentence structures used. Notice the effects of each sentence. Then select a section and rewrite in a totally different style by changing the sentence structure. What differences did you make to the balance, emphasis and tone?

2. The following sentences are grammatically correct. However, they are inappropriate for professional writing because of ambiguity and/or wordiness. Restructure the sentences to make them more suited to a professional context.

    (a) This program has a graphics design capability.

    (b) The security guards working at night have the responsibility of checking all offices.

    (c) There is a possibility that they will try to buy us off.

    (d) We opened the project to suggestions with a view to being able to get some ideas on the improvement of the security of the building.

    (e) The Department Manager was not told of the decision, which was foolish.

    (f) Since we hired the new technical assistant, the quality of the equipment has improved.

(g) His project will involve a big investigation into how the monetary economy has evolved.

(h) There are several organisations that are concerned with the destruction of rainforests.

(i) The inspecting officer cannot do a verification of the data until the issuing authority has made a decision on a suitable methodology.

(j) The media could not provide the public with a justification of their manipulation of the information in the news story.

(k) Before submitting the proposal, we must conduct a marketing action analysis.

(l) We may have to check the obsolete operator's manual.

(m) When logging in, the data must be completed fully.

(n) Financial improvement is the greatest effect of the policy change.

(o) The need for more university-educated personnel in government agencies exists.

(p) Due to recent financial fluctuations, we have decided to hire a stability evaluations manager.

(q) Non-computer background personnel can do this task.

(r) To find the committee room, signs have been posted along the corridor.

(s) The possibility of creating bit-map graphics for this project is to be noted.

(t) A detailed analysis of trends and an evaluation of the relations between state and corporation is the purpose of this report.

3. Write as many versions as you can of these sentences, changing the style but leaving the information content the same. Change both sentence structure and word choice:

   (a) Music has been found to have healing properties.
   (b) Scientists have found that if you live in high altitudes, you have a bigger chance of living longer.

4. Here is an extract from a report on the development of a computer game, written by one of the developers to the project manager. The writer follows a 'write as you think' approach, which gives the text a muddled and wordy presentation. Also, the style combines specialist techniques (extensive use of technical terminology) with journalistic elements (chatty tone). Revise and edit the text following the guidelines for clear, precise and concise writing outlined in this chapter.

The game was a drag and drop style board game involving one person directing another person's actions using a set list of verbal commands. The game also recorded moves made during a game for reviewing, either as a textual description or as real-time playback. As well as implementation, documentation of the system was a big part of the project with documents on five major aspects of the system produced. P1, the project plan, described the overall project, what was involved in the current system and our plans to implement a new system. P2, the requirements document, detailed the current system and our proposed solution to the problem presented to us by the client. P3, the architecture document, presented how we intended to develop the system and how it met the requirements determined in the previous document. P4 detailed the user interface of the document and also how it met the requirements of P2. P5, the detailed design document, contained the specifics of the implementation of the system and was intended to be used when coding the system. The documentation was intended to guide the implementation process in order to produce better quality software. I think that the software produced during the project was superior to previous software used for the same reason and I think this can be entirely attributed to following the project software development process.

When I say that the software produced during the project was superior to the software previously used I don't mean that the software produced was a superior piece of software. I think the overall design of our project was a good design that could've been implemented successfully but I do think it was lacking in some areas due to not enough time spend during this phase. It was initially intended that the interfaces would respond to users' commands and pass the responsibility of performing the operations on to various other modules. Little consideration was given to how a textual review would be displayed with regard to getting the information from the storage system to the interface so we ended up with the interface extracting the information from a stored round object.

5. Rewrite the following sentences so that their structures are parallel:

(a) He has the ability both to choose a suitable course of action and he can implement his decision wisely.

(b) Walking quickly burns as many calories as you burn when you run slowly.

(c) Buying a new computer every couple of years you spend a lot of money but it helps you keep up with technological development.

(d) It has been found that *Homo sapiens* has not changed anatomically in the last 10,000 years, and also our intellectual capacities are about the same.

(e) The court found him guilty of insurance fraud and he has been sentenced to two years' imprisonment.

(f) From this report it is recommended that the following initiatives be adopted: links with the Chamber of Commerce and Industry, the viability of an information technology school should be examined and also a scheme, which assists small business with accounting matters, should be established.

6. Improve the cohesion in the following paragraphs by using some of the devices shown above:

(a) The intelligence report is clear: an informer has tipped you off that a terrorist organization is planning an imminent attack on a key military base this week. What should you do? Ignoring the tip-off could be disastrous. The base is very well defended, making any attack pretty suicidal. Taking action is not without its problems. Resources would be diverted from other vulnerable targets. The terrorists could be alerted to the informer in their midst.   (Adapted from Matthews, 1998, p. 29)

(b) Romantic individuality may have something to do with the sport's popularity – the fact that one undertakes a kind of Byronic solo adventure when one jumps. The jumpers do their thing in groups and form little outlaw societies in which they approve of and cheer one another. It could be the illegality of the sport that pumps them up. In an interview last April, Kappfjell said he delighted in playing outlaw and 'fooling the authorities' as he gained access to his perches.   (Adapted from Rosenblatt, 1999)

(c) Complex systems are particularly good for modelling the complexities of the natural world. During the Gulf War, large quantities of oil polluted the sea. This damaged the ecosystem – but how do you go about measuring that damage and monitoring the ecosystem's recovery? Researchers needed to disentangle a complex web of interrelationships.   (Adapted from Stewart, 1998, p. 37)

(d) Explorative graphics enable the user to move about a website by selecting a graphical object. This is an alternative to using text to navigate the website. They make the website more attractive while increasing download time. Excessive use of exploration graphics can confuse a user.

4 Business and Technology Journalism

Focus on:

▶ Types of journalism
▶ Journalistic style
▶ Writing press releases
▶ Writing feature articles

The ability to develop new products, invent new methods for doing things or discover how the universe works also requires the ability to communicate your results to various groups for support, funding or publicity. In such cases, your audience could comprise people who may not have the same level of technical knowledge as you, but who may have an interest, financial or social, in learning about your findings. This chapter looks at techniques that will help you to write an appealing and informative article for a specialist magazine or company newsletter.

As opposed to other kinds of journalistic writing that address the wide public or the general consumer, high-level specialist journalism addresses an audience that is more versed in subject-specific terminology, and that is more motivated in acquiring the information presented. Business journalists, for example, may well promote the marketability of products, but they must also present more detailed and accurate information than consumer advertisers.

In advertising jargon, the language directed to the general consumer is **marketese**: direct selling in a sensational and highly emotive tone – the language of television commercial scripts and popular consumer magazine advertisements. Direct commands aiming to sway consumer preferences are examples of marketese. Because it addresses the wider public, or the consumer in general, marketese lacks specificity and is characterised instead by frequent use of generalities focused on highlighting the benefits of a product for the lowest common denominator of the population. In contrast, high-quality business and technology journalism uses language with a strong informative content, which not only entertains, but also educates. The targeted audience are those who know what their specific needs are, and who can communicate in the jargon of the industry – at least on a basic level.

⬤ A journalism primer

Types of articles

Journalists divide news into hard and soft varieties. **Hard news** is the information that readers need to know: the 'breaking' or 'hit off the press' news of events that happen suddenly and affect a great number of people or a whole community. Hard news is ephemeral. Although the information presented may have serious and long-lasting consequences, the actual news itself becomes outdated quite rapidly. Examples of hard news are reports of war outbreaks, earthquakes or stock market changes. **Soft news**, on the other hand, is the kind of information that people want to hear and its relevance or popularity does not disappear as rapidly as that of hard news. Examples include technological developments, profiles of leaders and fashion research.

These are the basic formats of articles, in the order in which they would generally appear in a magazine.

Editorial

This is an opinion article written by the editor(s), dealing with a current news topic, usually one that is covered at more length later in the issue. Depending on the publication, editorials can be provocative and/or strongly opinionated, with a 'call to arms' approach intended to increase awareness of an issue. In more formal journals, editorials introduce the theme of the issue and briefly present each of the contributors' articles.

News stories

These present the facts in current events and developments. News stories are generally not long – a one-page story would be long; most news stories take up a quarter to half a page. They describe the facts in the event by following the 5W's and 1H questions (what, where, when, who, why and how). News stories follow the inverted pyramid format (see Figure 4 on p. 81), and, in business and technology journalism, they are largely based on press releases (more on this below).

Features

These articles elaborate on topics that may have been news stories weeks or months before. They describe the topic in terms of its history, constituent parts, applications, relevant people, possible benefits and/or dangers. They come in different lengths, and are based on secondary research as well as primary research, such as interviews. The cover story of the magazine is a feature, usually located close to the centre of the publication.

Opinion articles

An issue may have two or three opinion articles of different lengths, and scattered throughout the issue. These present an analysis of a topic in terms of the argument(s) it generates. In some cases, a slot where an opinion article appears (a 'column') becomes associated with a particular writer and his/her style (the 'columnist'). In other cases, opinion articles are written by scholars who specialise on the topic, and who can, therefore, present an expert opinion.

Interviews

This is an article following a question-and-answer form. These articles focus on the contribution to a topic of an individual, and present this topic through the direct words of that individual, spurred by the writer's questions.

Profiles

These articles balance information on a topic with a personal narrative of a key individual associated with the topic. They are similar to interviews in some ways, since, if the profile is of a living person, they are largely based on an interview with that person, with additional or background information from secondary sources.

Reviews

These articles describe and comment on the quality and innovation of a book, film or game. They often compare their object of analysis with others in the field, showing its advantages and drawbacks. For writers, producers and developers, getting a favourable review in a reputable publication is a much desired achievement.

Layout considerations and page design

Magazine layout is pivotal in editorial decisions about length and presentation of articles. Magazines have a set layout, which determines content choices – not the other way around. In other words, a magazine will not change its layout and the space it assigns to each type of article, to accommodate a particular article, no matter how interesting or how important this article may be. The article will be edited and formatted in the magazine's standard manner. This is analogous to buying furniture. It is unlikely that you would demolish walls and restructure the building to fit particular pieces of furniture. It is much more likely that you would measure the space you have and then buy furniture to fit that space. Printing is costly, and changes to templates would make it even costlier.

The following are the main layout considerations:

- *Space* Word limits are required for each article in relation to the space allotted for the article in the magazine template layout.

- *Paragraph length*   Magazine articles generally have shorter paragraphs than reports or essays. Paragraphs would need to be even shorter if printed in columns (more on this below).
- *Visuals*   some articles are graphic-intensive, and others are more verbal. In general, visuals complement effectively documents written in journalistic style. Visuals are chosen to convey meaning more accurately to target audiences, and are designed with the target audience's assumed needs and expectations in mind.
- *Sections and headings* ('crossheads' in journalistic jargon).   Space determines sectioning. Crossheads are used, generally, in longer articles as a form of signposting to direct readers' attention. They are also effective in cutting down on transitional sentences and paragraphs and are used when brevity is required. For example, a sentence or even a paragraph can be deleted if space requires it and its content summarised in a phrase that becomes a section heading. As regards organising content into sections, the general rule for journalistic articles is that they are 'top-heavy', that is, they place important and/or catchy information at the beginning.

Page design is divided into four aspects: **proximity**, **alignment**, **repetition** and **contrast**.

Proximity

This refers to the spatial layout that displays related objects. For example, you should leave more space before a heading than after it. Headings belong to the text that follows them and should be closer to that text. Also, photos and captions should relate to each other and come close to the relevant text. Different elements should be separated by space to create a hierarchy of information.

Alignment

This refers to the horizontal and vertical elements on the page being placed in balanced positions in relation to each other – as opposed to thrown together at random. For example, keep unity on a page by aligning every object with the edge of some other object. In a table, for instance, you could align the objects on the left with the left edge of the page, and the objects on the right with the right edge of the page.

Repetition

This refers to repeating elements that tie different sections together. Bullet points, colours and typefaces can be repeated to provide visual impact and help the reader recognise and scan through the pages quickly and easily. By repeating certain elements, you reinforce the uniqueness, or personality, of a publication, as readers become aware of the characteristic motif of the publication – a bit like a signature.

Contrast

The opposite of repetition, contrast refers to putting together elements that are different and thus creating a visual impression on the reader. The use of contrasting elements acts as an information hierarchy and increases scanning ability. Contrast adds a dimension to the page, introduces an element of surprise, and shows that it has depth and variety. Contrast can be used in colours, fonts and direction. To create an effective and impressive publication, balance repetition and contrast.

Here is some terminology that journalists use to talk about layout of articles and pages:

- **Title** is used for all articles except news stories; **headline** is used for news stories. Titles can be creative and cryptic; headlines are not: they are structured in sentence form, present tense, leaving out articles. For example, a title could be *Swept Away* (an actual feature article in *New Scientist* on tsunami); a headline could be *Largest Tsunami Ever Recorded Hits Country*.
- **Pullquote** is text pulled out of the article and used as a highlighting device – the pullquotes of an article should themselves tell a story (i.e. summarise main points of the article).
- **Subhead** is the text that comes under the title and is used to give more information on the article's topic. Subheads are useful when the title is too enigmatic and needs explanation.
- **Crosshead** is the journalistic term for 'heading.'
- **Caption** is the text that accompanies a visual.

● Organisation of content

Paragraphing

As a researcher and writer, you will find that paragraphing offers a powerful tool for articulating and critiquing your ideas. As a communicator, you will find that paragraphing helps you to keep your reader focused on your topic and line of logic. It enables you to divide your material into units that readers can readily cope with and assimilate into their understanding.

The purpose of paragraphs and sections is to divide and prioritise information into meaningful chunks. This helps to highlight points and issues and to encourage a sense of sequence and development. Bear in mind that people assimilate and commit to memory 'chunks' of information that comprise between about five and seven items. This should guide your paragraphing style, especially in journalistic documents where a direct and conversational approach is favoured.

Magazine article paragraphs tend to be short, often running to two or three sentences. Even one-sentence paragraphs are acceptable in articles as long as they do not run in succession. Like short sentences, short paragraphs have a more intense effect than long ones because they concentrate meaning in a few words that stand out from the rest of the text. This is why in magazine articles one-sentence paragraphs are often placed at strategic places to provide a striking effect.

Also, magazines tend to work on the assumption that the reader will have a relatively short concentration span and may not necessarily want to follow an item in detail. In many cases, magazines are read at hours of leisure – coffee and lunch breaks, while riding the bus, etc. Writers, therefore, cannot assume that the reader will invest the time and attention necessary to absorb a complex document. Accordingly, the writer has to present the information succinctly and directly without elaboration and in-depth analysis. The tone should have a conversational impact rather than conceptual density. Finally, magazine articles also compete for attention. As opposed to a formally commissioned report, which can assume that the reader has a vested interest in reading it closely, a magazine article often needs to grab the reader's wandering eye. In this situation, having long paragraphs would be daunting and discouraging.

As noted above, the layout of magazines also influences paragraphing. Most magazine articles are printed in columns. Even a short paragraph will look longer in a narrow column format than it would if allowed to spread right across the page. Also articles are allocated a small space. Many articles are a page or less in length with only cover stories and major features exceeding two pages. Short paragraphs allow the information to be spread out evenly in a small space.

The inverted pyramid

News stories conventionally follow the inverted pyramid format. To understand this format, keep in mind that the length of an article is determined not only by its content but, more significantly, by the amount of space available on the page. Conventionally, editors cut down sentences from the end of the article to make it fit. Journalists are therefore required to write in inverted

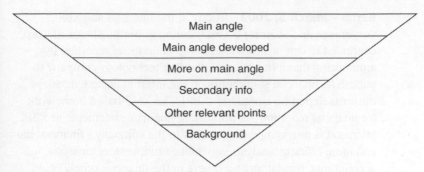

Figure 4   The inverted pyramid

pyramid format: the most important information in the article is placed first. Non-essential information appears in the middle and end of the news item. Although this is the rule in news reporting, it is also a generally followed guideline in other types of journalism and journalistic editing, making this type of writing top-heavy. The inverted pyramid is shown in Figure 4.

Press releases

Another document type that follows the inverted pyramid format is the press release. Press releases target an audience of local news professionals, working either in print or broadcast, and announce new and important work or events. Sometimes press releases are sent to specialty audiences, such as convention organisers. At other times, they are placed on the company's website, on the 'press', 'public relations' or 'journalism' page. Often they are mailed to target press representatives as part of a press kit, which may include testimonials, quotations and product features – anything a journalist would need to know to write an article.

Press releases vary in length from half a page to three or four pages, depending on the significance of the announcement and on the number of people or companies involved. Press releases are 'uncontrolled' information. That is, the writer and issuing organisation have no control over the final version in which the news will appear. Therefore, clear organisation and adequate facts are important. The first paragraph gives all the information the press wants, structured around the 5W's and 1H. It states what the situation or product is, who is involved, where and when it was produced, launched or used, why it is interesting or important and how it is different from others or from its predecessors. The subsequent paragraphs give more background and details in descending order.

For example, notice how the first paragraph of a press release published on the Microsoft Home Page fulfils these requirements:

> **Berlin – March 5, 2002** – Today at the International XBRL
> Conference and Steering Board meeting in Berlin, Microsoft Corp.
> continued to demonstrate leadership in financial reporting by
> announcing that it has become the first technology company to
> publish its financial statements on the Internet using Extensible
> Business Reporting Language (XBRL), an XML-based framework
> for financial reporting. By publishing financial statements in XBRL,
> Microsoft is providing easier access to the company's financial data
> and more efficient analysis capabilities to investors, analysts,
> accountants, regulators and others in the financial supply chain.
> (www.microsoft.com/presspass; retrieved: 18 March 2002)

In just 90 words this extract gives specific facts about the product that it is
promoting:

When? 5 March 2002.

Where? The International XBRL Conference and Steering Board in Berlin.

Who? Microsoft Corp, investors, analysts, accountants, regulators etc.

What? Extensible Business Regulating Language (XBRL).

Why? To provide more efficient analysis capabilities in financial reporting.

How? By publishing its financial statements on the Internet; by providing
easier access to the company's financial data.

In addition, the extract promotes the image of the company by emphasising
its demonstration of leadership and innovation.

The press release from the Disney Corporation on the next page illustrates
the main components. Some items that are essential in press releases are:

- Clear presentation of names, dates and titles. If you use acronyms,
  make sure you explain what they stand for. Do not take for granted
  that readers will understand them, no matter how famous they are.

- Easy-to-find contact details of people that the press can contact for
  more information. Ideally, include phone numbers, email
  addresses, fax numbers and physical addresses.

- At least one relevant quotation. This makes the release more
  specific, by focusing on the direct words of responsible parties. It
  also gives the press an indication of the opinion of key figures and
  a lead to follow if they want to investigate further.

February 08, 2007

DISNEY-ABC TELEVISION GROUP RENAMES TELEVISION STUDIO ◄

Headline in the characteristic present tense.

Touchstone Television Becomes ABC Television Studio, Aligning Content Studio with Network Brand ◄

Subhead explaining the headline by providing specifics on the new name and its implication.

The Disney-ABC Television Group will rename its in-house production company, Touchstone Television, as the ABC Television Studio, it was announced today at the 2007 Disney Investor Conference by Anne Sweeney, co-chair, Disney Media Networks and president, Disney-ABC Television ◄ Group. The announcement was made as part of a company-wide strategy to focus on three core brands. Disney, ABC and ESPN. ◄

The first sentence summarises the content of the news release. It encompasses *what*, *where* and *who* in just one sentence.

The new name reflects the studio's critical role in building a brand that viewers identity with quality television on any platform. The newly named ABC Television Studio will continue to develop and produce premier programming for network, cable, web, VOD, mobile and broadband platforms for The Walt Disney Company, as well as other outlets. ◄

The second sentence gives context to the information presented in the first.

In a related announcement also made at the conference, the business unit formerly known as Buena Vista Games will now be known as Disney Interactive Studios ◄

'Over the past few years, the studio has delivered some of the highest quality, most successful programming on television, including international franchise hits "Lost" and "Desperate Housewives", as well as this year's Golden Globe winners, "Grey's Anatomy" and "Ugly Betty".' said Sweeney. "The new name ties this success more closely with the ABC brand that viewers have come to value and trust." ◄

This paragraph describes the implications of the developments, and mainly answers the questions *why*. Note the promotional touch in the factual exposition, evident in the phrases 'critical role', 'quality television', and 'premiere programming'.

The formerly-named Touchstone Television has emerged as a leader in television development and production The studio currently has 18 series on broadcast and cable networks, including ABC, NBC, CBS, ABC Family, Lifetime and FX. The studio's current slate includes the top three scripted shows on television in the key A18–49 demographic – 'Desperate Housewives', 'Grey's Anammy' and 'Lost' – a feat no other studio has achieved in the history of Nielsen People Meter rating system. In addition to its contributions to ABC's schedule, the studio's programming also includes the Emmy-nominated comedy 'Scrubs' on NBC and hits 'Ghost Whisperer' and 'Criminal Minds' for CBS. For cable television, the studio produces ABC Family's best-performing original series of all time. 'Kyle XY,' as well as 'Dirt,' the new FX series starring Courteney Cox. Another series, 'Army Wives,' will launch on Lifetime in June. The studio also produces ABC's late-night talker 'Jimmy Kimmel Live' and is a distributor for 'The Amazing Race' on CBS.

Goes on to provide additional relevant information.

Quotation providing a further promotional tone to the news, and linking the developments to information the readers are assumed to already possess (currently running television programmes).

'It is incredibly rewarding that the company recognizes the strength of the studio as an asset to build overall brand perception,' said Mark Pedowitz, president ABC Television Studio. 'Under the ABC Television Studio banner, we will continue our strategy to create quality programming that makes a connection with consumers through a multitude of platforms.' ◄

Comment: Consistent with inverted pyramid style, the last two paragraphs provide supplementary information that reinforces the main facts presented at the top.

Accessed 26 March 2007 from
http://corporate.disney.go.com/news/corporate/2007/2007_0208_disney-abc_television_group.html

● A zesty, active and concise style. A press release is still a promotional text targeting publicists (it promotes to the promoters, so to speak). Therefore, follow the guidelines for business journalism given in this chapter. Although marketese and pompous exaggeration must be avoided, press releases are not supposed to be modest.

For broadcasts timing is very important, so, if your press release is to be broadcast on the radio or television, time it accurately. The average reader can read about 150 words in a minute. Broadcasts are on average about 30 seconds. So, for a 30-second announcement, you will need about 60–70 words. Practise reading out your announcement to make sure it fits comfortably within this time frame while still providing the main information. Also, note that broadcast press releases tend to begin with location. This is an influence from drama, where a scene is described before the dialogue begins. Unless you have reason to improvise, start your announcement by stating the scene. Because broadcast announcements are spoken, avoid abbreviations and acronyms, unless they are well known (e.g. NASA). Finally, incorporate quotations in your own words (that is, paraphrase them) to fit with the reading voice.

Organisation of content in features

Most business and technology magazine articles tend to be organised using one of three methods of organisation:

1. The **descriptive** method focuses on an analysis of the product or development in terms of its constituent parts. When following this method, describe product qualities and benefits, and explain possible applications and examples of use.

2. The **comparative** method describes and evaluates the product in relation to competitors in the market. When following this method, discuss advantages and disadvantages of the products for different users, and evaluate their position in the market.

3. The **progressive/historical** method focuses on the qualities and functions of a product in terms of how they developed from a previous form. When following this method, tell a story, comparing the current market situation of the product with parallel cases in the past and pointing out analogies. Focus on innovations and on the specific attributes and benefits that make the product a novelty.

In the Quest for Youth: Understanding Botox®

In the battle against aging, Botox® has emerged as the world's favourite weapon to fight wrinkles and fine lines. Botox users are rumoured to include celebrities such as American former presidential candidate John Kerry and pop Diva Madonna – among thousands. But what exactly is this Botox®? How does it work? And are there side effects that need to be considered before selecting this method for regaining a youthful appearance? ◄

Sets the scene.

Highlights popularity of product.

Introduces the article by indicating its sections in the form of questions to be answered.

Botox® is an easy and affordable treatment. In fact it is nicknamed the 'lunch-hour face-lift,' because it is a simple injection costing on average $400 and taking 10 minutes – very different from the traditional 'face-lift,' a major and expensive plastic surgery which requires the patient to undergo anesthesia, long-recovery time, and potential scarring, However, unlike plastic surgery, in order to maintain wrinkles at bay with Botox®, treatments need to be repeated every 4–6 months. ◄

Description of product showing user benefits. Last sentence acknowledges limitation.

Botox® is Allergen Inc.'s trade name for botulism toxin type A, a neurotoxin produced by the bacterium *Clostridium botulism*. Botulism toxins, of which there are seven distinct types, attach to nerve endings and reduce the release of acetylchoine, the neurotransmitter responsible for generating muscle contractions – and resulting wrinkles. Cosmetic Botox® injections are a diluted form of this neurotoxin, and work by temporarily relaxing the muscles into which they are injected. ◄

Simple scientific description of the Botox process.

In the 1950s, researchers discovered that injections of botulism toxin type A into overactive muscles decreased muscle activity for 4–6 months. However, it was only in the 1980s that ophthalmologist Alan Scott discovered that the toxin could be used to treat blepharospasm, an eye muscle disorder characterized by uncontrollable contractions. Allergen Inc., then a small pharmaceutical company specializing in eye therapies, bought the rights to the product in 1988. The drug was renamed Botox®. Further clinical trials continued and in April of 2002, Botox® was approved for cosmetic treatments including temporarily eliminating wrinkles, facial lines caused by excessive muscle contraction. ◄

History of the product, linking it with research and experimentation.

Botox® is generally considered safe by medical authorities, and has been approved by the US Food and Drug Authority (FDA). However, side effects are possible, although all known ones are temporary, and no cases have been documented of systemic complications. Clinical trials reveal that the most statistically significant side effect, observed in 3.2% of patients treated with Botox® versus 0.0% placebo, is blepharoptosis, or 'droopy eyelid,' which results from either injection of too much toxin or injection into the wrong facial area causing paralysis of eyelid muscles. Other common side effects include headache, respiratory infection, nausea, and redness at the injection site. The FDA has also recently issued a warning against popular 'Botox® parties,' at which patients combine Botox® with alcohol in a non-medical setting. This may be dangerous for two reasons: (1) alcohol thins the blood, allowing it to more easily pass into the skin, increasing bruising, (2) since, as with all medical interventions, complications are possible, the patient needs to be at a location equipped to handle an emergency. ◄

Introduces side effects; emphasises their low risk.

Objectively lists side effects.

Focuses on one possible problem in using the product and explains it in more depth.

Today, Botox® is used in over 70 countries, and the popularity of the treatment is growing. Clinical trials continue, and novel uses for Botox® are emerging for controlling side effects. ◄

Ends on a high note, suggesting the future looks good for the product.

Depending on the length of the article, select one method or blend the three. Consider which organisation of information would allow you to present your object in the most appealing and effective way. Also, bear in mind that the order in which information is presented in a text is a strategic device providing the writer with the means to manipulate information so as to produce the most desired effect. For instance, if you are attempting to motivate readers to try out a course of action, it would be counterproductive to begin with the cost or the disadvantages. This would be beginning with a weakness that could well defeat your intention. Instead, include the cost or disadvantage at a strategic position, after you have highlighted advantages and qualities. For example, the article on p. 85 on Botox is objectively informative and balanced. However, it avoids emphasising the possible downsides of the drug, that would discourage the reader, by describing them towards the end of the article, and placing them in an appropriate context.

● Journalistic style revisited

Chapter 3 looked at style in terms of sentence structure. Here we revisit it in terms of content. Business and technology journalism makes unfamiliar concepts and developments familiar, by presenting information that is clearly relevant to readers in a creative and zesty way. This involves skills of analysis and synthesis: of combining innovation and the new in a framework that also contains assumed shared knowledge between writer and readers. When popularising your topic, choose language and techniques that are:

- **Factual**: Give as much factual information as possible, while avoiding a 'dry' tone. Use the 5Ws and 1H questions to guide you.
- **Rational**: The business reader is usually interested in making an evaluative judgement. Therefore, rational descriptions of an economic, technological or business nature are best. Emotional appeals may fall flat unless they are supported by a rational basis.
- **Specific**: Give specific examples where possible. People love to read about other people, so include quotations, success examples and testimonials. Also, describe experimental data where possible to provide some evidence for your statements.
- **Technical**: While avoiding tediously technical jargon that may alienate the more uninformed readers, use the jargon and dominant metaphors of the industry that you represent. Business and technology journalism is 'cult' writing: it should be both innovative and popular. Show that you can speak as an 'insider' who knows

the concerns, strengths and needs of the industry, and with whom your readers can identify as 'one of us'.

The following article compares two (fictional) operating systems: the corporate OpenEye and the open source Salter. The first version of the article is a draft where the writer describes plainly the pieces of information that will make up the final. The second version is an example of how a plain listing of facts can be 'spiced up' to produce the creative and energetic style characteristic of 'insider' technology journalism. The target audience are IT enthusiasts.

Version A: Draft

OpenEye vs. Salter

For the last few years, OpenEye has been the strongest company in the computer operating system market. This has been because of a lack of real alternatives, but now OpenEye is being challenged by Salter. This system was created by Mark Salter and it is becoming famous. It is based on the source code of an older system, called Marcus. OpenEye beat Marcus, but now Marcus is getting stronger by making another system very similar to it on a basic level. It is cheaper than OpenEye and also has some qualities that OpenEye does not have.

First, Salter costs very little. Its only expenditure is in the side effects of its implementation. It was made this way in order for users to continue developing it as they are using it. On the other hand, OpenEye costs about $700 to start with, and would require much more money if used as an investment.

Second, Salter is faster than OpenEye and it has more functions. Because Salter has been built by engineers all over the world in an open format, it has a variety of functions. For example, it is very easy to network using Salter and this is a serious consideration for IT experts.

The drawback for Salter is that, like Marcus, its predecessor, it is difficult to use. Only specialists with considerable expertise can understand its use, since it uses many of the same commands as Marcus. Also, as Salter was made to run from a command line based shell interface, it is not as visually impressive as OpenEye. OpenEye, on the other hand, uses a graphical user interface, or GUI, as its method of control, which is easy for non-experts to use.

In conclusion, OpenEye is easier and is visually more pleasing than Salter. Salter, on the other hand, is more advanced and gives expert users the satisfaction of control. Increasingly, it is overcoming its weaknesses and becoming more and more competitive for OpenEye.

Version B: Revision

OpenEye vs. Salter – The Contest

For the last few years, OpenEye has dominated the computer operating system market. This has been because of a lack of real alternatives, but times are changing and the OpenEye empire may be brought to its knees by a man called Mark Salter. Salter has developed an operating system that has gained mention worldwide. And the name of the new heavyweight? You guessed it – Salter.

Salter was developed from the source code of an older system called Marcus. OpenEye has ruled supremely ever since it overthrew Marcus, but now Marcus is making a comeback with a clone of itself. But why would OpenEye have cause to be afraid? After all, it has already defeated Marcus once. What does Salter have to offer that OpenEye does not?

First in most people's minds is the question of price. How much is this going to cost to implement? Salter has the perfect answer to this question – nothing! Well almost nothing. There is always going to be some outlay when implementing a new operating system, but Salter takes a long step forward by offering itself for free. Salter was made so that it would be openly available to everyone, thus making it possible for anyone to help develop the system. With this in mind, most applications and other such software are available for free on the Internet, which is more than can be said for the popular OpenEye system. Not only are you looking at a large outlay for the initial purchase of the product, which starts at around $700, but you could be looking at thousands of dollars being invested in software titles.

A determining factor in whether or not an operating system will be successful is likely to be the expertise required to use it. This is where Marcus lost out to OpenEye. While Marcus was and still is a more powerful operating system, it required a highly skilled technician to run it. Like Marcus, Salter was originally made to be run from a command line based shell interface, and so it lacks the lustre of the beautiful graphical interface that OpenEye provides. At first glance, Salter even looks like Marcus as it uses many of the same commands and thus is almost as difficult to use. OpenEye, on the other hand, uses a graphical user interface, or GUI, as its method of control. This means that almost anyone can use it, and it provides a great introduction to the world of computers for complete novices.

There is no debate as to which system is faster. Salter is light years ahead of OpenEye as far as speed goes. Functionality? Salter wins the race hands down. Because Salter has been built by engineers all over the world in such an open format, there is almost nothing it cannot do. Networking is a breeze, and anyone in an IT position would have to seriously consider Salter over OpenEye. While OpenEye may be more aesthetically pleasing and simpler to use, it does not have the same degree of mastery that Salter has when it comes to making the computer do what you want it to. The fact remains that until Salter becomes easier to use, OpenEye will still be the juggernaut. But Salter continues to grow in strength, and so the war rages on.

● Accuracy in journalism

As a scientist or technical professional, you are faced with a dilemma when popularising a complex concept: how accurate can you be while also avoiding jargon, equations and formulae? How appealing and entertaining can you make your article without betraying the complexity and seriousness of your topic? By creating a lighthearted approach will you not also be sacrificing depth? In short, will you be misleading your readers into thinking there is an absolute truth where in fact there are only conjectures and hypotheses? Such doubts have plagued science writers for a long time. Einstein, for example, describes this situation quite neatly in 1948:

> Anyone who has ever tried to present a rather abstract scientific subject in a popular manner knows the great difficulties of such an attempt. Either he succeeds in being intelligible by concealing the core of the problem and by offering to the reader only superficial aspects or vague allusions, thus deceiving the reader by arousing in him the deceptive illusion of comprehension; or else he gives an expert account of the problem, but in such a fashion that the

untrained reader is unable to follow the exposition and becomes discouraged from reading any further. If these two categories are omitted from today's popular scientific literature, surprisingly little remains.   (Cited in Barnett, 1948, p. 69)

There is no simple answer to this predicament. Three factors, especially, must be considered. First, as noted earlier, space is a major consideration in journalism, and it is impossible to do justice to a complex topic by examining it from different angles and analysing it in depth within such space constraints. In this respect, popular science books have an advantage because they have the length necessary to expand and elaborate. Second, audience is another major consideration. People still need and want to be informed about technological developments even if they do not have the same expertise as the initiators of these developments. At the same time, it would be unrealistic to expect them to understand terminology and methods that have taken professionals years to learn. Therefore, an interpretation becomes necessary. Third, the market and general social context should be taken into account. Technology develops hand in hand with the evolution and diversification of society, in which market forces and commercial interests are major factors. Connecting technology and science with its social relevance – the theory with the application – is, therefore, important, as is identifying the links between scientific endeavour and commercial practice.

Within this framework, popularisations of science and technology can be fruitful if the writer:

- understands that s/he cannot be as thorough in a popular document as in a specialist or scientific document, and must, therefore, be carefully selective
- has a sense of visualisation and narrative and can explain concepts in terms of images and stories, keeping in mind that being simple does not mean being simplistic
- can resist the temptation to exaggerate, generalise or sensationalise in ways that would mislead the reader into thinking that a debatable and inconclusive topic is certain.

Hedging (using terms that mitigate certainty and absolute constructions) is a major difference between academic/scientific writing aimed at specialist, peer, audiences, and journalistic/popular writing aimed at a wider public. One of the reasons that professionals are often suspicious of journalists is the tendency of the latter to simplify and generalise from inconclusive results, and thereby to discourage or raise the hopes of the public inappropriately. Science writing scholar Jeanne Fahnestock gives some interesting examples of this. In the debate about whether the sexes are equally endowed with mathematical ability, she quotes scientists' statements and compares them with their interpretations in popular publications.

Here is the scientists' claim:

> *We favor the hypothesis that* sex differences in achievement in and attitude toward mathematics result from superior male mathematical ability, which *may* in turn be related to greater male mathematical ability in spatial tasks. This male superiority is *probably* an expression of a combination of both endogenous and exogenous variables. *We recognize, however, that our data are consistent with numerous alternative hypotheses.* (Benbow and Stanley: Sex differences in mathematical ability: Fact or artefact? *Science* 1980, cited in Fahnestock, 1986, p. 284; my emphasis)

Here is one popularisation of the claim:

> According to its authors, . . . Benbow and . . . Stanley of Johns Hopkins University, males inherently have more mathematical ability than females. (The gender factor in math – *Time Magazine,* cited in Fahnestock, 1986, p. 285)

And here is another:

> The authors' conclusion: 'Sex differences in achievement in and attitude toward mathematics result from superior male mathematical ability'. (Do males have a math gene? – *Newsweek,* cited in Fahnestock, 1986, p. 285)

The dangers of this kind of misrepresentation of scientific results, common in public, general interest, magazines and newspapers diminish with specialist popular science magazines that target a more informed and discriminating audience. Table 5 shows some common communicative strategies that characterise the styles and content choices of academic/scientific writing and journalistic/popular writing:

As an example of how these strategies work on the textual level, consider the extracts dealing with the topic of movement in humans and robots. Both are introductions to their respective articles: extract A is taken from *Nature*, (a scientific journal for scientists); extract B is taken from *New Scientist*, (a popular science magazine for non-specialist science enthusiasts). As is the norm, the article from where extract A comes was written before the article from where extract B comes, with the latter being a popularization of the findings presented in the former.

Academic style	Journalist style
Concentrates on objects, events and outcomes. Credibility comes from showing that a claim stands objectively, independently of personal merits of specific persons.	Concentrates on people, their intentions, thoughts, hopes and reactions. Interest comes from showing the human interest aspect of professional endeavours.
Uses jargon and specialist terminology. Shows that writer is a member of the scientific community.	Avoids jargon. Instead 'translates' technical terms into everyday language. May give examples to illustrate the meaning of specialist terminology. In specialist, 'cult' journalism, writer uses 'insider' language to establish peer – audience dynamics.
Uses specific claims or statements that are testable and falsifiable. Supports these claims with specific and detailed evidence, such as facts and figures.	May rely on general observations when explaining a phenomenon. May appeal to imprecise constructs such as 'common sense' and 'people'.
Avoids certainty. Uses 'hedging' to modify the certainty aspect of statements ('might', 'appears to be', 'it seems', 'evidence suggests').	Describes events with more certainty. Does not need to look at different sides of a hypothesis, but may present one view only. Uses imperatives (command-type structures).
Avoids emotional evaluation of observations. Instead uses words that specify and quantify. Concentrates on factual information rather than on feelings about this information.	May use evaluative adjectives, such as 'terrible', 'fantastic', etc. Shows relevance of abstract data for personal experience, for example, through examples of everyday life.
Appeals to scientific community and not to individual readers. Avoids excessive use of personal pronouns and may not use any ('I', 'you', 'we').	Appeals to ideal, personalised readers, using techniques such as direct questions and use of pronouns.

Table 5   Common strategies of academic and journalist writing

Extract A (academic/specialist style)

Although people's legs are capable of a broad range of muscle-use and gait patterns, they generally prefer just two. They walk, swinging their body over a relatively straight leg with each step, or run, bouncing up off a bent leg between aerial phases. Walking feels easiest when going slowly, and running feels easiest when going faster. More unusual gaits seem more tiring. Perhaps this is because walking and running use the least energy. Addressing this classic conjecture with experiments requires comparing walking and running with many other strange and unpractised gaits. As an alternative, a basic understanding of gait choice might be obtained by calculating energy cost by using mechanics-based models. Here we use a minimal model that can describe walking and running as well as an infinite variety of other gaits. We use computer optimization to find which gaits are indeed energetically optimal for this model. At low speeds the optimization discovers the classic inverted-pendulum walk, at high speeds it discovers a bouncing run, even without springs, and at intermediate speeds it finds a new pendular-running gait that includes walking and running as extreme cases. ◄

One way of characterizing gaits is by the motions of the body (Fig. 1a). In these terms, walking seems well caricatured (Fig. 1b) by the hip joint going from one circular arc to the next with push-off and heel-strike impulses in between. Similarly, running could be caricatured by a sequence of parabolic free-flight arcs (Fig. 1c), with impulses from the ground at each bounce. ◄

Why do people not walk or even run with a smooth level gait, like a waiter holding two cups brim-full of boiling coffee? Why do people select walking and running from the other possibilities? We address such questions by modelling a person as a machine describable with the equations of newtonian mechanics. The basic approximations are: first, that humans have compact bodies and light legs; second, that gait choice is based on energy optimization; and third, that energy cost is proportional to muscle work. We use a simplification of previous models, perhaps the simplest mechanical model that is capable of exhibiting a broad range of gaits that includes walking and running. Although the model is a mechanical abstraction that is not physically realizable, it is subject to the laws of physics. Because of its simplicity, the model is amenable to interpretation. It can also be studied with exhaustive and accurate simulation experiments, far beyond what is possible with human subjects. ◄

Adapted from: M. Srinivasan and A. Ruina (2006). Computer optimisation of a minimal biped model discovers walking and running. *Nature* 439(5), pp. 72–5. Reprinted with permission.

Side annotations:

First four sentences set the scene, indicating the issue that the article discusses.

Introduces the main topic: mechanics-biased models.

Explains the choice of the minimal model used in the article.

Refers to three figures that show in schematic form the information presented verbally in the paragraph.

Describes the type of gait in technical terms.

Questions that draw attention to the significance of the problem. This makes this piece less technical than others, but that is consistent with the style of the Letters section of *Nature*, which tends to publish work in progress or less formal articles than other sections. Note that the 'you' pronoun is avoided in these questions.

Explains how the questions will be answered in technical terms.

Lists approximations to clarify assumptions and measurement scales.

Gives extensive justification of choice of method.

Extract B (journalistic/popular style)

They're everywhere. From the Imperial Walkers of Star Wars to the alien tripods from War of the Worlds, there's something about walking robots that captures the imagination. Maybe it's that they look alive. Maybe it's that machines with two legs look human. Whatever the reason, they have given engineers a headache for decades: making robots that walk well has been an enormously difficult trick to pull off.

Until now, that is. It seems walking robots are finally up and running. Surprisingly, we may have toymakers to thank for this. In 1938, the American inventor John Wilson filed a patent for a toy that, when placed on a gentle slope, would walk on two pivoted legs with a comical waddling motion that served to lift the swinging feet clear of the ground. Wilson's 'Walkie' waddled its way to success, and its descendants can be found in toyshops to this day. These gizmos don't need batteries or clockwork. Gravity alone is enough to set the legs in motion.

We humans don't waddle like the Walkie because we can bend our knees to ensure our swinging feet clear the ground. But the toymakers' observation has nonetheless proved a vital one for engineers trying to recreate the human gait. Until recently, robot designers had a tendency to pack their devices' legs with even more motors and stricter controls to direct the movements of the joints. That approach led to machines like Asimo, built by Honda. They are remarkable feats of engineering but they walk with a slow, plodding gait that is nothing like a human's. What the Walkie showed was that natural walking can arise from the way gravity acts on a body supported by freely hinged legs, not from precise motor control of the legs' movements. In short, walking is not active but passive. 'I am appreciating more and more the insights that the inventors had,' says walking-robot researcher Andy Ruina of Cornell University in Ithaca, New York. 'I think they perhaps deserve more credit.'

Adapted from: P. Ball (2006) Walk this way. *New Scientist*, 4 February, pp. 40–3. Reprinted with permission.

Begins with creative generalisation. The referent of the pronoun 'they' is enigmatic, inducing the reader to read more.

Makes reference to widely known popular texts.

Speculates using examples from everyday life.

Last sentence introduces the topic of the article. Note also the informal phrase 'trick to pull off'.

Sentence fragment acting as transition to the second paragraph. As noted in Chapter 3, fragments are inappropriate for formal writing, but work well in more creative styles.

Play on words 'up and running' is a literal description of the robots' movement as well as an idiom meaning 'operational'.

Brings in the toy example to ground scientific research in a popular activity.

Brings in engineering example.

Gives a specific example of this.

Quotes researcher's words. Andy Ruina is one of the authors of the previous extract.

● Developing a feature article

When writing a feature article you are explaining how something works or how something has developed over time, informing the public of something new and/or important, and interpreting complex information in an understandable and appealing way. In effect, you may be doing one or more of the following:

- describing the parts of your object and their interrelationships
- tracing the history of the object and describing its changes
- describing the object's qualities and characteristics
- analysing the object's value.

To achieve this effectively, use a combination of the following strategies.

Define terms and differentiate them from other similar ones This is very useful when you are writing about a large topic with many subdivisions, aspects and categories. By defining it, you are specifying the parameters in which you will explain it. Consider using sentence or paragraph-length definitions for complicated topics, and parenthetical definitions for less complicated ones (see below for examples).

Give an analogy, for example: 'using the same principle as an overhead projector, an epidiascope projects three-dimensional images onto a screen using a magnified beam of light.' This gives the reader the gist of what you are saying and makes complicated terms and processes easier to grasp. In the same light, you can contrast the term to what it is opposite to or different from. This is useful if you think the reader may misunderstand a topic by confusing it with something that looks similar but is actually very different.

Give examples that illustrate the functions or properties of the topic you are explaining. This helps the reader put the topic in context and thus relate to it better.

Compare the topic with others to show its special features or common attributes. As with analogies, comparisons are useful in helping the reader classify the topic in a category with which s/he is familiar, and/or to understand the innovation or specific nature of the described object.

Describe the properties/qualities of an object or situation and detail how it works or how it occurs and under what circumstances.

Suggest reasons for a situation or development. This is useful when you think the reader is likely to ask the question 'why'. It justifies a current state of affairs by explaining what caused it to come into being.

Tell a story that illustrates your discussion. This is useful in making conceptual information more concrete by describing a 'physical' situation where the ideas you are talking about were at play. Stories are very effective in assisting the reader to visualise and, therefore, to better understand, your description.

Describe a process. This is a way to show how something is done, a protocol or procedure. Describing processes also comes into play when giving instructions on how to carry out a task.

Describe applications. This emphasises the practical aspects of research, by showing how inventions and discoveries can be used in everyday life.

Use visual aids, such as a diagram or photograph. If you choose this strategy, make sure you explain in your text what the visual is intended to show and how it fits in your written explanation. To avoid digressing from your text to explain a diagram, consider using side-bars that contain visuals and text, and provide self-sufficient information that complements the information presented in the body of the article.

Here are some examples of these strategies in action.

Defining

You can give an extended definition of an object or phenomenon, a sentence definition or a parenthetical definition. An extended definition takes one or more paragraphs, and includes explanations of the meaning of terms, as well as a description of the general category in which the defined object belongs.

Be careful that your definition does not contain terms that will themselves be obscure to your target audience. If you have to use such terms, ensure that they too are explained or defined. Lead the audience from the familiar to the unfamiliar. Sentence definitions are condensed versions of this, while parenthetical definitions explain the meaning of a term without disrupting the sentence in which they are found.

Here is a one-paragraph definition of 'presence' in virtual reality. Notice how the writer justifies the choice of 'presence' in a discussion of virtual reality, by pointing out that it is one aspect of virtual reality when seen in terms of human experience rather than of technology. The writer leads gradually to a one-sentence precise definition of 'presence' by first describing some of the attributes of the term:

> The key to defining virtual reality in terms of human experience rather than technological hardware is the concept of presence. Presence can be thought of as the experience of one's physical environment; it refers not to one's surroundings as they exist in the physical world, but to the perception of those surroundings as mediated by both automatic and controlled mental processes. Presence is defined as the sense of being in an environmen.
> (Steuer, 1995, p. 35)

The following is a form of parenthetical definition, using a dash (dashes are generally preferred to parentheses in journalistic articles for layout reasons).

> Dating back to Newton's laws of motion, the equations of physics are generally 'time symmetric' – they work as well for processes running backwards through time as forwards.   (Barry, 2006, p. 36)

Giving an analogy

Analogies are useful when you are presenting a difficult topic or a topic that the reader has little knowledge of. The advantage of analogies is that they can clarify and explain a topic by tracing a parallel pattern with another topic that may be easier to grasp. The disadvantage of analogies is that, if not used carefully, they can confuse the reader by understating or overstating a topic. You use an analogy by juxtaposing two situations and showing their common features and qualities. Rhetorically, an analogy is equivalent to a simile. For example, here is how writer Flannery O'Connor addressed a class in writing:

> I understand that this is a course called 'How the Writer Writes', and that each week you are exposed to a different writer who holds forth on the subject. The only parallel I can think of to this is having the zoo come to you, one animal at a time; and I suspect that what you hear one week from the giraffe is contradicted next week by the baboon.   (From Kane, 1984, p. 89)

Giving examples

A paragraph of example/illustration could lead off with a topic sentence that states the general principle or idea. Your second sentence will usually contain the phrase 'for example' or 'for instance' or variations on this. If you have a lot of example paragraphs to write you could introduce variation by employing some substitutes for 'for example' and 'for instance'. You might perhaps write, 'An interesting case of X is . . .'.

Another way to exemplify is to define or describe the example in theoretical terms in one sentence, and then go on to elaborate by means of more visual language or by recounting a story that would make the conceptual description more understandable to non-specialists. This extract exemplifies these principles. The first sentence states what the example represents. The second sentence describes how it does this and leads into a more vivid story to get the point across. The third sentence provides a link to a second example, created by the linker 'similarly'. The fourth sentence once again describes what the example stands for theoretically; and the last sentence illustrates the concept by creating a more tangible image:

> One notable early example of an attempt to provide great sensory breadth in a mediated presentation is the Sensorama device, developed by Mort Heilig. This arcade game-style simulator utilizes four of the five senses to simulate a motorcycle ride: Users see the Manhattan streets go by, hear the roar of the motorcycle and the sounds of the street, smell the exhaust of other cars and pizza cooking in roadside restaurants, and feel the vibration of the handlebars. Similarly, many park theme attractions, particularly those at Walt Disney World and Disneyland, use a high degree of breadth in order to simulate a sense of presence. The addition of changes in orientation, haptic sensations, smells, and tastes, in combination with auditory and visual sensation, are particularly effective in this regard. For example, the Star Tours and Body Wars simulators combine a motion platform with multi-channel sound and film to simulate space travel and a tour through the human body, respectively.   (Steuer, 1995, p. 43)

In the following extract, novelist Stephen King explains the importance for writers of reading. To illustrate this, he gives examples of the many occasions available for people to read in the course of a day. Notice that the writer adopts a first-person perspective in presenting his examples. This is effective because the writer is an expert in the field he describes (writing), and so his personal experience is directly relevant.

> Reading is the creative center of a writer's life. I take a book with me everywhere I go, and find there are all sorts of opportunities to dip in. The trick is to teach yourself to read in small sips as well as

in long swallows. Waiting rooms were made for books – of course! But so are theatre lobbies before the show, long and boring check-out lines, and everyone's favorite, the john. You can even read while you're driving, thanks to the audiobook revolution. (King, 2000, p. 114)

Comparing

When comparing, select some qualities from an object and describe how they compare with qualities of another object. Create a balance between similarities and differences. Two objects that are completely different cannot be compared – it would be like comparing an artichoke and an elephant. Similarly, two objects that are identical do not have enough distance between them to allow comparison – this would be like comparing yourself with your image in a mirror. In such cases, other strategies of description and explanation would probably be more effective.

Adverbs and adjectives of comparison are useful in this strategy 'More', 'less', 'fewer', and words ending in -er or -est show comparison. In addition, there is a range of signpost words and phrases that express the relation of comparison/contrast, for example, 'similarly', 'conversely', 'also', 'in the same way', 'after all', etc. The following extract compares two cameras. Notice that the writer chooses to base the comparison on user needs and skills.

> Both model X and model Y are great cameras, containing features for the beginner as well as for the more advanced photographer. However, model X's ease of use and limited extra features mean it is more targeted towards the amateur or novice photographer who occasionally wants to dabble in manual photography, but still needs an automatic camera. Model Y, in contrast, with its more powerful system and additional features, is more for the serious photographer who occasionally wants to take photos without setting up the scene. Financially, it sets you back a bit more, especially if you purchase all the extra gadgets, but you can take it further – which is great if you get serious about your photography.

The following extract compares science and art.

> The scientist works mainly at the level of very abstract ideas, while his perceptual contact with the world is largely mediated by instruments. On the other hand, the artist works mainly on creating concrete objects that are directly perceptible without instruments. Yet, as one approaches the broadest possible field of science, one

discovers closely related criteria of 'truth' and 'beauty.' For what the artist creates must be 'true to itself', just as the broad scientific theory must be 'true to itself'. Thus, neither scientist nor artist is really satisfied to regard beauty as that which 'tickles one's fancy'. Rather, in both fields structures are somehow evaluated, consciously or subconsciously, by whether they are 'true to themselves', and are accepted or rejected on this basis. So the artist really needs a scientific attitude to his work, as the scientist must have an artistic attitude to his.   (Adapted from Bohm, 1998, pp. 32–3)

Describing qualities

Here you detail the features or aspects of the object. This is a spatial strategy, so remember to chunk qualities in categories, and prioritise information if appropriate. You can list qualities or describe them in paragraph form. The following example lists some aspects that make up the quality of a virtual reality system. The writer first lists the aspects, and then explains each by asking a question from the user/reader's perspective.

To the layman's eye, the quality of the VR system is based on the following:

1. The details of the graphic. Does he really look like a relatively believable robot? Is this an aesthetically pleasing and compelling environment?
2. The responsiveness of the image. Do objects move in real time to match my gestures? When I reach out, is there a delay before my computer-generated hand reaches out?
3. The safety and comfort of the helmet. Does it fit? How dirty is it? Can I get out of it if I get claustrophobic?
4. The ease of use of the input device. How coordinated do I have to be to use this thing? (Adapted from: Hawkins, 1995, pp. 178–9).

Suggesting reasons

When adopting this strategy, present your topic as something whose existence requires justification or explanation. Then describe one or more possible causes. You can begin by describing the causes leading to a phenomenon and then describe the phenomenon itself, or you can describe the phenomenon and then go to its possible causes. In the following example, Bill Gates speculates on the reasons for revolutionary software. He achieves this by listing several possible causes, and leading to his answer.

What does it take to create revolutionary software? Does it mean being first to come up with a new idea, or being first to turn that idea into a product? Does it mean carrying out pioneering research, or making incremental improvements to what's already there until you get it right? Does it mean becoming a giant, or standing on the shoulders of giants? Usually, the answer is a bit of each. Most software blends innovation, inspiration, and incremental improvement in equal measure. (Gates, 2002)

The following extract presents a reason why roboticists do not build more life-like robots. Notice how this paragraph also leads to a definition of a phenomenon.

One reason researchers have shied away from building more sophisticated androids is a theory put forward in 1970 by roboticist Masahiro Mori. He proposed that our feeling of familiarity increases as robots appear more and more human-like, but that our comfort level plummets as slight defects in behaviour and appearance repulse us, as if we are watching a moving corpse. Mori called this the 'uncanny valley'. The term is widely used by roboticists and has spread to the animation industry, where it describes people's reaction to increasingly realistic digital characters. (Schaub, 2006, p. 43).

Telling a story

When telling a story, decide how much of your story your target reader is likely to be able to absorb without a break and how much they want to know. Also, make sure that your story clearly relates to the topic that you are attempting to explain, by explicitly making connections between the two. For example, the following extract tells a story to explain why many people find the concept of evolution difficult to understand. Notice how the writer begins the paragraph by stating his main topic. Then he asks two questions constructed from the perspective of 'most people'. He then recounts a story, which becomes a story within a story, giving 'most people's' version of why evolution is difficult to grasp. He ends the paragraph by extrapolating that it is the time element in evolution that 'most people' find difficult to conceptualise.

Most people find evolution implausible. Why is my spine erect, my thumb opposable? Can evolutionists really explain that? Once I attended a lecture by the writer Isaac Bashevis Singer, and one of the many biologists in the audience asked Singer about evolution –

did he believe in it? Singer responded with a story. He said there was an island upon which scientists were certain no human being had ever been. When people landed on the island they found a watch between two rocks – a complete mystery. The scientists when confronted with the evidence of the watch stuck to the view that the island was uninhabited. Instead they explained that although improbable, a little bit of glass, metal, and leather had over thousands of years worked its way into the form of a watch. Singer's view differed from that of the scientists – as he summarized, 'No watch without a Watchmaker.' This story reflects the feeling many people share that random chemical interactions cannot explain the existence of life on earth. The reason it is hard for such people to grasp the evolutionary viewpoint is the difficulty in grasping the immense time a billion years actually is. (Pagels, 1983, p. 196)

Here is the beginning of a story created to describe the development of sun- and wind-operated boats. Notice how the writer dramatises the situation by describing a realistic scene where events took place, and even the thoughts and emotions of the main character.

The solar sailing story began a decade ago when Robert Dane, a doctor in the fishing town and seaside resort of Ulladulla in New South Wales, found himself on the shores of Canberra's Lake Burley Griffin. He was watching the city's annual race for solar powered boats, and, as a keen sailor, was sorely disappointed by the spectacle. As far as he could tell, it was nothing more than a bunch of boffins piloting boats clumsily loaded with banks of solar cells. There was no feel for sailing, no integration of the solar technology with the boats and no understanding of what it takes to push a vessel efficiently through water. (Thwaites, 2006, p. 52)

Describing a process

The principle behind presenting a process is quite similar to the principle behind storytelling. When presenting a process, divide it into stages going from the beginning of the process to its intended result. Sentence openers such as 'first', 'next', 'then' and 'finally' are useful in describing processes, and so are numbers and lists. If the process includes technical terms, remember to adapt them to the technical level of your target audience. The following paragraph describes a process for extracting titanium.

The process takes place in an electrolytic cell. The cathode is connected to a pellet of titanium dioxide powder, while the anode is made of an inert material such as carbon. The two electrodes are immersed in a bath of molten calcium chloride, which acts as the electrolyte. When the power is switched on, electrons at the cathode decompose the titanium dioxide into titanium metal and oxygen ions. The ions flow through the electrolyte to the anode, where oxygen is released as a gas.   (Hill, 2001)

The following extract describes how to recharge a battery, using an instruction-style process, with the writer directing the user's actions.

To recharge Moixa's nickel metal hydride battery, you flip open its top and plug it into the USB socket. A circuit inside lowers the supply to around 1.4 volts, and a sensor detects the temperature rise when the battery is charged and switches off the power (*New Scientist* 30 September 2006, p. 29).

Describing applications

When describing the applications of a discovery, you are, in effect, listing possible future or present situations where the discovery is put into action. Applications show different uses of a product or method, so you could describe them by listing ('first', 'second'), or adding ('also', 'another application'). Here is an extract from an article describing how science defines the feeling of love as the result of biochemical and genetic processes. The extract outlines some ways in which such research may be useful.

Is this useful? The scientists think so. For a start, understanding the neurochemical pathways that regulate social attachments may help to deal with defects in people's ability to form relationships. All relationships, whether they are those of parents with their children, spouses with their partners, or workers with their colleagues, rely on an ability to create and maintain social ties. Defects can be disabling, and become apparent as disorders such as autism and schizophrenia – and indeed, as the serious depression that can result from rejection in love. Research is also shedding light on some of the more extreme forms of sexual behaviour. And controversially, some utopian fringe groups see such work as the doorway to a future where love is guaranteed because it will be provided chemically, or even genetically engineered from conception.   (*The Economist*, 2004, p. 10)

● Analysis of example

Read the following article on the planet Mars, and notice how some of the strategies described above are used in its composition.

Life on Mars

Can Mars contain life? Is there any possibility that we are not alone in this solar system? Close examination of these questions has led scientists to propose that the following characteristics (rare for any planet) are necessary for Mars to support life:

● The planet must have a strong magnetic field which is created by the spinning of liquid metals deep inside. This magnetic field acts like a force-field to prevent the harsh winds and energies of the Sun from stripping away atmosphere and clouds like a gas-powered leaf blower.
● The area in which life evolves must be relatively stable. Life is delicate and would not survive repeated bombardments by meteors and other objects, which would cook any developing organisms in hot gas and magma.
● Water is necessary for all life. It dissolves almost any compound and allows organisms to produce energy for their own growth and survival.
● Life needs an atmosphere with enough carbon dioxide to allow the surface of the planet to be warmed by trapping the Sun's rays much like the Greenhouse Effect. ◄——— *Lists qualities necessary life on a planet.*

With the explosive growth of spaceflight technology, examining Mars for these planetary characteristics has finally become a reality. The Mars of today, unfortunately, does not meet these criteria. The planet's core is not spinning anymore leading to the lack of a magnetic field and an atmosphere. All of Mars's water is either deep underground, out of the Sun's reach, or frozen in the ice caps. Finally, Mars is a very cold planet with frozen carbon dioxide that cannot be used by living organisms. ◄——— *Gives reasons why Mars cannot support life.*

Thus, for all you ET fans out there, the chance we find any living organisms on Mars is very small. 'What's the point of exploring Mars for life?' you may ask. Mars may be cold and dead now, but it wasn't in the past. ◄——— *Transitional paragraph leading to a historical rep on Mars's atmosphere.*

About four billion years ago, Mars was a stable planet while Earth was still in its infancy. New data analyzed from the Mars rovers shows that Mars had an active core resulting in a magnetic field comparable to present day Earth – enough to maintain an atmosphere of carbon dioxide, oxygen, and water. Analysis of Martian canal-like structures reveals a cloud system similar to Earth's and vast oceans several kilometers deep. During this time, Mars was also volcanically active, theoretically providing organisms with energy that could be harnessed for life. Four billion years ago, Mars met all the criteria for a living world. In fact, many scientists have a difficult time arguing *against* life on Mars! ◄——— *Tells a story about Mars' situation in the past.*

Why do we care about fossils billions of years old? Evidence of ancient life on Mars has very important consequences for our understanding of how life begins. In 1984, scientists working in Antarctica discovered a meteorite from Mars approximately 4.6 billion years old. This Mars object created controversy, as many scientists suggested the meteorite contained evidence of bacterial life. If such meteorites indeed contained Martians, as could be confirmed by our expeditions on Mars, all living organisms on Earth may have evolved from Martian hitchhikers. We might be, in fact, the last traces of Martian life. ◄——— *Gives reasons for an inte est, and leads to a specu tion that further supports the reasons.*

● Integrating quotations

An important difference between specialist and journalistic documents lies in use of quotations. In formal reports, as in academic writing, quotations have a secondary function: they are there to provide credibility or lend support to an idea. In journalistic writing, on the other hand, ideas or facts are often crafted around quotations, foregrounding the immediacy of spoken language. For this reason, specialist documents avoid extensive use of quotations, which give the document a choppy or fragmented appearance. This is not the case for journalistic articles, however, where it is generally expected to attribute opinions, facts and ideas directly to people by reporting their speech.

This difference in emphasis is highlighted in the way quotations are integrated in the text. In specialist documents, lead to a quotation so that the sentence begins in your own words and ends with the quotation. Reverse this technique in journalistic writing: begin the sentence with a quotation and end it with your comment. Compare these extracts. The first is appropriate for a report and the second for a magazine article.

1. Conservation International, North Motor Company and Nielsen Engineering have agreed to collaborate in three 'walkway projects' in the Amazon Valley and Indonesia. These projects involve creating walkways that allow visitors to traverse densely forested areas without the need of roads. This is an important step in promoting both tourist activity and the safety of the forests. As the Public Relations Manager of Conservation International points out, 'tourism can boost an economy, but it will bust it if it destroys the environment'.

2. Conservation International recently joined forces with Motor and Engineering companies for a series of ventures promoting tourism in environmentally safe ways. 'Tourism can boost an economy, but it will bust it if it destroys the environment,' says Tim McIntyre, Public Relations Manager of Conservation International. 'Ecotourism can be as, if not more, profitable as a logging-based tourism industry, especially in our era of environmental awareness,' he adds.

Another difference in the integration of quotations and attributed knowledge in specialist and journalistic documents is the kind of referencing to sources. In specialist documents, such as reports and academic articles, references follow one of the formal styles, APA, Chicago, etc. This means that the full source is named either at a footnote, or at an end-of text reference list. In journalistic articles, on the other hand, the convention is to include the person's name and affiliation within the body of the article, preferably in the sentence that includes the quotation. References to journals where research was initially published are placed in brackets at the end of the sentence or paragraph that describes this research. Notice how this is achieved in the following examples.

Example A

According to Jeremy Gruber, legal director of the National Workrights Institute based in Princeton, New Jersey, US companies can legally watch everything employees do – and only two states require employers to tell workers they are under surveillance.   (Newitz, 2006, p. 30, my emphasis)

Example B

Stephen Britland at the University of Bradford, UK, and his colleagues applied extracts of maggot juice to layers of cells that mimic skin. When circular 'wounds' were created in the cell layers, those exposed to the maggot extracts healed fastest (Biotechnology Progress, DOI: 10.1021/bp0601600). Closer analysis revealed that protease enzymes in the juice caused specialised repair cells to move more swiftly and freely to the wound site. 'They all march in unison and fill the hole significantly quicker,' *says co-author David Pritchard of the University of Nottingham.*   (*New Scientist,* 14 October 2006, p. 18, my emphasis)

● Leads, hooks and ties

In contrast to reports, scientific and business magazine articles do not develop in a linear fashion. Also, they do not state assumptions and background, or give justifications for assertions. They are subjectively descriptive in that they describe an object from the point of view of the mental and/or physical state of the reader – they tell the readers what they want them to see.

A linear, or developmental, model of writing would start by describing the background, overview and assumptions guiding the essay or report, and then go on to detail different aspects of the topic, leading to a conclusion and, possibly, a set of recommendations. Instead, a magazine article plunges straight into the description of the product or discovery that the article discusses, immediately showing its relevance to the interests or needs of the reader. It then goes on to present different facets of the topic, beginning with the most crucial and continuing in diminishing importance. It may end quite abruptly, or it may end with one or two sentences that tie in a comment, opinion or evaluative remark to the preceding discussion.

A corporate client needs less invitation or hook to read a report, and expects more precision from the outset. A magazine reader, on the other hand, wants to be seduced into reading the article. The lead is the opening statement that should attract the reader to the article. Its job is to relate your main topic to what you believe your reader's general interests and experience are. For instance, if your marketing department has told you that your clients are concerned about the graphic user interface aspect of your company's software, you might, in a newsletter article, begin with a sentence that throws a question at the reader about graphic user interface. Or you might briefly mention some annoying glitch you had personally experienced. A hook is similar to a lead, although it is usually more 'spicy' or provocative. A hook should be well baited, so that your reader is tempted to carry on reading. Avoid abstractions and densely technical language at this point. The following article on 'virtual banking', for example, makes lively use of an opening question:

> How long would you spend queuing in a bank before storming out? The American bank technology company NCR wanted to find out what really goes on in customers' heads when they enter a high-street bank. So it commissioned CyberLife to breed surrogate people that could wander around inside a virtual bank and test the layout of machines and services – without the time and expense of real-life tests.   (Davidson, 1998, p. 40)

The sentences following the hook in the first paragraph add background to the topic or issue. As with formal report introductions, you may also add a sentence that states what it is that the ensuing article will do, although this is not necessary. The following extract, for example, leads by stating a fact and asking a question about this fact from the reader's point of view. It then goes on to overview the specifics that the article will discuss in more detail, and ends with a statement on the purpose of the article:

> The two market leaders in non-professional cameras are the Canon X and the Pentax Y, but what makes them so good? The X leads the market by being so jam-packed with features. However, the Y holds its own with its ease of use and a slightly better price.

Here we set them head to head and pull them apart for our
readers.

If you have more space to expand, you may also consider using a short
narrative as the lead. As people respond more strongly to narrative information than to any other form, your chances of intriguing and capturing your
audience are increased. This is the strategy chosen by the writer of the
following extract on Massive Multiplayer Role-Playing Games. He begins
with a story that will pique the reader's curiosity, then goes on to give the
name and background of the product he is describing. The rest of the article
will be a detailed description of one type of game in relation to how it is
similar to and different from others:

> The two moons of Dereth had already risen, illuminating the sky
> in a bright pale light. In this light it was impossible to miss the
> great hole in the ground, and even if it was masked by the shadow
> of night, you would still be able to smell the acidic stench that
> emanated from it. The figure emerging from the shelter of the
> trees to the clearing strode purposefully towards the entrance, and
> entered the cave. He travelled downwards a few metres and
> waited for his vision to attune to the darkness. He could now see
> a figure rushing towards him from deeper inside the cave, and he
> positioned his shield and hammer to best hinder the creature's
> attack.

> Today we have three well-known and popular Massive Multiplayer
> Role-Playing Games (MMRPG). This long-winded name describes
> what it is; you play with hundreds or thousands of people, and you
> assume the role of a fictional character in this world. The above
> scene describes what a lot of players would imagine when playing
> their game, whether it is fighting Goblins in *Ultima Online*, Dragons
> in *EverQuest*, or Olthoi in *Asheron's Call*. All three games lure you
> with the excitement of living in another world, forging friendships
> with other players, and vanquishing monsters.

Here are three more examples of leads and hooks.

> What goes ding in the night? Apparently the space shuttle Atlantis,
> which last month sustained one of the largest debris hits in the
> history of NASA's shuttle programme.   (*New Scientist*, 14 October
> 2006, p. 7)

Scientists are finding that, after all, love really is down to a chemical addiction between people. (*The Economist*, 28 December 2006)

There are nine planets in our solar system. Or there are eight. Or there are ten, or maybe even twenty-three. No one knows. A planet is an arbitrary thing, a notion. In a matter of weeks, however, the International Astronomical Union, meeting in Prague, is likely to issue a definitive description. (*The New Yorker*, 24 July 2006)

The tie is an optional device that ends the article with a comment or question summing up the writer's attitude towards the topic. More attention is paid to introductions in articles because of the aim of capturing attention, and the fact that most readers look at the opening sentences of an article before deciding whether to invest any more time in it. If space allows, however, a good tie does have the effect of emphasising the main message of the article and making it more memorable for the reader.

Figure 5 shows the magazine layout of the article *Life on Mars* presented earlier in this chapter. Notice the formatting sections, as they would conventionally appear in a print publication, and their terminology.

● Submitting an article for publication

When you decide to submit an article to a magazine for publication, make sure you are familiar with the topics and styles of your chosen magazine. You have a higher chance of having your article accepted if it fits with the 'culture' of the magazine. All magazines have details of the editor, so if you cannot find submission guidelines, contact the editor to request them– this is the editor's job and, besides, most magazines are looking for fresh ideas and new writers. In most cases, you will be required to submit a proposal summarising your article, and noting its significance and the types of readers it is likely to interest (more on proposals to editors in Chapter 6).

In order to familiarise yourself with the stylistic conventions of your chosen magazine, follow these steps:

1. Read carefully each article in recent issues of the magazine. Note the basic question or issue that they deal with and trace the ways that they answer it. How do they use the 5Ws and 1H? What new knowledge do you learn from the articles? What facts do you learn?

Life on Mars ◄

The potential of the red planet to sustain living beings ◄

Can Mars contain life? Is there any possibility that we are not alone in this solar system? Close examination of these questions has led scientists to propose that the following characteristics (rare for any planet) are necessary for Mars to support life:

First, the planet must have a strong magnetic field which is created by the spinning of liquid metals deep inside. This magnetic field acts like a force-field to prevent the harsh winds and energies of the Sun from stripping away atmosphere and clouds like a gas-powered leaf blower.

Second, the area in which life evolves must be relatively stable. Life is delicate and would not survive repeated bombardments by meteors and other objects, which would cook any developing organisms in hot gas and magma.

Third, water is necessary for all life. It dissolves almost any compound and allows organisms to produce energy for their own growth and survival.

Fourth, life needs an atmosphere with enough carbon dioxide to allow the surface of the planet to be warmed by trapping the Sun's rays much like the Greenhouse Effect.

The Exploration of Mars ◄
With the explosive growth of space-flight technology, examining Mars for these planetary characteristics has finally become a reality. The Mars of today, unfortunately, does not meet

Title – fonts for the title, subhead and pullquote are Lucida Bright. The rest of the article is in Palatino fonts. Therefore, there is enough contrast (two fonts for this length article are sufficient for contrast) and repetition (there is enough consistency to prevent distraction).

subhead

visual – notice how the visual is aligned with the text

caption

hook

pullquote

crosshead

tie

Figure 5 Magazine layout of article

Mars at its 2001 opposition.
Reproduced courtesy of NASA and the Hubble Heritage Team
(STScI/AURA; www.stsci.edu/institute); Acknowledgemnt: J. Bell (Cornell University).

still in its infancy. New data analyzed from the Mars rovers shows that Mars had an active core resulting in a magnetic field comparable to present day Earth – enough to maintain an atmosphere of carbon dioxide, oxygen, and water.

Analysis of Martian canal-like structures reveals a cloud system similar to Earth's and vast oceans several kilometers deep. During this time, Mars was also volcanically active, theoretically providing organisms with energy that could be harnessed for life. Four billion years ago, Mars met all the criteria for a living world. In fact, many scientists have a difficult time arguing *against* life on Mars!

these criteria. The planet's core is not spinning any more leading to the lack of a magnetic field and an atmosphere. All of Mars's water is either deep underground, out of the Sun's reach, or frozen in the ice caps. Finally, Mars is a very cold planet with frozen carbon dioxide that cannot be used by living organisms.

'Mars had an active core resulting in a magnetic field comparable to present day Earth'

Thus, for all you ET fans out there, the chance we find any living organisms on Mars is very small. 'What's the point of exploring Mars for life?' you may ask. Mars may be cold and dead now, but it wasn't in the past.

About four billion years ago, Mars was a stable planet while Earth was

Why do we care about fossils billions of years old? Evidence of ancient life on Mars has very important consequences for our understanding of how life begins. In 1984, scientists working in Antarctica discovered a meteorite from Mars approximately 4.6 billion years old. This Mars object created controversy, as many scientists suggested the meteorite contained evidence of bacterial life.

If such meteorites indeed contained Martians, as could be confirmed by our expeditions on Mars, all living organisms on Earth may have evolved from Martian hitchhikers. We might be, in fact, the last traces of Martian life.

2.   Notice the tone of the articles. Is it humorous? Serious? Technical? Chatty? This will give you a hint on what tone to give your own article.

3.   Notice the use of research. Have the writers conducted primary research, such as interviewing people, or are most articles based on secondary research – the consultation of written sources? How many quotations do the articles use? How much information is paraphrased, that is, written in the writer's own words? List the sources. Check some of them to see how the writer used them in his/her article.

4.   Notice the use of pronouns ('I', 'you', 'we', etc.). Are articles written mostly in an impersonal, objective style or do they rely heavily on personal comment? How does the writer refer to him/herself? Does s/he use personal pronouns?

5.   Notice the leads and ties. How long and snappy are they? Do the articles rely strongly on leads to 'bait' the reader, or are other elements, such as pictures or quotations of famous speakers, more prominent?

6.   Underline the first sentence in each paragraph. They should form a step-by-step sequence. Then note the cohesion that the writers have used: the linking words and phrases within paragraphs and the transitions from one paragraph to the next. Often the same words or ideas will be repeated in the last sentence of one paragraph and the first sentence of the next.

7.   Notice how the articles develop their theme. Is the article structured chronologically, developmentally, by alternating examples, point by point? How did the writer build the organisational structure to answer the title's question?

8.   What techniques does the writer use to make the article both informative and appealing? For example, does s/he use analogies, anecdotal examples, metaphors, personal stories, rhetorical questions, direct questions to the readers, etc.?

9.   Notice the title. It may have been changed by the editor; nevertheless, how does it reflect the article? Does it tease, quote, state facts? What technique does the writer use to make the reader want to read the article?

10. Look at para-textual elements, such as visuals, pullquotes, subheads, etc. Although the editor may have produced these, you can still get an idea of the type of 'framing' that the magazine requires, and this will give you some tips on what types of information the editors consider important.

Submitting an article for online publication

Writing for online magazines shares many characteristics with print journalism, most notably the inverted pyramid format. Also, as with print publishing, it is essential that you are a reader of your magazine of interest before you become one of its writers. Reading carefully all the articles in recent issues of the magazine will give you invaluable tips on what the editors and the readers expect. Other than the content of the articles, a good way to analyse the audience of the magazine is through its advertisers. Many online magazines have narrow bars, called banners, at the top or the sides of the page, which contain ads. The type of ads you find there will tell you much about the demographics and psychographics of the target audience.

By browsing many sites, you will eventually become familiar with the professionally produced and well-funded electronic magazines that offer a good market choice for your article. In many cases, there is a link to 'About Us', or something similar, where you can go to learn about the editorial slant and the audience, as well as about submission requirements. To be sure, it is always a good idea to email the editor to run your idea by him/her, and to determine your fee (if applicable), deadlines and such issues.

As regards style, on the whole, online articles are written in a more casual style than print publications. This includes quite a few coined words, that is, words that the writer has created by mixing different contexts or the metaphors of different industries. Online articles tend to be more 'hybrid' (a mix of different genres and styles, and pop culture analogies) than print publications, allowing for more experimentation in word choice. Also, they need to contain shorter sentences and paragraphs because of the limitations of the screen-based interface. In all, there is an economy of style, coupled with an attention-grabbing playfulness, in electronic articles that is not often expected for the printed page.

Activities

1. Read an article in a specialist magazine of a field that interests you and answer these questions:

   (a) Most articles contain an answer to a basic question (the main message of the text). Identify that question here. How does the article use the 5W's and 1H to answer the question?

   (b) Study the writer's use of facts, quotations and anecdotes. How effective is it?

   (c) List every source used. Where do you think the writer found this information? How was research undertaken to write this article?

   (d) Focus on the quotations. Why is each used? How does it carry the theme forward? Note how the sources of the quotations are introduced. How much does the reader need to know of the topic to place these sources?

   (e) Usually, the point of view adopted in an article is determined by the usage of the magazine to which it is submitted for publication. What point of view is used in this article? Is it a first-person perspective? 'You'? 'We?' 'It?' Is this consistent or does it change?

   (f) What new knowledge did you get from this article? Were you also motivated to do something?

2. Research the business or scientific magazines that publish in an area you are interested in. Find out the submission requirements of each magazine, and make a style-format analysis of the types of articles each magazine publishes. Then write a memo to your instructor detailing your findings.

3. Analyse a feature following the guidelines presented in this chapter. Bring your analysis to class for discussion. Concentrate on what impressed you about the article and what areas you think could be improved. Did the writer answer the questions you had on the topic? Could s/he have been clearer and more accurate within the space limitations?

5 Writing for the Digital Media

High visibility and low cost make the Internet the most effective and fastest means of global communication. A functional knowledge of the Internet as a medium of advertising, information design and application is now essential for most business environments. This chapter

looks at important aspects of the human–computer interface, and at the uses of language in electronic contexts. We concentrate on multimedia in Internet writing, the differences between electronic and print writing, elements of an effective website, and elements of an effective PowerPoint® presentation.

This chapter gives the basic terminology and concepts needed to develop an informed opinion on web-based information. For those who are already skilled in web and multimedia design, the guidelines offered here will give support in concerns of audience dynamics and text adaptation. As this chapter consists of hints and examples that include a strong visual aspect, you will gain more from it if you work through it while connected to the Internet.

Be aware that the guidelines offered here are rapidly evolving and will need to be frequently updated and revised to keep abreast with Internet developments. These developments are so fast that sometimes printed information on the Internet is out of date by the time it is published. For similar reasons, this chapter makes minimal reference to any actual websites for analysis. This aims to avoid both contention and the risk that the site will have changed or disappeared completely by the time you try to access it. The best way to understand the concepts described here is to apply them to data that you discover yourself.

● The framework: servers, browsers and hosts

For those that approach the digital medium for the first time, a brief description of the terminology will help to clarify the framework in which IT writers and designers work. This section is quite basic, so those with more experience in the field can skip it.

Think of your computer as divided into three parts: the **hardware** (also known as the part that you can kick!), the **operating system** and the

software. The hardware is the actual electronics and wiring of the computer together, and includes memory, hard drive capacity, the presence of different drives (e.g. CD-ROM, DVD, etc.), and type of screen. The hardware gives the computer its inherent power, so, for example, if you want to run multimedia applications, you need a computer with a certain size of hard drive and a minimum of megabytes (MB) of memory. Otherwise, the computer will not be able to handle the programs you try to feed it. The next step from hardware is the operating system (OS), or platform, that you choose, and this determines general **functionality** (how the computer works) and **interface** (what the design of the screen looks like). It also determines the kind of software you can install and run. Currently, the two most common platforms are Microsoft Windows® and Macintosh.

Software refers to the programs, or applications, that you install. There is software for different purposes: for example, Microsoft® Word is a very widely used word processing program, and Adobe Photoshop® an equally popular graphics program. Most software programs come in two formats, for either Windows or Macintosh platforms.

To connect to the Internet, you need a **browser** and an **ISP** (Internet Service Provider). The browser is the software that allows your computer to access data on the World Wide Web; for example, Internet Explorer and Firefox are two very popular browsers. The Internet is actually a huge, centreless network of computers connected through individual *servers* – the part of a company's computer network that connects directly to the Internet. If you are an individual user, you need a provider that has a server in order to connect (usually at a set fee). Companies and institutions have their own servers. What is known as a web address (or *URL, Uniform Resource Locator*) is actually a link to a server. If you want to publish any material on the Internet, such as a website, you need a server, which will *host* your site. Your network administrator or your provider will tell you how much space there is on the server to host your site; this will determine whether you can include elements that take up a lot of space, such as video.

● Internet and World Wide Web

Everyday talk often confounds the Internet with the World Wide Web. A distinction is, however, necessary. The Internet includes the web; in fact, the Internet is the infrastructure level of the medium, and includes such services as email. The web is the public face of the Internet medium, where users access information on products and services by visiting websites (allowing for the existence of secure pages, of course, which make the web not so public!)

As noted in Chapter 2, it is important to remember that the Internet is a medium – not a document type. In other words, it provides the means of transmission and exchange of information presented in different document types. For example, you can sent a report via email as an attachment, or post it as a **Portable Document Format (PDF)** on a site. The document would still be a report, regardless of its medium of transmission. In other words, when composing it, you should still follow the conventions and expectations of report writing. Microsoft® Word, for instance, creates documents that are generally intended to be read in printed form or hard copy, even though they have been created and maybe sent in a digital medium.

● Print versus electronic writing

This takes us to the next point, the strengths and weaknesses of electronic writing in relation to print writing. As things stand, print still has some considerable strengths over digital:

- Printed documents are much easier to read than electronic ones. Reading off a screen increases reading time significantly – up to 25 per cent. The visual resolution of a typical book is about 250 times sharper than that of an average computer screen. Therefore, if you want to present a lot of factual or detailed information to be fully read (instead of skimmed), or kept on record, print is still the best option. For example, corporate annual reports to stockholders are still generally published in print form. Also copyeditors print copy for proofreading and editing, as it is very difficult to carry out such tasks accurately on digital copy.
- Print is more portable. You can read a book, magazine or leaflet at the doctor's waiting room, the hairdresser's, on the bus or in bed – without any investment in hardware.
- Print is reliably WYSIWYG (What You See Is What You Get). Mostly, a page layout program, such as *Adobe PageMaker* or *Reader*, shows you a page the way it will look on paper. Web page authoring has to deal with the fact that people view the pages on different platforms, using different browsers that interpret and display the pages differently.
- Print is faster to skim through and scan (although not faster to access in many cases). Web pages take longer to download and are not as easily scannable as print. It is always easier to shuffle

printed pages than screen images. It is also easier to underline or highlight text on paper and to scribble notes on the margins.

In other areas, however, writing in digital form has some clear advantages:

- Web publishing is in most cases much cheaper than print publishing. This allows you to experiment more with style and space.
- The web makes a much more effective use of colour than print. Most colour printing on paper uses the CMYK process (cyan, magenta, yellow and black). Other colours are simulated by overlapping these colours in varying percentages. Computer monitors use the RGB model (red, green, blue), which represents a larger percentage of the visible spectrum and means that colours are more vibrant.
- Web writing is easier to update, edit and revise. There is no need for out-of-date material on the Internet. The disadvantage of this, however, is that it is often difficult to keep track of digital publications as they can be altered or even disappear suddenly.
- Interactivity is much enhanced in web writing. When conducting surveys, for example, you will generally find that people tend to respond more readily to a digital request than to printed texts that would require them to use stamps, envelopes, etc.
- As noted above, the web can make use of multimedia and, therefore, can present information in a more dramatic and entertaining way.
- The web enhances complex communication through **hypertext** – by linking different sites, sometimes on different subjects. A historical parallel to this phenomenon would be the creation of the encyclopaedia in the seventeenth century.
- Finally, as regards collaborative work, another advantage of the digital medium is its lack of national boundaries. Different team members can live in different countries while contributing to the same project.

● Email

Email has one definite quality: it is fast. For professional situations, this is both an advantage and a drawback. The advantage is that your message can reach a number of recipients in different parts of the world in seconds –

saving you both time and the cost of courier or airmail. Also email can make a message public (read by many readers simultaneously) thereby opening it up to more constructive feedback. The drawback is that, because of its ease and simplicity, email often tends to be associated with speech rather than written language, which can lead to bad audience dynamics and miscommunication. When sending email as part of a professional communication, keep in mind these two points:

1. *An email message is a written text.* It is, therefore, bound by the conventions of writing, as discussed in this book. That is, your audience and purpose should determine the relative formality of style and the amount of detail. Contrary to what is sometimes assumed, the Internet does not level status distinctions; you are still writing to someone with a specific position of power and authority in relation to your own. Reflect this in your writing. Also, the ease with which a message can be transmitted and deleted does not justify sloppy composition, with misspelt words and ungrammatical sentences. In fact, a very common complaint with business email is that writers seem abrupt and disrespectful and messages hastily put together. Therefore, implement the guidelines for revision and editing given in this book also for email text.

2. *Email does not replace hard copy.* Printed and signed documents are still considered more binding and formal than soft copy. For example, although you may email a report for fast transmission, make sure you also send a hard copy to formalise the communication. One reason for this is that it is still easier to lose documents in cyberspace than if they are in tangible form. Another reason is that electronic communication depends on availability of software and hardware, whereas print can fall back on the universality and reliability of paper. Your best option for certain transmission is to send your document in both forms.

The closest hard document to an email message is the memo. Email headers, for instance parallel memo headers, comprising From, To, Subject and Date. Therefore, construct your email message like you would a memo. This means you should:

1. *Begin with an opening address*: This could be 'Dear . . . ' for more formal correspondence, or 'Hello . . . ' for less formal. You can omit an opening address if the message is one in a series of reply exchanges on a topic.

2. *Place your main message as close to the beginning as possible.* Do not force the reader to have to read the whole message to understand what it is about. Give as much information as possible about you (if necessary), and your main point at the beginning to put the reader in perspective. Any details you then give will be more meaningful.

3. *Write in full words and sentences.* Do not use abbreviated words, unless they are acronyms – email is not text messaging.

4. *Do not use upper case to emphasise.* Words and sentences written in upper-case fonts are perceived as equivalent to shouting, not emphasis. If you want to emphasise, do so by using appropriate terminology.

5. *End by clearly stating what action you request or expect the reader to take* in response to your message, and close the message politely.

6. *Revise the message before you send it,* paying close attention to spelling, word choice and repetition.

7. *Sign your message* with your name and affiliation as appropriate: often, the e-mail address is not enough for the recipient to know who you are.

In addition to this general framework for email writing, here are some more specific guidelines:

- *Write short paragraphs* (no more than three sentences). It is more difficult to read from a computer monitor than it is from paper, so you facilitate communication by making the text as simple as possible.

- *Do not use headings, tables or formatted text in the body of the email.* The reason for this is that email text is based on code – HTML (Hypertext Mark-up Language). This means that layout and formatting may not display as you intended.

- *Include attachments for longer documents.* If you want to send formal documentation, such as a letter or a report, write an introductory message, memo style, and attach your letter or report in an easily printable format. Your best options are Word® documents or PDF files. Find out which is preferable, or save and send in both formats. The current convention is to use Word for shorter documents and PDF files for longer documents. Do not copy your letter or report in the body of the email message since fonts and layout appear differently in different operating systems and browsers. Make sure you say in the message that a document is attached, and perhaps give a summary of the attachment, if appropriate. Of course, also make sure that you actually do attach the document. Saying you attach a document and then forgetting to do it is a very common problem!

- *Use email if your message may be deleted when action is taken.* Use email instead of letters (for external communication) and memos (for internal communication) if your purpose is to:

  - notify of a change or development
  - ask a question
  - make a formal request for documentation to be sent to you
  - express an interest to be considered for a task or be put in a group
  - complain about a situation
  - negotiate a change
  - make an announcement, such as the completion of a project or the acquisition of a new product.

In cases where your message is a binding contract, or includes information that should be recorded, consider submitting it in a different document, such as a letter, a contract, a written agreement or a report. Submit these as PDFs or Word® documents (which are easier to store in folders on a hard drive), or in hard copy. For formal, developmental procedures where the actual document is important, and not just the action it recommends, make sure a hard copy is available – and maybe signal its existence by an email message.

Public writing on the web

Multimedia

Before anything else, remember that websites are addressed to users rather than readers. This means they must provide information in a way that is consistent with the nature of their medium, and in a way that makes full use of the medium's resources. Digital capabilities are often grouped under the umbrella term 'multimedia', which includes **text**, **graphics**, **sound**, **video** and **animation**. The potential of multimedia is increasingly being recognised and used in most areas of communication: in education, entertainment and business. In fact, new fields of communication have emerged through the use of multimedia applications, such as the creative combination of educational, information and entertainment techniques that has come to be known as 'edutainment' and 'infotainment'.

The fact that the digital medium is actually a collection of different media capabilities gives the web designer a singular task: to coordinate the different media and produce, through their combination, an effective and compelling result. As the technology for graphics, sound, video and animation is constantly changing, the next section focuses on text.

Text

Content is still the most important factor in website development. A website is, in most cases, not just an ornamental piece used for decoration. It should provide specific information that will attract and interest readers and motivate them to take some form of action (such as contacting the company, buying a product, etc.) in response to the information presented. This makes text the fundamental element in website development. Surveys of product marketing on the web, for example, generally find that there are more return visits to sites with substantial text content than to those that rely on other multimedia elements. This suggests that most users still expect the graphic elements to complement the text rather than the other way round.

The writing strategies outlined throughout this book are valid also for web design. The fundamental principles of clarity, conciseness and accuracy are as important in websites as they are in other types of professional documents. In addition to these, text that is read on a computer monitor requires some other considerations:

- **Balance text with other media**. The visual nature of electronic communication should be acknowledged by blending verbal information with visual or aural components to produce a multi-sensory effect. Sites that rely too much on verbal language exhaust users and are not likely to have a strong appeal. If you have a lot of written information to communicate, it is best to include Portable Document Format (PDF) files in your site. These can be printed out as complete, numbered pages, becoming much easier to read.
- **Begin with most important information**. Although this is valid also for other types of journalistic documents, it is of special significance in websites. Pages load from top to bottom, so the users need to read something compelling in the first eight seconds or they might leave. As graphics take longer to download than text, make sure the users have something substantial to read while waiting – preferably some information on the purpose of the site or on the function of the company hosting it. The most common form of information distribution on the web is the inverted pyramid style, described in more detail in Chapter 4. The conclusion or

central point of the document goes first, followed by information in descending order of importance.

- **Organise text into small chunks**. Words, sentences and paragraphs should be shorter in electronic format than in print, and they are better presented in columns balanced with other media, rather than across the screen. In all, layout considerations for web writing are more similar to journalism than to other professional writing, such as reports. In fact, website layout was initially modelled on magazine layout. Visual information is processed faster than verbal information, so try to make electronic text as visual as possible.

- **Select font, colour and size carefully**. Fonts are divided into *serif* and *sans serif* (serif fonts have little 'tails' on the edges while sans serif fonts have sharp edges). Sans serif fonts are easier to read in multimedia format, which may include colours and graphics. An example of serif font is Times New Roman, and an example of sans serif font is Arial:

Times New Roman
Arial

See the section on typography at the end of the chapter for more tips on fonts.

- **Restrict the use of upper case to major headings**.
Experiments have shown that upper case fonts reduce the readability of text and increase reading time by about 12 per cent. Reading from a screen increases reading time by about 30 per cent, so text has to be made as easy as possible to read.

- **Be aware of the aesthetic that your audience values**. Online articles that show an 'elitist hipster attitude' (a term coined by the editor of the online magazine *Charged*) tend to be more easily recognisable as a distinctive Internet style, and, therefore, are more appealing. This suggests that there is a trend for online writing to be informal, and playful, although still grammatically correct and well informed ('cool' does not equal 'sloppy'). Comparing this with print formats shows that the electronic text is closer to creative journalism than to academic writing. In fact, as noted earlier, many web writers are increasingly using the inverted pyramid format, inherited from journalism, for their content. However, the Internet is too diverse to be bound by one aesthetic. There are as many styles in cyberspace as there are cultural communities in the physical world, so audience and purpose analysis techniques are as important here as in other forms of document production.

- **Cater for international audiences**. One thing to remember when choosing words and phrases for your web content is that your audience will be international. This means that many local terms and symbols may be misunderstood by outsiders. For this reason, most multinational corporations employ technical writers and language specialists to localise products; that is, to research and recommend appropriate, inoffensive, memorable and pleasant-sounding terminology for international audiences.
- **Use colour effectively**. Colour is useful for:

  - emphasising important information
  - grouping related items
  - reinforcing site structure
  - increasing comprehension and recall.

When using colour, be aware that it can change the appearance of objects, including text type. For example, warm and bright colours make things look larger than cool and dark colours, so, for example, if you use a black screen use bigger text. Also be aware that people cannot look into bright colours for long, so avoid dense text on a bright screen. Shape also affects the appearance of colours. Use blue for large areas and backgrounds, but not for text type, thin lines or small shapes, as it is difficult to focus on blue. To remember the impact of colour on the user, think of the colour spectrum (ROYGBIV) running from the front of the screen to the back. For example, red, orange and yellow will stand out the most; blue, indigo and violet will recede into the background. Keep in mind also that colour and shape carry symbolism that varies from culture to culture. This is of particular relevance if you are aiming for an international audience. For example, Euro Disney initially used purple extensively in their site only to find that for some cultures purple is considered a taboo colour, linked with death.

● Website development

In developing websites or in evaluating currently existing ones, consider, in addition to content, two other factors: **page design** and **navigation**. Design and navigation should be developed at the same time as content. This gives balance and consistency to the website and makes an overall better impression of an integrated product.

Page design

Page design on the web takes its cue from magazine layout, which was covered in Chapter 4. The main elements of page design, you may remember, are proximity, alignment, repetition and contrast.

Navigation

Navigation on web pages is equivalent to turning the pages in a book. As the users do not have all the pages in front of them and cannot skip rapidly through them, designers should be careful to create a navigation structure that follows a logical organisation, in accordance with number of pages and amount of information. Navigation takes place through links, and in designing links, the considerations are similar to those involved in paragraphing and sectioning written texts. For example, questions to be considered are:

- how many links to make and what to call them
- what information to put in each linked page
- how to cross-reference pages so that the user does not have to go back to the Home Page in order to access another link. Appropriate navigation bars at the side and/or top of pages are effective in achieving this.

Navigation involves the information architecture of a website. There are three basic architectural designs:

- *Sequential.* This involves simple navigation and is suitable for sites that describe products. This involve scrolling down a page or 'jumping' to a section within the page, usually by means of devices called anchors. Sequential navigation is not advisable if there is a lot of information to communicate, because it comes across as one big chunk of unprocessed writing, and tends to lose the interest of the user.
- *Hierarchical.* Commonly used in company websites, this navigates through static taxonomies (i.e. broad categories, equivalent to chapters in a book: 'Company History', 'Recruitment Procedures', etc.). Hierarchical navigation takes the user from one page to another by clicking on links and involves minimum scrolling.
- *Network.*This navigates through associative links and is suitable for research or exploring (search engine websites are an example of this). Network navigation takes the user from one site to another rather than from one page to another in the same site.

Writing web content

The strong visual aspect of websites creates many similarities between web content and copywriting. Therefore some copywriting guidelines would be useful. Copy is the text that accompanies products as part of the packaging, and the text that goes with images, logos and photos in advertisements. Copy is short and intense. The place where the copy is to be published determines the length of copy as well as the length of paragraphs and/or sections, and formatting. Generally, copy is between one word and a couple of paragraphs long. In many cases, copy goes with what is known as the 'three-way power' of **headline**, **illustration(s)** and **text**, so formatting involves blending these three elements in a compelling and attractive way. 'Headline' indicates the importance of interesting and attention-grabbing titles and captions, 'illustration' draws attention to the skill of integrating suitable and impressive visual information with verbal text, and 'text' brings in the role of the written word in communicating meaning. It is the effective balance between these three elements that accounts for the success of the copy.

In both print and digital contexts, quality copywriting is not 'conning' people into buying things and bringing you profit; it involves expressing your enthusiasm and motivating others to see the world from your point of view. Sincerity is transparent and good promoters are those that can create a desire in other people by showing this desire in themselves.

When writing content for a company website, first decide on your focus: will the most effective means of communicating your message be by detailing qualities of the product, by explaining how the product works and what you can do with it, by showing its novelty with regard to its predecessors in a historical framework, or by positioning the product in relation to others in the market? According to your choice of focus, apply one of the following three strategies:

Product-centred strategy

This looks at features of the product and builds a message around them. Often used in brand advertising, this strategy turns the product into an object of value by using signs of prestige, power, high status, aesthetic appeal or authority. If the selling focus is an organisation, this strategy is called corporate or public relations advertising. For example, this extract from the IBM web site uses this strategy:

> IBM Global Services is the world's largest information technology services provider, with 2000 revenue of more than $33 billion. In

addition to consulting, IBM Global Services is the world leader in IT outsourcing, hosting and systems services (www.ibm.com).

Prospect-centred strategy

This focuses on needs and wants of the target audience and turns product attributes into client benefits. It emphasises the functional aspects of the product in relation to their practical effects on clients. It usually achieves this by giving examples of people who have used the product successfully, or outlines uses of the product in specific circumstances. For example, this extract from Apple's website promoting their new version of Final Cut Pro (a video editing program) uses this strategy:

> And just as QuickTime gives Final Cut Pro the ability to work with a variety of capture hardware, the new QuickTime real-time architecture enables Final Cut Pro 2 to work with a variety of real-rime hardware, allowing video professionals to choose the format and features most suited to meet their needs (www.apple.com/finalcutpro).

Unique selling proposition (USP) strategy

This constructs a benefit statement that is unique to the product in relation to competing products, and that is also important to the client. Copy implementing this strategy usually begins with a statement about the uniqueness of the product. It then goes on to explain the reasons for this uniqueness, maybe by indicating the attributes that contribute to it. A short example is:

> X magnesium tray is the only way to polish silver without rubbing. X magnesium contains a unique gel-based lubricant that allows smooth cleaning without scratches.

● **Website evaluation: content, aesthetics and usability**

How much credibility you give to a website depends on **purpose** and **intended audience**. For example, if the site was designed for entertainment purposes, factors such as accuracy of factual information and in-depth analysis of topics would not be suitable criteria for evaluation. Similarly, a promotional site should be evaluated according to advertising, as opposed to scholarly, criteria. For example, does the site attract attention through graphic design and text that is appealing to its target audience? Does it provide information that anticipates the users' questions and concerns?

According to usability expert Jakob Nielsen (2000), ineffective web writing is characterised by:

- long blocks of prose, without paragraphing or headings, making it difficult to scan quickly
- overly wordy expositions of concepts, with more than one idea per paragraph
- obscure or confusing headings rather than ones that are immediately understandable and informative
- little or no hypertext or links
- hypertext that takes the user to another page rather than linking discrete blocks of related material
- indirect or delayed exposition with main points or conclusions presented near the end of the text (as opposed to inverted pyramid style, which is more effective)
- marketese or exaggerated language
- technically complex elements (such as animations, unnecessary special effects, etc.) that expand file size and slow page loading
- inadequate site search functions that limit navigation
- inadequate site maps that limit navigation

The following is a checklist of the most important aspects of an effective website. Refer to this checklist both when you design your own site and when you evaluate others' sites:

Website Evaluation Chart

Relevance
- [ ] Does the site provide information relevant to its topic?
- [ ] Does the content reflect the title of the site, and are all headings and sections useful in determining content?

Timely/current information
- [ ] Does the site include a date for the information it presents?

Objective
- [ ] If it is a commercial site, has an exaggerated promotional writing style, or marketese, been avoided?
- [ ] Is the language and style used appropriate to the content, purpose and audience?

Scannable

☐ Do users have the option to scan tables of contents, sections of summaries, bullets and boldface, short paragraphs?

Concise

☐ Is the text clear and concise?
☐ Is text organised in small chunks?

Writing

☐ Is spelling and grammar correct?
☐ Is there introductory text where necessary?
☐ Do multimedia elements support the task?

AESTHETICS

Audio

☐ Does the music evoke an appropriate emotion?
☐ Does the audio help to set the scene?

Video

☐ Is it useful?
☐ Is the quality adequate?
☐ Does it load quickly?

Animation

☐ Is it useful?
☐ Is the quantity suitable?

GRAPHICS

☐ Do they complement the text?
☐ Are they stored for maximum compression (in other words, do they take the least space possible for their size and therefore decrease downloading time)?

Colour

☐ Is the choice appropriate for the site?
☐ Is the number of colours suitable?
☐ Are colours used consistently?

Typography

- [ ] Is the font appropriate to the content of the site?
- [ ] Are there sufficient margins?

Layout and design

- [ ] Does the page fit on the screen?
- [ ] Is the layout consistent throughout the site?
- [ ] Does the site appear pleasing?

USABILITY

Download time

- [ ] Does the content download fast enough (up to 10 seconds)?

Ease of use

- [ ] Are options visible without scrolling?
- [ ] Is it possible to compare all options at the same time?

Links/image map

- [ ] Do link names match page names?
- [ ] Are link headings easy to understand?
- [ ] Do all the links work?
- [ ] Is there a clear link to the Home Page?
- [ ] Are clickable areas obvious in the image map?

Navigation

- [ ] Is the navigation scheme obvious?
- [ ] Does each page include information on the site?
- [ ] Can the user go from one page to another without returning to the Home Page?
- [ ] Is hierarchical and/or sequential navigation used effectively?

Platform

- [ ] Does the site work with all major browsers?
- [ ] Does the site work on small and large monitors?

● Designing your own website

Keeping the above discussion in mind, here are ten steps to guide you when designing your own website. These highlight the basic considerations, especially as regards the writing component, but, of course, they are not exhaustive.

1. Planning

As with other types of writing, the planning stage is vital to conceptualise your project. Visualise your project in terms of your goals and your audience. Be specific because this is your guiding light. What do you want the site to offer? What kind of presentation and information does the target audience expect? For example, are they likely to be impressed with a high-tech presentation or would a low-tech presentation concentrating on factual information be better? Do you think your audience would have access to high-tech hardware and software? Or should you play it safe and use more standard technology that anyone with a 54k modem and a simple browser with no animation would be able to access? Use the pre-writing techniques outlined in Chapter 1 to generate ideas about the content and format of your site.

2. Storyboarding

Map out the organisation and structure of your site before commencing any work on the site itself. A constructive way to do this is by storyboarding (see also Chapter 1). To understand the function of this, remember that a fundamental characteristic of the digital medium is that it is non-linear and works according to the principle of random access –users can skip from one section to another easily.

An oral text is linear. The hearer perceives it one sound at a time. Print writing uses the two-dimensionality of the page, but it rarely takes advantage of this spatiality – most texts can be transcribed on a very long line. Hypertext has developed another way to construct a reading space: the multiplication of parallel linear sequences. This means that you can access information in a non-fixed, or random, order: there is no inherent sequential structure, and you can skip or repeat sections, and pick any section at any time without the limitations of temporal, linear, order.

However, as there is no structure as such, this situation is difficult to conceptualise in the planning stage. This is where storyboarding comes in. Storyboarding is the design of numbered and sequenced screens, each screen representing a section of the project. Each screen contains information on the contents, problem areas, research sources and other relevant information of each section. Storyboarding is useful because it imposes a structure where there is none, so that you can see better what you are doing.

3. Creating a content inventory

After planning and storyboarding your project, consider what content should be included. Where is the text that you intend to include? Does it exist in a print document, or do you need to create it from scratch by doing more research and new writing? Also, remembering that electronic text is more difficult to read than printed text, even if it exists already in print, you may still need to edit it to shorten sentences and restructure content to make it suitable to the digital medium.

Similarly, do photos and graphics exist or will you have to create them? Photos, for example, will need to be scanned and digitised. Display text, artwork or other graphics might need to be created, then saved as certain file formats.

4. Organising content

The way you arrange content will determine how easy it is for users to access and navigate your site. Often it helps to use flow charts and other diagrams to list content categories, organise things by topic, refine topic groups, and arrange groups into a workable structure that you can manipulate and change as you progress on the project.

5. Considering navigation controls

Navigation controls should be functional, useful and easy to understand. As noted earlier in the section on navigation, good navigation minimises travel from page to page inside and outside the site to get the information you need. It also minimises redundancy: by thinking carefully about how many pages to include, what to call them and what information to include in each, you have less risk of repeating the same information on different pages or misleading the users about where to go to get what they want. Think of navigation as signage in a zoo. Which way to the elephants? Which way to the lions?

6. Choosing a style or personality

Users will remember and recognise your site by its personality. Therefore, choose your style carefully. For example, do you want to project a serious or an irreverent image? Do wild colours or sedated grays represent your services better? Create a style and personality for your site, by using consistently repetition and contrast: for example, if you choose to use a type of font for a heading and another for text, make sure that you follow this through consistently for all headings and text. The same goes for choice of words and phrases. As happens with magazine layout, websites have basic design constants (number of columns per page, body/text size or style, graphic styles) but also many variables (headline styles, colour treatment, etc.).

7. Creating the site

You can create your site by using code (HTML) or you can use one of the many web authoring packages of software that are available. You do not need to know any HTML to create a site, although it is useful to have a basic knowledge, even if using software, to have more control over your work. If you are using authoring tools, it may be useful to design your site first in a word processing or image editing program (such as Microsoft® Word, Adobe Photoshop®, or Macromedia Fireworks®) – or even with pen and paper. Also, it often helps to create a template page. It saves you from having to reformat every new page with your layout specifics.

8. Reducing the size of graphics

The key to a fast loading site is the size and format of the graphics. Everything on a website, text included, may be saved as a graphics file (not only images and pictures). Remember, though, that graphics take more space than HTML, so it is best not to overuse them. Three important tips to keep in mind when designing and saving graphics are:

- Images are measured by 'pixels' so direct your software to keep the image size/resolution to no more than 90 pixels per inch, preferably 72 pixels per inch.
- Use a browser-safe colour palette (this comes with web application software, such as Macromedia Dreamweaver®). If you use your own colours, you may find they come out different on different browsers and ruin the effect you intended.
- Use the ALT tags. The words placed in the ALT tag describe the graphic. These words are important for people who surf with images turned off, or who do not have access to graphic browsers, or those who have limited vision and use text readers to read web pages.

9. Naming pages

Name carefully each page that you create, remembering that page names are not the same as the name of the site. Search engines will scan these page titles, so the more descriptive they are, the more hits you will get from people using search engines. Also, page names link the pages, so if you change the name of a page, you must remember to change it everywhere else where it is linked, so that the browser knows how to access it.

10. Testing

Web design is unreliable. What you create on your screen will look differently on other screens and different browsers. This is especially true with regard to tables, but it is also true for text and graphics. That is why it is important to test work–in–progress regularly, at least on major browsers such as Microsoft Explorer and Firefox. Also, test your completed site on different computer platforms (especially Macintosh and PC) and with at least two browsers on those platforms.

PC and Macintosh (Mac) platforms are currently the most common operating systems. These two platforms have differences that you should take into account when designing a site. At this moment, the more important differences are:

- Mac typefaces are about 10 per cent smaller than PC type. Your text, if created on a Mac and viewed on a PC, will look very large.
- PC monitors have a higher screen resolution (90 pixels per inch as opposed to 72 pixels per inch for Macs). Because the visual difference is small and smaller file size is important, it may be best to reduce to 72 pixels per inch.
- PC monitors are darker than Mac monitors. Photos will appear darker on a PC, especially if the photos were created on a Mac.

● All in the (type) family: what fonts to use

This section looks at typography: the study of writing characters, or fonts. Fonts are arranged in generalised groupings known as 'type families'. Type families are divided into individual and specific. For example, Arial is a member of the sans-serif family, which can include specific groups such as 10 point Arial, 12 point Arial Bold, 8 point Arial Italic, and so on. Some of the more common families are as follows:

Serif

Serif fonts have little 'tails' on the end of letterforms. These 'tails' help the eye to quickly define letters and words and are easier to read in print than other families. They have an ancient history: the Romans chiselled serif typefaces on their buildings. One serif font is Century Schoolbook, which was designed in the USA in the early twentieth century for use in primary school textbooks.

Century Schoolbook

Sans serif

The art and literary movements of the early twentieth century, particularly those following the First World War, brought sans serif typefaces. As the name implies, the 'tails' are missing, giving a stripped down, unemotional, nihilist typeface reflecting the ideologies of that era. Today, sans serif fonts are the favourites of advertising designers and transportation signage creators. They are the preferred font for electronic writing as they are easy to read on a computer monitor.

Verdana

Script

Originally designed to put feeling back into the mechanical world of printing, scripts are used to imitate handwriting. Never use all uppercase letters in a script typeface. It is incredibly difficult to read.

Lucida Calligraphy

Decorative

Some type is not meant to be read in large text blocks. Decorative faces are great for headlines, signage and other uses, but use them sparingly.

Curlz

Engraved

Engraved fonts have a classical, sophisticated and elegant look. They are based on the work of John Caxton, the founder of the British printing and typography industry in the seventeenth century.

Colonna MT

Black letter (also known as Fraktur)

In the sixteenth and seventeenth centuries, printing and type design were wrapped up in the political and economic birth of European nation states. A few examples of these 'nationalistic' typefaces remain in Cyrillic (Russian alphabet) and Black Letter. This typefont has a Gothic touch to it and is associated with horror movies, prison tattoos and Nazis! Because of these connotations, use with care. Once again, avoid setting words in all upper-case in this font.

Lucída Blackletter

Dingbats

Dingbats are symbols masquerading as letters. Use very, very sparingly and only for fun. Definitely avoid if precision and clarity are your aims!

✳❂❑❖❖❖■✳❂❂▼▲ (this is meant to read ZapfDingbats)

● PowerPoint® presentations

Since Microsoft® PowerPoint® is a software program, operating in the digital medium, and producing text that is mostly read off a screen, this chapter is a suitable place to discuss oral presentations that are accompanied by PowerPoint slides. PowerPoint presentations are used in countless business situations, from presenting a business plan to potential investors, to presenting progress on a project to management, to presenting the findings of an investigation to a committee – to name just a few situations.

What makes a good presentation? In the final analysis, the best way to answer this question is by attending presentations and seeing which stand out as impressive, which are competent but unexceptional and which are downright boring and confusing. You can then analyse the characteristics of each, emulate the ones that produce effective results, and avoid the ones that lead to failure. Being an attentive member of the audience will give you invaluable tips on being a master speaker. The following guidelines are based on tested observations.

PowerPoint is associated with two 'diseases': **Death by PowerPoint**, and **PowerPoint Karaoke**. Death by PowerPoint occurs when the speaker 'kills' the topic (not to mention the audience) by over-reliance on slides. Some speakers seem to think that every word they utter must come off a slide and, therefore, write slides to fill an hour's talk – which can make up about 90 slides! The fact to remember here is that an oral presentation is a speech, and that PowerPoint is an aid in delivering this speech – a means to an end, not the end itself.

A related 'disease', PowerPoint karaoke, occurs when the speaker uses the slides as transcripts and reads them out to the audience. In this case, the slides become the centrepiece of the talk, not the speaker. However, although focusing on one or two slides to analyse information is acceptable (especially if the slides contain financial data or other important graphical information), depending on the slides to carry the whole interaction is not. If you expect the audience to read a lot of data during your talk, consider giving handouts or sending out some written information before the talk, to prepare the audience.

Such considerations of balance and timing are not just cosmetic touches. They can have far-reaching consequences. For example, after the space shuttle Columbia burned up upon re-entering the atmosphere on 1 February 2003, a committee, the Columbia Accident Investigation Board, was put together to find out if the accident could have been prevented. This found that there was evidence that an accident might occur, but that this evidence was not communicated effectively to appropriate parties who could make decisions and implement preventative action. In particular, the Board concluded that a presentation by engineers to NASA officials was partly responsible for the confusion. Evidently, the engineers had used so many disorganised data on their slides that their analysis was obscured and the officials were misled as to the level of danger (Gurak and Lannon, 2007, p. 219).

And the NASA officials did not, apparently, do a much better job themselves. The Board stated:

> At many points during its investigation, the Board was surprised to receive similar presentation slides from NASA officials in place of technical reports. The Board views the endemic use of PowerPoint briefing slides instead of technical reports as an illustration of the problematic methods of technical communication at NASA. (Cited in Gurak and Lannon, 2007, pp. 219–20)

Such incidents support the claim that PowerPoint slides are a visual medium with verbal elements, rather than the other way around. For complex arguments, elaborate explanations and detailed justifications, presentations should be complemented with written material that does not have to be read off a screen.

So, what are the **differences** between oral and written presentations of information? These are some:

- *Spoken information is more difficult to retain.* This is why listeners need to take notes or be given written material to summarise, highlight and reinforce the main information presented.
- *Attention tends to fluctuate when listening.* Distractions are more pronounced in oral communication contexts than in written. When

reading, one can always reread information; when listening, this is not always possible.

- *Spoken information is coloured by the speaker's physical presence.* In fact, the speaker him/herself may be a distraction, which is why speakers should take care to dress, speak and move in ways that complement the content of their speech, not in ways that draw attention away from it. When delivering an oral presentation take care to present a strong and confident presence (unassuming speakers tend to diminish the importance of what they are saying), with enough control over mannerisms and voice projection so that you do not become the centre of attention, drawing attention away from the content of your presentation.
- *Speaker's presence enables clarification.* This is an advantage in speaking because listeners can ask for explanations and otherwise interact with the speaker. However, a presentation should be clear enough to avoid the need for many clarifications and repetitions.

However, oral and written presentations contain also some **similarities**. Both should:

- *Take the audience from what they know to what they do not know.* People become involved in the interaction if the presentation begins with common ground (i.e. information that is shared between speaker and audience) and then presents the new information or findings against this background.
- *Have an overall message sustained throughout.* A presentation is a document. Therefore, do not try to cram too much information in it, especially if it does not relate directly to the main message of the presentation. If you have a lot to say, produce different documents with a main message in each, or give a series of presentations. At the end of your talk, the audience should be able to clearly summarise what the talk was about.
- *Establish a pattern of organisation.* Be consistent through the presentation, so that the audience can recognise your logic of organisation and follow it better. For example, if you decide to present a topic in its chronological development, sustain this throughout, or indicate and justify the point where you change. Similarly, if going from most important to least important, sustain it and do not suddenly include an important point towards the end, where it is more likely to be misunderstood as a minor detail because of its position.

- *Balance innovation with expectation.* People generally listen and read to learn something new that they can understand. Therefore, make sure your content is original enough to be compelling and interesting, and understandable enough so that the audience do not lose their way.

Here are some facts about visuals that were mentioned earlier in the chapter, and which could be reinforced here:

- It takes longer to read off a screen
- It takes even longer to read uppercase fonts
- Colour is not just ornamental – it communicates
- Colour creates illusion when used as background or foreground
- Numbers in graphs are hard to read.

For these reasons, when preparing PowerPoint slides avoid:

- visual clutter: include ample white space; in fact, five points or fewer on a slide is a good way to go
- blaring colours and contrasts
- images that are just ornamental and have no relevance to the topic
- backgrounds and slide designs that are just ornamental and have no relevance to the topic
- animation that has no relevance to the point and is used only for clever effect
- small fonts: 18 point font or larger is advisable; use smaller fonts for secondary points.

Ordering information in PowerPoint® presentations

What you say and how you say it depends on your purpose, audience and time limits. An analysis of these should give you the background and confidence necessary to create an effective talk that answers the audience's questions and wins them over. Here are some general guidelines that would be valid for many occasions.

1. Begin with 'bottom line' in business contexts and with hypothesis/objectives in research contexts: this puts the audience in perspective and directs their attention – they know why it is important to listen.
2. Give only as much background as necessary: since listeners cannot

retain as much information as readers, limit background details to the essential.

3. Avoid an overly linear sequence: especially in longer (one hour or more) presentations, divide your content into sections. At the end of each section, summarize briefly and introduce the next section. This is useful because listeners may get distracted and lose your thread; by including appropriate section endings and beginnings within the talk, you allow them to catch up

4. End on a high note: chances increase that the audience will remember your presentation if it ends on a strong point rather than just fade away or end abruptly, especially if you are competing with other presenters for attention.

Bullet points in PowerPoint® presentations

Bullet points are the raw material of PowerPoint presentations. To use them effectively, you should be aware of their function in writing. Bullet points list information that belongs to one logical category. Accordingly, they should not be a random itemisation. Ideally, they should follow from a lead sentence or title, and be structured as endings of that sentence, with each point suggesting an alternative completion of the sentence. They could be individual sentences, but again, the rule of being part of a logical category would apply: they should present different aspects of the information in the title.

Some common problems to avoid when using bullet points include:

Confusing levels of hierarchy. Being part of the same category, a list of bullet points should not introduce information on a different level. For example, the following bullet-points show this error. Notice how each point develops from the previous, making these individual sentences, rather than a list of items:

- Confusing levels of hierarchy
- This disrupts the flow of information
- Points should follow from lead or heading.

Using narrative sequences. This is related to the previous, in that each bullet point is a sequence of action, with all the points making a section or story. In this case, a paragraph structure would be more appropriate to present this kind of information:

- The project investigates the high staff turnover in the company
- We collected data from surveys and interviews conducted over a period of two years
- Exit surveys showed a dissatisfaction with promotion opportunities
- It is obvious that measures need to be taken to prevent such staffing issues.

Neglecting parallel structure. The fact that points are part of one category should be reflected in their grammatical structure. Try to make your points as parallel as possible. Here is an example of lack of parallelism:

Suggestions for improvement include:

- More incentives for initiative should be given
- Salary increase
- We should review current recruitment methods
- Developing a mentoring scheme.

This problem can be corrected by choosing one structure and keeping it consistent in all points, for example:

> Suggestions for improvement include:
>
> - Giving more incentives for initiative
> - Increasing salary
> - Reviewing current recruitment methods
> - Developing a mentoring scheme.

Activities

1. Find three sites, from corporate, news and entertainment contexts and discuss their differences. Focus on layout, naming and aesthetic aspects, such as colour. Note how appropriate the design choices were for the target audience and purpose.

2. Find some websites that make effective use of page design and navigation and some that do not. How well integrated is navigation with page design? How do the sites make use of the four elements of publishing:, proximity, alignment, repetition and contrast? Could they be improved?

3. Make a list of documents that would be more effective in print form and a list of documents that would be more effective in digital form. Discuss your reasons. Find some examples of these documents to analyse and discuss in your group.

6 Reports and Proposals

This chapter looks at longer business document types, in particular proposals, business plans and investigative reports. The guidelines and formats outlined here are based on standard, international conventions where English is the medium of communication. Keep in mind, however, that format and structure of reports vary to a certain extent to suit the needs of the particular company, writing situation and audience. Similarly, many companies have in-house templates that should be used. In all, however, the framework presented here will alert you to the factors that you should take into account when writing reports, and when creating templates and style guides for others to use.

Focus on:

▶ Reports, research articles and essays
▶ Types and functions of reports
▶ Proposals
▶ Report layout

● Essays, research articles and reports

As a professional in a business or industry context, you are generally required to produce two types of documents: reports on various issues to management and/or clients, and research articles for professional associations and journals documenting the data you discovered in your experience. If you decide to develop your writing talents further, you might also publish popular interpretations of your work for non-specialist audiences, such as essays for creative non-fiction publications. Therefore, an overview of the differences between these document types would be useful. We start by looking at essays, then research articles, and end with reports, which will lead to the main part of the chapter.

Essays

An essay discusses a topic from different angles, synthesises ideas, and develops the ramifications of an issue. Essays are generally evaluative and may include a subjective approach, which, when the essay is expertly written, is a deliberate choice. Essays are usually composed of continuous and well-developed (four to seven sentences long) paragraphs. Cohesion and flow from one point to the next are important for the readability of an essay, especially in the absence of headings, bullet points and other highlighting signals. Essays tend to follow a linear development, building on points indicated in the introduction, and should not be repetitive. Although, to a certain extent, clarity and conciseness are valued in most document types, essays are allowed a more convoluted style and idiosyncratic expression to reflect the complexity of the topic with which they deal.

For example, consider the following paragraph, in relation to its essayist patterns, from an essay by David Bohm on creativity in science:

Example of Essay Paragraph

Could it be that a scientist deeply wants to discover the laws of nature, so that he can predict natural phenomena, and thus enable man to participate intelligently in nature's processes so as to produce results that he desires? Of course, such prediction and intelligent participation can sometimes be very interesting. But this is only in a context in which these activities are determined by something else that is more deeply significant, such as, for example, a common goal of great importance. Generally speaking, however, there is hardly ever such a common goal. Indeed, in most cases, the content of what the research scientist predicts is in itself actually rather trivial (the precise paths of particles, the precise number of instruments that will register a certain phenomenon, and so forth). Unless there were something beyond this that could give it significance, this activity would be petty, and, indeed, even childish.   (Bohm, 1998, p. 1)

The writer reflects on the nature of the scientific process by posing a question and then explaining certain implications of this question. The topic of the text is itself suited to an essay, as opposed to, say, a business report, since it can only be developed by means of speculative reasoning rather than experimental or empirical data. In addition, the answer to the question is not given in this paragraph, suggesting that this paragraph is one 'move' in a spiral of ideas leading to a conclusion that itself may be open-ended. The style is explorative and comprehensive, rather than 'bottom line', direct and concise, as would be the style of a business document.

Research articles and papers

Each topic of research involves different issues, problems and concerns, and requires a methodology suited to its specific qualities. In general, research is classified into two categories. **Qualitative research** is typified by cultural and conceptual studies where findings are more commonly expressed in words and logical reasoning rather than in numbers and statistical frequency. In such cases, a hypothesis is substantiated by consistent argument. **Quantitative research**, on the other hand, is typified by experimental studies in scientific disciplines where findings are usually expressed in numerical, or measurable, form. In such cases, a hypothesis is substantiated by quantifiable evidence, such as statistics.

When composing a research article that describes experimental data and statistical frequency, include the following information:

- **Hypothesis**. State hypotheses clearly and describe their relationship to previous research. Often, especially for the purpose of statistical testing, hypotheses are expressed in the *null* form: 'There is no difference between . . . ' or 'There is no relation between . . . '

- **Assumptions**. If you make assumptions, state them clearly. Do not take anything for granted.

- **Limitations**. State clearly limitations on time allowed, restrictions on length of document, or lack of resources.

- **Scope**. Set the parameters of the study by describing the elements it includes and those it excludes to make the study manageable and coherent. By delimiting the scope you set a focus and establish the big picture that justifies the details.

- **Definitions**. Define all keywords and variables. The interpretation of the findings of a study depends to a large extent on the way major terms are defined. Define variables operationally in terms of how they are measured in quantifiable form.

- **Research design**. Describe and justify the statistical or experimental methods for testing hypotheses. Also, indicate if the application of a certain statistical test or experiment will lead to the acceptance or rejection of the stated hypotheses.

- **Description of population and sample**. Describe and justify the population from which a representative or random sample is drawn. Show that you are not biased in your choice of population and/or sample.

- **Control of error**. Show how you control the variables that are operating in a given situation. In laboratory work it is usually possible to control major variables. In field studies it is usually only possible to control key variables. In either case, state clearly how variables are controlled.

> **Reliability and validity**. Describe the reliability and validity of test instruments. Ensure that tests provide consistent measurements.

Reports

In business contexts, you may be required to produce three types of reports: **descriptive**, **technical** and **analytical**. Descriptive reports inform the reader of events that have happened in the past or that are planned for the future, and are detailed and factual. Analytical reports usually deal with a problem by identifying the issues involved, investigating solutions, and recommending action. Technical reports describe and explain specifications, components of equipment, and system applications. Whereas descriptive and technical reports may be based entirely on facts, analytical reports include elements of persuasion and logical reasoning.

Descriptive and technical reports are the topic of Chapter 8. Here, we consider analytical reports.

● Analytical reports

Here are some major types of analytical reports and their functions:

Proposals and submissions show the highest level of persuasion. A proposal argues for a particular course of action and often takes the form of requests for funding or formal authorisation to pursue a particular project. While an investigative report researches a problem and suggests solutions, a proposal sets out a detailed project and in most cases includes a budget and resource requirements. Submissions argue for or against an issue to be decided by a responsible body. Members of the business community, for example, might make submissions for or against a new taxation bill under consideration by a government select committee.

Investigative reports analyse a problem and methodically recommend a specific course of action to solve this problem. Such reports often require specialist knowledge and are commissioned by a client or management, who requests the writer to expertly judge certain actions and comment in detail on issues and events that relate to a particular situation.

Feasibility studies investigate a possible plan of action and advise on whether the action should be taken. For example, a software company might request a feasibility study to decide whether there is market potential to invest in a new virtual reality game. A feasibility study weighs projected costs against projected income, taking into account such aspects as demographic factors, market demand, the actions of competitors, and resource requirements.

To understand better the difference in approach among these types of reports, consider this scenario. Assume you are the Director of Facilities Management in a company, in charge of ensuring security and smooth operation of building facilities. You are confronted with a problem of high electricity costs and inadequate heating. At the moment, the building uses electric heating. You could become aware of the problem in different ways, leading to different forms of communication.

For example, you could become aware of the problem through your own observations, and decide to propose a change in heating from electric to gas. In this case, you would communicate your idea in the form of a proposal, which would support the claim that it would be more cost effective to replace the current electric heating with gas. Alternatively, you could be led to believe that the problem is serious and long-ranging and requires more research to find an appropriate solution. In that case, you would undertake an investigation leading to a recommendations report, based on the problem that heating costs are high and the building is not warm enough. In your initial stage of research you are aware of the problem, but not the solution: you do not yet know if gas would be more cost effective. Finally, you could begin with the question, 'Should we convert to gas heating?' and base your research and analysis accordingly, in order to answer it. Your results would then be presented in a feasibility analysis. This would analyse the problem and recommend action but its scope would be more limited than in an investigative report, because you would be considering only one possible solution to the problem.

These alternatives would take the following forms:

> *Proposal claim*: it would be cheaper and more effective to replace the current electric heating with gas.

> *Trigger for investigation*: heating costs are high but, at the same time, the building is too cold.

> *Feasibility analysis*: would our heating situation work better if we converted to gas heating?

General guidelines for effective reports

All analytical reports share some common compositional and structural characteristics:

- *Include all the information the readers need.* Pay special attention to the problem or situation that triggered the report, the methods used to gather information and the findings of the investigation or data gathering. In design reports, include information about why you made specific design decisions and justify your choices.

- *Structure your report so that readers can easily locate the information they want.* For example, some readers will be interested in one or several sections. This is why reports should be divided into titled and numbered sections. The executive summary and the section headings act as signposting showing readers where to go to get what they want. Also, it is advisable to include a header or footer with identifying information on each page (such as the title of the report and your name or the title of the project). Report sections may be distributed, so readers should know where each section came from.

- *Write as clearly and concisely as possible without sacrificing content or detail.* Chapter 3 provides guidelines on how to achieve this. Keep in mind that clarity comes not only from style but also from the organisation of information. The pattern you create in sequencing information communicates as much as the data you present. For example, presenting information in chronological order suggests that time and progression or change are important aspects; similarly, prioritising and listing information shows the degree of importance attributed to each item in the list.

Paragraphing in analytical reports

Report paragraphs tend to be longer than in web content or magazine articles, but shorter than in essays. A length of four to six sentences is generally appropriate. By committing yourself to that kind of length you are serving the following objectives:

(i)   The paragraphs need to be sufficiently short so that crucial pieces of information catch the reader's eye. Reports generally contain section headings for this reason.

(ii) But equally, the paragraphs need to be long enough to allow elaboration and analysis of issues. Enough space must be given so that cause and effect, chronological, comparison/contrast and other relationships between ideas are clearly and fully expressed.

When composing report paragraphs, follow these guidelines:

1. Avoid a succession of very short (one to two sentences) and very long (eight sentences or more) paragraphs. The problem with short paragraphs is that they read disjointedly and present the reader with difficulties in linking your ideas together into a main message. With very long paragraphs the reader needs a pause so as to feel that s/he or she has read and understood a unit of the message. If you rush on without a paragraph break, the reader will soon feel overwhelmed and stop assimilating the ideas and interacting with the text.

2. Present one main point or idea in each paragraph. Avoid crowding a paragraph with too much vital information. If you have a large amount of reasoning or supporting examples to give for a point, break them into two paragraphs. Bear in mind that people are adapted to taking in and committing to memory chunks of information that comprise between about five and seven items.

3. Make sure there is enough cohesion within the paragraph. That is, avoid listing a set of disconnected sentences. Similarly, provide adequate transition signals between paragraphs in one section. Show the reader how the idea of one paragraph is connected to the idea of the next paragraph in that section.

There are three main problems writers have when composing paragraphs:

- The paragraph could contain too much information, which can confuse the reader as to what the main point is. This is a bit like a song with discordant rhythm or beat.

- The paragraph could be abrupt, containing incomplete information on the main point. This again loses the reader, who may find it difficult to follow through a point and understand its relevance.

- The paragraph could give enough information on the main topic, but the sentences are disconnected and the paragraph lacks unity. This reads like a list of items with no connection and can be quite dull for the reader, who is forced to provide all the links.

Sections and section headings

As opposed to articles and essays where headings are optional, reports require division of paragraphs into sections and headings for all sections. Headings summarise the point(s) of each section and make reading under pressure easier. Readers can scan a document and find information without having to read all the text. In reports, this is an important asset because, often, different people read different sections of the report. Also, headings give readers some breathing space, as they indicate where a section has ended. Finally, sections give depth and dimensionality to the report by adding levels. The main sections constitute the main level, subsections introduce subordinate levels, etc. When sectioning:

- Balance the sections so that information is distributed effectively across the report. Avoid short, one-paragraph sections; also avoid putting the whole report in one long section. Use subsections for details or subordinate points of the idea of the main section. If information is important, do not bury it in a subsection, but devote a main section to it. On the whole, avoid sub-sub-sections, for simplicity and clarity. Sub-sub-sections add layers and therefore introduce more complexity in what could already be a complex report topic. Reduce the layers by analysing information, and thereby spreading it across fewer levels.

- Think carefully of the quantity and quality of the information you want to include in a heading. If a heading is too vague or general, it defeats the purpose of signalling to the reader the content of its section. Correlatively, if a heading is too long and detailed, it can slow down the flow of reading unnecessarily.

- Make sure all your headings of the same level are parallel in structure. When you choose a structure for all your headings, remain consistent throughout the report. For example, if you begin one heading for a main section with a gerund (an –ing form), the rest of the headings in main sections should also begin with a gerund. If you begin a heading with a noun, all headings should begin with nouns, and so on. Parallelism is discussed in more detail in Chapter 3.

The importance of headings becomes clear in the report outline. A report outline lists the sections and sub-sections that you intend to use in your report. A client or project manager often asks for an outline to monitor the progress of the report, to consider extra funding, and similar reasons. It is important, therefore, that your headings are worded and structured in a way that highlights the content and significance of your project.

Numbering of report sections

Headings and subheadings are conventionally numbered according to alphanumeric or decimal numbering methods.

Alphanumeric numbering:

I. First main idea
   (A)   First subdivision of main idea
   (B)   Second subdivision of main idea
      1. First example
      2. Second example
         (a) First detail
         (b) Second detail
   (C)   Third subdivision of main idea
II. Second main idea

Decimal numbering:

1. First main idea
   1.1   First subdivision of main idea
   1.2   Second subdivision of main idea
      1.2.1   First example
      1.2.2   Second example
         1.2.2.1   First detail
         1.2.2.2   Second detail
   1.3   Third subdivision of main idea
2. Second main idea

The outline of a business plan is on the following page.

Bullet points and numbered lists

Points are a powerful device to condense and highlight information in reports. They make a text more concise while allowing you to cover a wide area. Points also stand out from the rest of the text and draw the reader's attention to the issues you are discussing. They enable you to show your awareness of issues without needing to discuss them in depth. Use bullet points for items of roughly equal value; use numbered lists for items with priority ranking.

As explained in the section on PowerPoint presentations (which rely heavily on bullet points), in Chapter 5, bullet points chunk and itemise information on the same level of hierarchy; they do not connect items in a developmental sequence, which is the function of cohesion and transition signals. Bullet points are additive rather than procedural devices. When you include bullet points in your document:

Outline of Business Plan

1. Company Description
   1.1　Name and legal form
   1.2　Location
   1.3　Financial highlights
   1.4　Shareholders

2. Management and Organisation
   2.1　Organisation chart
   2.2　Key management
   　　　2.2.1　Board of Directors
   　　　2.2.2　Consultants and collaborators
   2.3　Other shareholders, rights and resolutions

3. Market and Competitors
   3.1　Market statistics
   3.2　Competitor data
   3.3　Market and customer surveys

4. Product
   4.1　Technical specifications
   4.2　Competitive advantages
   4.3　Patent, licence and trademarks
   4.4　Industry standards
   4.5　Research and development plans

5. Marketing and Sales
   5.1　Marketing plan
   　　　5.1.1　Marketing vehicles
   　　　5.1.2　Marketing materials

6. Financial Information
   6.1　Financial statements for last five years
   6.2　Financial forecasts and projections
   6.3　Amount and timing of needed funding

- *Use them sparingly*: overuse of points makes your writing choppy and leaves the reader without a strong grasp of your main message

- *Use them consistently*: use the same punctuation in bullet point lists throughout the document, and make sure that all items in one list are parallel.

- *Introduce them in a full sentence*: sections and paragraphs that begin with a list of points without any introduction look awkward. Headings describe the content of a whole section and should not be used as an introduction to a list of bullet points.

Compare the following extracts; the first is written in a block paragraph, and the other uses bullet points. Both are correctly written, so their appropriateness is determined by context and purpose. For example, the bullet-pointed version lends itself more readily to a document where each point is taken up and discussed further in subsequent sections.

Example A: block paragraph

The agency must make a reasonable effort to make the individual aware that information is being collected and the purpose for which it is collected. Also, the agency must indicate who the intended recipients are as well as provide details on its own structure. Another responsibility of the agency is to notify the individual of the legal requirements of the information (i.e. whether it is mandatory or voluntary), and the consequences of not providing it. Finally, the agency must clarify what access the individual will have to the information to correct it, if necessary.

Example B: bullet points

The agency must make a reasonable effort to make the individual aware of the:

- Fact that information is being collected
- Purpose for which the information is being collected
- Details of the agency collecting the information
- Legal requirement of the information
- Consequences of not providing the information
- Rights of access and correction of that information

● The proposal

Proposals are an extremely common type of document in professional settings. Even if your line of work does not put you in a position to write reports – say, if you are a trade journalist or a computer programmer – chances are that the time will come when you will need to submit a proposal in order to get approval and/or funding for a project. The following guidelines give an overview of the standard format and type of information associated with proposals. Many companies and funding agencies have set templates that need to be filled in when submitting a proposal. If that is the case, follow the instructions (they will not be too different from the ones outlined here). If no guidelines are offered, use the model presented here.

Proposals are initiated in two main ways: you either have an innovative idea that you believe will benefit an organisation or company and want to sell it to them, or you respond to a request for ideas that an organisation or company publicise. In the first case the proposal is **unsolicited**. In the second, it is a **request for proposals** (RFP). Unsolicited proposals are investigator initiated, and, therefore, there is often a greater need to sell the concept because it is novel and innovative. On the other hand, a request for proposals (RFP) or a programme announcement (PA) calls for research in a defined area, or requests an answer to a specific question. Here, it is a matter of matching one's expertise, ideas and plans to the solicitation.

Preliminary work for proposals

To maximise your chances for success, follow these guidelines:

1. Work on the conceptual framework of your idea until you really have good control over it.
2. Articulate your conceptual framework. Sit down with friends and/or colleagues and practise explaining your idea to them in a brief manner. If it is well conceptualised, you should be able to articulate it in a matter of sentences, over three minutes. Entertain their questions and make notes of the questions that occur. Recurring questions are probably indicative of problems in your communication or weaknesses in the concept. Use this feedback to improve your concept.
3. Investigate the current and previous research. Make sure that no one has already done the work you have in mind, or, if they have, that there is something really different or necessary about your approach. You are going to have to convince the readers that your activities are unique and justified. A major 'howler' is to be

informed that your project has already been done, or that you have missed a fundamental piece of work in the research.

4. Do your homework on the agency or company. Make sure that your idea falls within the topics they are interested in. Also, get as much information as you can on their required document formats. This will determine what attitude and style you should adopt. Familiarise yourself with the culture of the company and choose your words and expressions so that they are in tune with this culture. If your proposal is unsolicited, find out about the funding capacity of the agency or company. Remember that small agencies cannot afford to fund high-budget projects, so it would be a waste of time submitting ambitious proposals to them.

5. Assess your need for collaborators. Sometimes, having collaborators can substantially strengthen your proposal. However, it is important that, from the project's inception, everyone understands their role. Make sure that the content of each member's contribution and time allocation is understood and accepted by all.

Proposal components

Most proposals contain the following elements. More or less space is given to each element depending on the nature of the proposal. Therefore, these topics variously would constitute sections in some proposals, and subsections in others.

Cover page

On the cover page include:

- project title
- information about the individual applicant or applicant organisation
- date of submission
- proposed project period
- amount requested
- project director's name and signature.

Project description

Identify the problem or question to be addressed, and describe its implications. Give some background on the proposed project, including results from prior research. Show a clear connection between the problem, lack or gap that you identified and the role of the proposed project in dealing with it. Visuals that depict the relationship of your work to the current knowledge base or model base are often helpful in getting your message across.

Objectives or specific aims

State concisely and in measurable terms the specific aims of the project and the hypotheses that underlie those aims or objectives. Distinguish between short-term plans and long-term goals. It is always useful to describe how the project can evolve and develop if the expected results are achieved (in other words, what the company or agency is buying in the long run).

Methodology or experimental design

Describe precisely how you will achieve your objectives through experimental or other procedures. Describe new methodology and advantages over existing methods. If several outcomes (or result scenarios) are plausible, describe them. Give alternative courses of action in the event that results occurring early lead you away from your original methodology – anticipate outcomes and have a plan to deal with them.

Evaluation

In certain proposals, especially in those for projects with long-term implications, describe plans for evaluating the project or analysing the data. Justify the choices made for evaluation tools and describe any post-hoc evaluation that may depend on the results of the initial analysis. Explain how you will know if the project is producing positive results.

Sources cited

If applicable, include a list of the sources cited in the proposal, using a method of referencing that is acceptable in the subject area of your topic.

Budget and justification

Work out your budget very carefully and give as much detail as possible. Itemise each cost and justify its relevance to the project. The budget is usually presented in cost sheet format. Items commonly included are: salaries and wages; fringe benefits; equipment; travel; supplies; publication charges; postage; telephone; consultants; subcontracts; and indirect costs. A justification section usually accompanies the budget, which explains how you arrived at your totals. Briefly explain how budget items were estimated and why these items are needed, if it is not obvious.

Personnel and qualifications and facilities

Identify who will perform the various activities or procedures described in the plan. Provide justification for each individual appropriate to his/her level of involvement, and include the qualifications of key project personnel. Make clear the reasons that make you or your team the best candidates for the project. Describe the resources that are already available for performance of the project.

Other current and/or pending support

If applicable, describe sources that have already funded your current project or other similar projects, or sources that you intend to solicit for funding.

Resumé/biographical sketch (optional)

In external proposals, you may need to 'sell' yourself as well as your concept. Include some details about your professional background if you think this will influence the reception of your proposal positively.

Appendices (optional)

Possible items include:

- facilities descriptions
- letters of support, illustrations
- maps
- extensive bibliography
- other material not easily incorporated into the body of the proposal.

Here is a short internal proposal written by the Director of a software company to a client on developing the latter's company website.

Proposal for Acme Machinery Website

1. Background

Acme Machinery and Tools is a small, but growing, business specialising in machinery, plant, equipment and tools used in the engineering, construction, woodworking, agriculture, horticulture, farming, catering, food service and many other industries.

The existing Acme website lists a selection of available goods, categorised by industry. We have identified the following problems and limitations with the existing website:

- *Content is incomplete*
  The content on the website lacks important information. Only a selection of Acme's full range of products is online. The site is also missing information on the company itself.

- *Website is static*
  Both finding products and navigating the website are tedious tasks.

Customer communication is still limited to traditional channels (phone, fax, post, etc.).

- *Design is basic*
  The existing pages are very basic in design, offering little visual appeal to the visitor. The layouts, colours and graphics are inconsistent from page to page.

- *Website is difficult to maintain*
  Maintaining the static lists of products is time-consuming and technically difficult.

2. Project Description

The proposed solution is a new database-driven website with a professionally designed interface. We examine the goals and objectives, the design, and the methodology used to construct the new website.

2.1 Goals and objectives
The goals of this project are to:

1. Publish Acme's company information and products online, and provide the tools to keep this content up to date.
2. Allow searching of all products and website content.
3. Design a visually appealing interface while enforcing structural and aesthetic consistency across the website.
4. Allow maintenance of every aspect of the website through a web browser by Acme staff.

3. Methodology

The following process will be used to complete the project.

1. Strategy and specification
   The first stage is to identify the business strategies and the purpose of the website. Detailed specifications would be written to determine the functional and technical approach to constructing the website.

2. Implementation
   At the implementation stage, the website would be constructed according to the specifications.

3. Testing and debugging
   While basic technical testing would be performed during implementation, thorough testing would be done once the website is technically complete.

4. Delivery
   The website would be staged to the production server. Final testing would be performed and final approval would be sought.

5. Training
   Training in maintaining the website and databases would be provided to Acme staff.

4. Design

To achieve the goals, a public website and a set of website administration tools would be created.

4.1 Public website
The public website would include the following pages:

- Company information, history, processes, policies and contact information.
- Enquiry forms, servicing request forms and feedback forms.
- Product search, list and detail pages.

The pages would be constructed using templates, to ensure consistency across the website. A visually appealing design metaphor would be developed for the website.

4.2 Administration tools
The administration tools are a set of password-protected web pages accessible to Acme staff. These pages have forms for updating and adding content and products on the public site.

5. Technical Considerations

5.1 Compatibility
It is important to assess the compatibility of the hardware and software used by customers. Currently, little is known about the hardware or software used by the businesses targeted by Acme. For this reason, it will be useful to conduct a survey of these businesses, to determine their hardware and software capabilities, and to design the website accordingly.

5.2 Hosting
During or on completion of the technical specification, the website hosting arrangements should be determined. There are several options, including virtual hosting, dedicated hosting, co-location or in-house.

6. Management Considerations

6.1 People
For this project, the team would comprise a project manager from Acme, and a producer, creative director, designers and programmers from the contractor.

6.2 Timeline
Below is an estimated timeline for the project. It assumes the contract is signed on 1 October 2007.

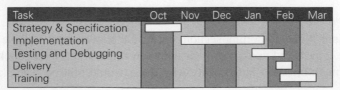

Task	Oct	Nov	Dec	Jan	Feb	Mar
Strategy & Specification						
Implementation						
Testing and Debugging						
Delivery						
Training						

6.3 Budget

Following is an estimate of the costs to complete this project:

Strategy & Specification	$10,000 – $15,000
Implementation	$40,000 – $70,000
Testing & Debugging	$15,000 – $25,000
Delivery	$2,500 – $5,000
Training	$5,000 – $15,000
Sub-total	$72,500 – $130,000
Total	$81,562 – $146,250

6.4 Resources

Acme would provide all copy, images and artwork – in electronic or paper form. The contractor would provide the development server and databases. However, on completion of the project, the website would be shifted to a production server. This server would be provided by Acme.

Proposal to an editor

If you decide to submit a feature article for publication in a specialist magazine, or have an idea for a book in your area of expertise, you will need to contact an editor for approval. Although similar, in general aspects, to the model outlined above, a book or article proposal differs in some respects.

Publishers' web sites include guidelines on how to submit proposals. In most cases, a book proposal is composed according to the following outline.

Description of subject of book and its position in the market

Describe the topic of the book, and explain why it is significant or worthwhile in the current market. Position the book in relation to interests, needs and debates in the wider social context. Propose a title.

Distinctive features

Explain the features of the book that distinguish it and give it a unique identity.

Primary and secondary markets

Describe the target readers of the book. Will they be reading it for entertainment, instruction or other purposes? Will the book interest one particular demographic or psychographic group, or will it have different types of readers? How do you know?

Main competitors

This is a very important section, because it shows that you have researched the topic and know what is available in the market. If the book has direct competitors, you must justify why there would still be a market for your proposed book. Select two or three competing books and describe them in some detail.

Comparison of proposed book with competitors

Following from the above, explain how your book differs from the competitors. Describe the distinctive features that would make the book marketable.

Qualifications of applicant

Attach a CV, or give a biographical sketch, highlighting the qualities that enable you to write a book on the proposed topic.

Summary/outline of chapters

Give an outline of the proposed chapters, with a description of each chapter, usually of about half a page. If you have a sample chapter, attach it to the proposal as an example of your approach and style.

If writing to a magazine editor to propose an article, follow this outline.

Description of topic

Describe your topic and its scope, explaining the angle, slant, or point of view that you will take. Remember to mention the proposed title (although the editor might change it).

Significance and innovation

Explain why your article will interest the target audience of this particular magazine. Why would the magazine benefit by including such an article in its repertoire? Remember that you need to convince the editor that your article will contribute to readers' interest in buying the magazine. Make sure you have investigated the magazine to be certain they have not already published on the topic.

Sources

List and briefly describe five sources of information that you will use. Justify your choices by explaining the importance of the sources in the relevant field of research. Will you be conducting interviews, or primary research, or will your article be based on secondary sources?

Personal information

Describe your qualifications for writing this article, including any special expertise or knowledge in the subject area. Explain also what has spurred your interest in the topic.

Here is an example of a proposal by a freelance writer submitted to *Wired* magazine, describing his idea for a feature article.

Proposal for a Feature – *Behind the Pretty Face*
Peter S. Jurgens

1. Topic

The June 2002 *Wired* contained an article called 'Why Is This Man Smiling?' The article addressed many of the complicated issues animators faced when they attempted to create lifelike characters on the silver screen. I believe it is time to write a follow-up.

1.1 Summary of article

'Behind the Pretty Face' will begin with a recap of some of the key issues in the original article: the complexity of facial features, the translucent quality of skin, etc. This will refresh readers of the original article, and serve as a foundation for new readers. It will also give them a context for understanding recent developments in the field. By interviewing an expert in the field, I hope to learn if any of these problems have been solved, or if a clever workaround has been found.

Often, doing a physically accurate simulation is too computationally expensive. Instead, a less accurate method is sometimes used. As long as the result looks 'right' the final viewer may never know. A good example of this is shadows. Early shadows were actually made by compressing the original object onto a 2D plane, painting it black, and putting it under the original object. This saved computers from having to do many calculations.

The remainder of the article will focus on existing and future uses of these technologies in the home. The prevalence of Media Center type PCs and the increasing complexity of On-Demand services from cable companies has started to blur the distinction between a personal computer and a television. Not surprisingly, video games have started to incorporate technologies previously reserved for big-budget movies. One of the best recent examples is the game *Half Life 2*. In addition to a complex realistic physics engine, the game features the most realistic character animation system to date. Characters show realistic facial expressions based on their speech, in real-time. The game engine that makes this possible has been licensed to several companies who are due to release new games next year.

Computer scientists are working on programs capable of processing human speech and even facial expressions and responding in kind. These technologies will continue to develop and will soon become mainstream. Imagine sitting down in front of your computer and having a conversation with it. The 'virtual pet' of the future will be incredibly lifelike.

2. Significance

Wired readers pride themselves on being tech savvy. They enjoy keeping up with the latest technologies and depend on your publication to keep them informed. Such informed readers would probably notice and appreciate the subtle technical differences between *Shrek* and *Shrek 2*. Characters like Yoda and Gollum have been entertaining audiences of all types. However, *Wired* readers will enjoy their performances that much more because they are privy to the technical knowledge and wizardry that imbued those characters with life.

Now we stand at the threshold of a revolution in home entertainment. Soon we will be able to interact with more than mere mouse clicks, and our computer opponent, or ally, will have a human face. But how will this face be designed? The proposed article will provide a first-hand account of this, and will contribute to *Wired* being at the cutting edge of computer technology news.

3. Sources

The article will be largely based on these sources:

1. www.wired.com/wired/archive/10.06/face.html
   This is the original article reposted on the Wired News website. I plan to use this as a springboard to introduce new developments and technologies.

2. Interview with Alan Barr
   Professor Barr has been at the forefront of computer graphics research for many years. It is difficult to find any academic papers on computer graphics that do not cite him in some form. He has done much work in the field of graphical simulations and is an expert on all areas of computer graphics. Professor Barr is an ideal interview candidate because he knows all of the developments that have occurred in computer graphics in recent years. I have already organised an interview with him.

3. Crawford, C. (1994): The coming revolution in entertainment software. *Digest of Papers,* Spring COMPCON 94 (Cat. No.94CH3414-0), 201–3.

   This article discusses the necessary factors for a dramatic change in computer games. This includes artificial personality, modelling of the human face, and a language of emotional expression to allow the player to interact with the game. This article will provide an interesting basis of comparison between current technology and projected technological development in '94.

4. Gustafson, J., Boye, J., Fredriksson, M. et al. (2005): Intelligent Virtual Agents. *5th International Working Conference, IVA 2005.* Proceedings, 37–51.

   This paper investigates the use of spoken dialogue technology within a computer game. It discusses the requirements that need to be fulfilled first and describes an implemented system.

5. Xiaoxu Zhou; Xiangsheng Huang; Yangsheng Wang (2004): Real-time facial expression recognition in the interactive game based on embedded hidden Markov model. *Proceeding of International Conference on Computer Graphics, Imaging and Visualization : 144–8.*

> This paper proposes a method of real-time facial expression recognition for a computer game. Being able to react to not only the player's words, but also their expression would greatly increase the interactivity of future games.

6. *http://www.steampowered.com/Steam/Marketing/June24.2005/*
   This is a press release by Valve software on the Lost Coast add-on featuring High Dynamic Range technology. This technology allows for greater realism in lighting not only detailed environments, but also characters.

4. Personal information

I am a PhD student in Computer Science at the California Institute of Technology, specialising in computer graphics. When I am not programming graphics projects, I spend time keeping abreast of the latest developments in the video game industry.

Convincing evidence in proposals

The main function of proposals is to persuade. Selecting the most appropriate evidence or reasoning, therefore, is vital. The best way to achieve this is to analyse the funding agency's mission, values, policies and expectations and to present your project in response to these. A project is acceptable and worthwhile or not depending on particular contexts of reception. Merits of the project are evaluated according to different sets of standards, and knowing these standards and responding to them maximises your chances of being successful. Internal (private) proposals have a different scope and impact than external (public) proposals, which may involve the welfare of the public at large. The range and duration of the project's impact, and the cost, are decisive elements in the persuasive force of a proposal, and you should take these into account when planning yor strategy.

Argumentation theorist Stephen Toulmin (2003), for example, found that 'logical' arguments are not universal, and different discourse communities have their own expectations of the reasoning process. What is convincing evidence for natural scientists, for instance, may not be convincing for marketing experts, and what is convincing for marketing experts may not be convincing for engineers. As Gerard Hauser says,

> When we seek a project extension, argue for a raise, interview for a job . . . we are involved in acts that require good reasons. Good reasons allow our audience and ourselves to find a shared basis for cooperating . . . You can use marvellous language, tell great stories, provide exciting metaphors, speak in enthralling tones, and

even use your reputation to advantage, but what it comes down to is that you must speak to your audience with reasons they understand. (Hauser, 1986, p. 71)

In addition to learning as much as possible about the funding organisation, there are two ways to increase your chances of producing a persuasive document. One is to run your proposal by peers and mentors, who are knowledgeable on the issues covered, especially if they have been successful in obtaining funding from the organisation to which you are applying. Since many projects in business and industry are collaborative, it should be easy to exchange ideas and get feedback. The second way is to consider your project from the recipient's point of view, and to brainstorm as many possible objections as you can. Play the 'devil's advocate', or get someone to play it for you, and criticise the proposed project from different angles.

From the information on the website of the National Science Foundation (NSF), which funds scientific and industrial projects internationally, we can trace these main reasons for rejecting proposals:

Possible objections to scientific and industrial proposals

- The problem is not important enough or is not original
- The study is not likely to produce useful information
- The methods are not carefully thought out or are not suited to the objectives
- The hypothesis and/or the sources cited are based on weak or unsubstantiated data
- The research plan is unrealistically ambitious
- The researcher seems too inexperiened , possibly because s/he shows no recognition of potential problems
- Alternative hypotheses or methods are not considered, and there is no contingency plan in case the initial experiments or procedures fail
- The issue is scientifically premature
- Rationale for experiments or tests is not provided.

Also, regarding publishing, here is a list of common objections to book proposals. Keep these in mind when structuring your proposal:

Possible objections to book proposals

- The topic is not in our range of interests
- There are enough books on the market that deal with this topic (or, we have already published on this topic)

- The target market is not well defined
- The topic is too specialised to interest a wide audience
- The scope (proposed content) is too broad or too narrow
- The proposed content contains a lot of irrelevant information
- The proposed time frame is not realistic
- The author does not seem qualified enough to write authoritatively on this topic.

● The business plan

When starting your own business, you need to attract investors, high-quality employees, collaborators and other desired relationships. To achieve this, you must persuade those groups that you are well organised, have a clear, realistic and ambitious vision, and are aware of competitors and market needs. The business plan articulates these elements and reflects your drive and professional competence. Like other important business documents, a business plan involves identifying the target audience, gathering accurate and convincing data, and carefully sectioning and organising the information in an accessible way. The key sections of a business plan are as follows:

Executive summary. This is a concise version of the entire plan, and, as it is read to determine the potential of your company, special care should be given to it, to make it appealing and comprehensive. As with other reports, write the executive summary last, when you are better prepared to confidently include all necessary information. More on executive summaries below.

Company description. This covers the company's mission, history, current situation, strategies and plans for the future. Divide this into subsections for clarity.

Management and organisation. This section describes members of the management team, their backgrounds and qualifications, as well as needs for new recruits. In this section, discuss also key outside advisers and collaborators.

The market and competition. This section defines the company's target market, the industry as a whole, current and potential clients/buyers, and competitors. The section should explain how buying decisions are made, how the market is segmented, what is your intended market position and what your defensive strategy will be to deal with competitors.

The product or service. This section describes the features, components and quality of the company's product or service. Include here the amount of research and development remaining to be completed, how the product or service will be made and at what cost, and how you will regulate service through quality control procedures.

Marketing and sales. This section describes the company's selling methods, how sales staff are trained, and how support is provided. This marketing plan should discuss results of market research and the value proposition of the product or service. Include also how the product or service will be marketed, such as advertising and public relations campaigns.

Financial information. This presents the financial forecasts, and is often, together with the executive summary, the most carefully scrutinised section. Include here balance sheets and statements of cash flow and income. If the business plan is designed to attract investors, this section should also include a funding request that states how much money is needed and for what purposes. Consider adding some information on the likely payback for investors and an exit strategy, if they wish to withdraw.

Entrepreneurial 'guru' Guy Kawasaki lists the following points in his advice to those starting out in business plan writing:

- *Do not exceed twenty pages in length*. As noted elsewhere in this book, conciseness is attractive in business contexts.
- *Select one person to write the plan*. Although the plan should reflect the spirit of the management team, the writing of the business plan should be coherent and not patchy.
- *Bind the plan with a staple*. Ornamental presentations do not add any value to the plan. Most readers will be looking for content, not window-dressing.
- *Simplify your financial projections to two pages*. Investors and other interested parties want to know your financial plans, but not in extreme detail, nor for more than the first five years.
- *Include the key metrics, such as the number of customers, locations and resellers*. For Kawasaki, this is even more important than actual financial projections because they give a better view of the organisation's plans.

- *Include the assumptions that drive your financial projections.* This gives more substance to the projections, because it explains the rationale on which you based them.   (Adapted from Kawasaki, 2004, pp. 70–1).

● The investigative report

As opposed to a research report, which is usually written to document and publicise research to peers, an investigative report may be written by a specialist or group of specialists to a non-expert audience. Situations leading to an investigative report include consultancies, where an expert, or team of experts, is recruited by an organisation to identify issues involved in a problem and to recommend solutions; and commissions, where an authority puts together an impartial investigation team to ascertain the reasons for a public disaster. Investigation reports may be written internally, when the investigator(s) is a member of the organisation, or externally, when the investigator(s) is recruited from a 'neutral zone.'

Planning the investigative report

An investigation follows the specifications of a **brief**. Basically, a brief (also known as **terms of reference**) is an instruction to perform a task. It may be a short and direct command: 'Write a report for Aviation International Corporation recommending whether it should submit a tender if X airport becomes privatised.' Or it may involve detailed specifications spread over several pages. The latter is often the case in briefs to conduct lengthy investigations after a major disaster. Formal consultancy reports, which involve hiring a specialist to solve a problem for a client, are based on a brief provided by the client, which indicates what is required and how the commissioned specialists should structure their report. Similarly, advertising companies that organise competitions on campaign skills issue a brief which candidates must address to win funding and/or a position in the company.

However, a brief is not only a formal document that presents issues to be discussed in a written project. It also sets the stage on which you will perform as investigator and writer. This is because writing itself is not, as is often assumed, a purely mental or even purely linguistic activity. Rather, it involves the whole sensory framework, which responds physically to the images evoked by the written signs. To make this clearer, think of the physical arousal produced by an action novel or a sexy story. Words can cause perspiration, a racing heart beat, laughter and tears. In fact, it could be said that understanding a text means having the sensation of being where the action takes place.

According to this, a brief gives the 'stage directions' for setting up and acting out the circumstances surrounding the professional writing task. It contains, explicitly or implicitly, the four aspects of all professional writing projects:

- Setting the scene
- Placing oneself as writer within this scene
- Tracing and identifying specific elements and players in the scene
- Deciding on tasks that ensure the smooth functioning of these elements.

A model for analysing the requirements of a brief, and planning an investigative report is as follows

Controlling scene: This encompasses the scope of the project, the audience(s), and the different parties involved. It consists of:

- the big picture
- the broad topic that you have to deal with
- the context in which the problem has arisen and the roles that exist in this context
- who you are writing for, and who you are writing about directly or indirectly
- the number of people affected by the context and the topic, and the extent to which they are affected. For example, decisions taken by government agencies (such as policy making and legislation) tend to affect a greater sector of the public than decisions taken by small businesses. In the first case, the influence of your task can be said to be general. In the second case, it is local.

Generally, the controlling scene involves the level of power and perspective your project involves. If your writing task is part of a top management strategy, it will have a larger scope and a more long-term planning orientation, involving more products or services and anticipating changes and developments. If it is part of a middle management strategy, it will involve more immediate concerns and specific products, services or issues. A top management perspective requires more research and analysis and tends to produce more complicated and lengthier documents than a middle management perspective, which looks at issues concerned with a specific product or service.

Role: This indicates your position within the controlling scene, your duties, freedoms and constraints, especially:

- Your position and status in relation to other participants in the controlling scene: are you a junior employee? a technical specialist? the CEO?
- Your relation to the problem: are you blamed for something and have to write to justify your actions? Are you an expert called in to solve a problem you are not personally involved in? Are you representing the company's interests and want to sway a consumer group's opinion on a product? Are you a technical expert wanting to warn a senior but non-specialist colleague of a problem?
- Your relation to the audience: are they your clients? Your peers?

It is vital that you understand your role absolutely. Keep in mind that even if you possess knowledge that will produce certain results, it is useless unless you can communicate it appropriately to the right audience and at the right time. Whether you should be assertive, modest, respectful, extravagant or whatever else, depends on a careful assessment of the controlling scene and of your role in it.

Note also that the title of your position and your role are not the same. As part of your professional position you will be asked to play different roles for different situations. For example, if you are the CEO of a company you would have top management responsibilities, such as making executive decisions on major financial initiatives and making long-term plans on new product development. However, when addressing shareholders in situations such as public relations speeches, conferences and product exhibitions, you assume the sub-role of equal, sharing the same values and working towards the same interests. The language you use should reflect this equality, or your audience will be alienated and discouraged.

Event: This encompasses the actual situation or question(s) that have created a problem needing a solution. It includes:

- The specific issues that should be addressed
- The details of the topic

- The aspects of the controlling scene that are immediately relevant
- The raw materials, sources and limitations that you are given to handle the task, such as funding, deadlines, access to resources, and equipment.

The event will also determine the role that you are invited to play. Much miscommunication occurs when communicators adopt a role that contradicts the event in which they act.

Treatment: This involves the actions and tasks that should be carried out to produce an appropriate result. It includes:

- The tasks that will solve the problem, address the issue, or provide some form of resolution to the situation. This includes physical and interactive actions, such as organising meetings and conducting interviews and focus groups, as well as mental operations that structure writing, such as describing, analysing, synthesising, assessing, justifying, etc.
- The type of documentation that you decide to produce for a situation. For example, a simple email message may be sufficient in some situations. In other cases, you may need to follow up your email message with a formal letter or maybe a memo, while a more serious situation would require the submission of a proposal leading to a full report. Choosing an unsuitable type of document is a tactical error and another common path to communication breakdown.
- The ways that you should present information according to audience needs. For example, if you decide a PowerPoint® presentation is enough to inform an audience of your progress on a project, what kinds of data will you use in the presentation? Would a verbal description suffice? Should you use tables, charts and graphs? Should you provide a full financial analysis of the situation?

The problems that can arise when the controlling scene, role, event and treatment of a task are not properly interpreted can clearly be seen in disaster situations. A famous and well-documented example of this is the Challenger space shuttle disaster in January 1986. It is now widely recognised that the explosion of the shuttle was largely due to misunderstandings that occurred in the exchange of written information between NASA officials before the launch. Although some officials had detected a functioning error in the shuttle and knew what had to be done to fix it, they did not communicate their finding in an appropriate way to the responsible parties (Herndl et al., 1991). Similar findings have emerged from the more recent Columbia shuttle disaster, in 2003 (Gurak and Lannon, 2007).

Many individuals in professional settings already have a determined role and a given scene, and need to concentrate on the event and treatment. However, even in this case it is useful to include both role and scene in your pre-writing planning and brainstorming notes – in other words, to deliberately write out what the controlling scene and your role in it are. This way you become aware of what you think others expect of you and what you expect to achieve. This, in turn, creates an objective distance between your professional role and any personal involvement in the given event, which allows you to take a broader view of the issues, unclouded by personal preconceptions.

Keep in mind that even if your professional role is 'real' (that is, you really are a marketing consultant, creative director or university lecturer), you are still acting out a role. Becoming conscious of this fact helps you to gain control over it and act it out more successfully.

Another point to consider is that a brief may be improvised to assist in the writing process even in cases when it is not handed out by others. For instance, if you find your progress in a project is hindered by some uncertain factor, or if you want to achieve an aim but have no idea how to go about it, you should find that conceptualising and writing down your situation in the form of a brief (i.e. a set of instructions or issue statement to yourself) may prove very productive.

A final point: recording and detailing your projects is vital in corporate contexts, where mobility is high and staff are transferred or change position often. The person replacing you should be able to continue your work without interruption. This is known, in IT contexts, as working in 'drop dead' mode, which means that if a team member or manager were to drop dead, s/he should leave adequate documentation and specifications on their work so that projects are not disrupted because they were wholly dependent on their initiator's habits and methods. Keeping notes on a project is, therefore, essential. Opposite is a template, based on the model described above, that you can use or adapt to help you document a writing task.

Components of the investigative report

Investigative reports generally contain the components listed in Table 6.

Document Planning Template

The event

1. Scenario (situation that triggered the task)
2. Purpose (s) of document
3. Target date for delivery

The controlling scene

1. The players
2. Internal, external or mixed audiences
3. Job titles
4. Technical, non-technical or combination
5. Level of technical knowledge
6. Level of subject knowledge
7. Attitude with which the document is likely to be received

The treatment

Format of document(s).

Main message to convey:

Key issues

1. ——

2. ——

3. ——

4. ——

Supplementary documents:

1. ....

2. ....

3. ....

Report component	Definition
Letter/memo of transmittal	The letter/memo indicates that you are formally delivering the report to the person who commissioned it, and who is responsible for taking action based on the report's recommendations.
Title page	A single sheet of paper stating the title of the report, the name and organisation of the author and the date of delivery.
Executive summary	A summary of the report body including main findings and recommendations.
Table of contents	A list of the sections and subsections of the report with their page numbers.
List of figures	A list of the visuals (tables, figures, charts, etc.) included in the report and their page numbers.
Introduction	The first section of the report, describing the project, objectives, assumptions and scope.
Methods (optional)	A description and justification of the methodology used to research the topic. If the research was based largely on secondary sources, the Methods could be incorporated as a subsection of the Introduction.
Discussion	A major part of the report presenting and discussing the facts or issues relevant to the subject of the report. This is divided into sections and subsections according to a logical pattern of organisation.
Conclusions	A set of inferences or opinions that the author has reached after analysing the evidence available in the Discussion.
Recommendations	A set of strategies and suggested actions for solving the problems that prompted the investigation.
References	A list of print and electronic texts referred to in the body of the report.
Glossary (optional)	A set of definitions for specialist terms used in the report.
Appendices (optional)	Supplementary material added in the end of the report.

Table 6   Terms and components of an investigative report

The front matter

The letter or memo of transmittal, title page, executive summary, table of contents and list of figures are known as **the front matter**.

LETTER OR MEMO OF TRANSMITTAL

The letter or memo of transmittal indicates that the report is being formally delivered to the person or organisation that requested it. Write a letter if the report is for someone outside your organisation, and a memo for someone within your organisation. The letter or memo of transmittal has these aims:

- To identify the report topic, and scope or extent of the investigation
- To identify the person who authorised the report, and the date of authorisation
- To communicate key findings
- To acknowledge any assistance in the preparation of the report
- To indicate willingness to provide further information in a courteous close.

TITLE PAGE

This gives details of the writer(s), the authorising organisation, the title of the report and the date of completion (or dates of commencement and completion for longer projects).

ABSTRACTS AND EXECUTIVE SUMMARIES

As these are often confused, it would be useful to explain their characteristics and the contexts in which each is used. Research articles and conference papers generally include an abstract. Abstracts serve several purposes; for example, they:

- summarise the issues included in the research
- describe the theoretical framework of the research and indicate the author's contribution within this framework
- list the methods and objectives of the research.

Abstracts are written in a block paragraph and often include a set of keywords, which are used for researching and indexing. They are written for completed articles as well as for work in progress. For example, the following is the abstract of a research article on the motion picture industry, published by the Harvard Business School (Eliashberg et al., 2005, n.p.):

> The motion picture industry provides a fruitful research domain for
> scholars in marketing and other disciplines. The industry has a
> high economic importance and is appealing to researchers because
> it offers both rich data that covers the entire product lifecycle for a

large number of new products and because it provides many unsolved 'puzzles.' Despite the fact that the amount of scholarly research in this area is rapidly growing, its impact on practice has not been as significant as in other industries (e.g. consumer packaged goods). In this article, we discuss critical practical issues for the motion picture industry, review existing knowledge on those issues, and outline promising research directions. Our review is organized around the three key stages in the value chain for theatrical motion pictures: production, distribution and exhibition. We discuss various conjectures, framed as research challenges or specific research hypotheses, related to each stage in the value chain, followed by a set of specific research avenues for each of those stages. We focus on what we believe are critical management issues.

Keywords: Motion Picture Industry, Entertainment Industry, Review, Research and Models.

Business reports generally include an executive summary. This accompanies the report as a completed document, and summarises its whole contents, from hypothesis to conclusions and/or recommendations. The executive summary should be a self-contained description of the research. In their composition, executive summaries reflect the 'bottom-line' approach of business writing, with an emphasis on the practical significance of the investigation and the applicability of its results. Executive summaries:

- describe the scope and objectives of the report
- summarize the findings
- outline recommendations or solutions, or extrapolate on future developments

Executive summaries may be written in a block paragraph, but may also include bullet points. For example, the following is the executive summary of the motion picture industry research cited above (Eliashberg et al., 2005, n.p.):

This paper reviews research and trends in three key areas of movie making: production, distribution, and exhibition. In the production process, the authors recommend risk management and portfolio management for studios, and explore talent compensation issues. Distribution trends show that box office performance will increasingly depend on a small number of blockbusters, advertising spending will rise (but will cross different types of media), and the timing of releases (and DVDs) will become a bigger issue. As for exhibiting movies, trends show that more sophisticated exhibitors will emerge, contractual changes between distributor and exhibitors will change, and strategies for ticket prices may be reevaluated. Key concepts include:

- Business tools such as quantitative and qualitative research and market research should be applied to the decision-making process at earlier stages of development.
- Technological developments will continue to have unknown effects on every stage of the movie-making value chain (production, distribution, exhibition, consumption).

TABLE OF CONTENTS
This identifies sections and sub-sections of the report and gives page numbers for each major section. Because reports are often subdivided, photocopied and distributed, take extra care to ensure that the page numbers in the table of contents correspond with the sections of the report.

LIST OF FIGURES
This gives the number, title and page numbers of visuals such as photographs, clip art, small maps, diagrams, etc.

The body

The body includes the introduction, discussion, conclusions and recommendations. The body of the report is divided into sections and subsections, analysing the different aspects of the issue(s) investigated. Although the report sections fall into categories of information distribution that the reader expects to find (such as Introduction, Discussion, etc.), this does not mean that the sections should actually have those names. As was noted earlier, headings can be very important as a signalling and summarising device, so there is plenty of room to be creative. As with everything else in professional writing, audience considerations are paramount, but you can definitely make a report more attractive and compelling by improvising on standard format and terminology within the bounds of the scene and situation in which you are writing.

INTRODUCTION (OR FIRST SECTION OF REPORT)
This should lead readers from information they already know to information they need to acquire. The introduction may be only a paragraph long, or it may be a major section in itself, depending on the length of the report. Start with an overview statement indicating the general subject matter and context of the report. Then answer the following questions, adapted as necessary for the specific nature of your report:

- *Background*: why was the report commissioned in the first place? What was the change, problem or issue that led people to believe a report was needed?

- *Purpose*: what are the specific objectives of the report?

- *Scope*: what issues are covered in the report? Refer to the brief given when the report was requested. Indicate the criteria used for evaluating the problem.

- *Research methods*: how were the data in the report obtained? What primary and/or secondary data were used? (If your methods were experimental and complicated, a separate section should be devoted to them, after the introduction.)

- *Structure*: preview the report structure.

- *Limitations* (optional): what issues are not covered in the report? What are the limitations of the research methods selected? What assumptions have been made?

DISCUSSION (OR MIDDLE SECTIONS OF THE REPORT)
The middle part of the report is the largest and most time-consuming section, and is further subdivided into subsections with headings. Use any one of the following methods, or a combination of methods, for organising the discussion section. Make sure that the method you choose is the most appropriate for presenting and explaining information to the target audience, and that it adheres to the expectations and logical patterns associated with that audience:

- General to specific
- More important to less important
- Comparison and contrast
- Classification and partition
- Problems and solutions
- Cause and effect
- Cost and benefits (advantages and disadvantages)
- Chronological
- Spatial.

When discussing aspects of a topic, issues in a debate, or possible solutions to problems, you can use a block form or point-by-point presentation. In the block form you combine all aspects, issues or problems together, and then analyse them or propose solutions. In the point-by-point form, you take each aspect, issue or problem and analyse it or propose a solution to it, before proceeding to the next. This is represented as follows:

Block form	**Point-by-point form**
Factor A	Factor A
Item 1	*Item 1*
Item 2	Factor B
Item 3	*Item 1*
Factor B	Factor A
Item 1	*Item 2*
Item 2	Factor B
Item 3	*Item 2*

CONCLUSION (OR FINAL SECTION)

This interprets the facts set out in the discussion. It answers the question 'so what?' Do not introduce new material here; instead, lead straight on to the list of recommendations. In fact, in some reports, conclusion and recommendations are included in one section.

RECOMMENDATIONS

Recommendations suggest specific actions. Again, no new material should appear in this section, and recommended actions need not be justified (their justification should be clear from the discussion part of the report). Recommendations may be numbered and placed in priority order. Most often they appear in bullet point form. This section is possibly the most important and should be very clearly set out. It is usual to recommend only one solution to each problem identified in the report. However, in some circumstances, you could suggest alternative solutions. In either case, recommendations must be realistic, taking into account factors such as cost, location, and current policy or practice within the organisation.

Effective recommendations not only state what action ought to be taken, but also specify who should be responsible for implementing it and within what time frame. Recommendations should address *what, where, when, who* and *how* (the *why* having been examined in the discussion section). Make sure all recommendations are grammatically parallel.

Here is an example of report recommendations. This list comes from a report written in response to a brief asking the writer to examine the reasons for junior lawyers' decision to leave the commissioning firm, Law Limited, after only a short term of employment.

Example of Recommendations

Following the results of the surveys discussed in this report, it is recommended that:

- Management implement a bonus scheme rewarding lawyers that surpass a given level of performance. The level of performance and the type of bonus should be decided by management in consultation with appointed junior lawyer representatives. Both type of bonus and level of performance should be reviewed every three years to ensure their relevance to changing industry standards.

- Human Resources organise a mentoring scheme where senior lawyers are paired with junior counterparts to discuss problems, aspirations and plans.

- Senior management organise formal briefing meetings with junior staff to discuss problems of concern. These meetings should take place at least twice a year.

- Changes be made to the budget to ensure that enough funds are available to maintain a regular orientation/professional development programme. The recommended time allocated to this programme is 15 hours per year for each staff member.

End matter

This includes references, glossary and appendices.

REFERENCES AND BIBLIOGRAPHY

These list the sources cited in the report. If a source has been influential, but you have not quoted from it or referred to it, list it under the heading 'Bibliography,' which should immediately follow the list of references. Use a referencing style suited to your field (APA, MLA, Chicago, etc.).

GLOSSARY (OPTIONAL)

This defines technical and specialised terms that are not likely to be familiar to readers of the report. Use audience adaptation methods to determine which terms will need to be defined and which will already be known by target readers. Items in the glossary are listed in alphabetical order.

APPENDICES (OPTIONAL)

An appendix is a part of your report that is relevant to the main theme of the report, but not essential. An appendix may include material that is too complex, specialised or detailed to be included in the body of the report. Material that supplements or illustrates points made in the body of the report is also suitable for an appendix. Keep in mind that the reader should be able to understand the main points of the report without needing to read the appendices. At the same time, appendices are useful in cases of primary and secondary audiences that may not have the same level of technical knowledge. In such cases you could include in an appendix specifications or explanations targeted to specific groups.

Examples of documents and data printed as appendices include:

- a copy of a questionnaire used in field research
- a list of questions used in interviews
- copies of letters or pamphlets
- maps, particularly if they take up a whole page
- detailed lists of raw data.

Always refer to the appendix in the body of the report and indicate its relevance to the reader. Letter appendices consecutively (Appendix A, Appendix B, Appendix C, and so on) and start each one on a separate page.

Pagination in reports

By convention, page numbering for reports is not a simple matter. Normally, these guidelines are followed:

- The letter of transmittal has no page number

- No page number appears on the title page

- The Executive Summary, Table of Contents and Table of Figures have roman numerals: ii, iii, iv. The tricky point is that the Table of Contents starts at ii, because the title page is regarded as the first page of the front matter, even though no page number appears on it

- The body of the report and the end matter have numbers: 1, 2, 3, 4, 5, and so on, starting from the first page of the Introduction.

Activities

1. You are documentation manager for XXX Software, a growing company, and you supervise preparation and production of all user manuals. The present system for producing manuals is inefficient because three different departments are involved in (1) assembling the material, (2) word processing and designing, and (3) publishing the manuals. Much time and energy are wasted as a manual goes back and forth among software specialists, communication specialists, and the art and printing department. After studying the problem, you decide that greater efficiency would result if the same desktop publishing software were installed in all computer terminals. Everyone involved would then contribute during all phases. To achieve this, you must write a proposal to be read by the General Manager, as well as by the three Department Managers.

   Brainstorm some reasons that you think these readers would find convincing for your proposal, remembering that they would have different concerns and interests.

2. The following are the actions you have to carry out to produce a quality report. Put them in order and discuss your list in your group. There is some flexibility in the ordering, but some tasks are fixed.

   Order your tasks under the headings: *Planning, Drafting* and *Revising.*

   1. Brainstorm
   2. Write glossary, references and appendices
   3. Write executive summary
   4. Plan time
   5. Proofread for organisation and cohesion
   6. Gain consents if necessary (e.g. for interviews and copyright)
   7. Check pagination and formatting
   8. Write paragraphs
   9. Arrange paragraphs
   10. Write table of contents, list of illustrations and title page
   11. Plan time
   12. Proofread for sentence construction, spelling and grammar
   13. Gather information
   14. Draft outline
   15. Establish a working bibliography
   16. Analyse audience needs and profile
   17. Write introduction, conclusion, and recommendations
   18. Establish research plan
   19. Proofread to cut out unnecessary or imprecise words
   20. Check references
   21. Draw graphics
   22. Revise outline
   23. Check validity of research sources
   24. Analyse scope of brief.

3. Interpret these briefs using the model outlined in this chapter. Identify the controlling scene, your role, the event and the treatment that you will need to apply. Determine what kind of research you have to do, and sketch an outline of your report:

(A) You are a travel industry expert.

A major airline, LibAir, has commissioned you to assess its competitive position in the travel industry. The airline executives want you to investigate recent developments in aircraft construction, security measures in the light of recent terrorist threats, and client services, and to evaluate their airline's advantages and disadvantages in relation to those of competitors. Write a report that identifies pertinent issues and recommends a practical course of action for the airline to follow in order to remain competitive in the current travel market.

(B) You are a security expert.

The Privacy Commissioner has asked you to investigate and write a report on contemporary issues concerning privacy. With developments in surveillance technology, the spread of Internet published information, and digitally stored personal information, there is serious concern that individual rights to privacy are being eroded. The increasing presence of computer hackers and state-owned satellite systems mean that individual privacy is being attacked from both private and public sectors. The Commissioner wants you to investigate the extent to which this fear is justified, to evaluate possible consequences and to suggest possible solutions. Write a report that identifies and analyses pertinent issues and puts forward a clear set of recommendations for action.

(C) You are the Human Resources Manager at Law Limited, a leading national law firm.

Law Limited has been having difficulties retaining its junior and intermediate level lawyers. This is an industry wide problem with law firms generally losing more than half of their junior lawyers before they reach an intermediate level (3-4 years experience). The Chief Executive of Law Limited has asked you to prepare a report investigating the problem both within the company and inter-company. Write a report that identifies pertinent issues while taking into account the interests of the company as well as the views of the junior lawyers. Outline a couple of alternative solutions, evaluate them and propose the best solution justifying your recommendation.

4. Here is a scenario that provides some information on the controlling scene, your role and the event of a professional situation that

require you to take writing action. Plan a treatment for the event by listing some possible types of research you would need to do and the people you would have to communicate with. Then decide on the kinds of written documents that you would need to produce as part of your treatment.

You are an investment consultant. You work in a middle management position and answer to the executive manager for investment options. Your company is experiencing a low period. You believe that the main reason is that many of your options are outdated compared with what is offered by competitors. Consider a suitable course of action to treat this event. How would you confirm that your belief is valid and who would you notify? What written communication would you produce? Into what steps would you organise your treatment

7 Critical Thinking

Focus on:

▶ Principles of critical thinking
▶ Common fallacies in reasoning
▶ Uses and misuses of statistics

The ability to reason logically and objectively is considered vital for professional success. In fact, 'objectivity', 'critical thinking' and 'problem solving' are key words in management positions. Together with skills in leadership, teamwork and communication, a demonstrated ability in dispassionate analysis of critical issues is highly sought-after in most professional positions. This chapter addresses this need by describing the main problem areas, especially as they relate to the communication tasks of professional fields.

The terms and ideas presented here form the backbone of all forms of research, investigative writing and objective interpretation of arguments and statements. They also form the basis for professional involvement in corporate policy and public relations. The main value of objective reasoning, as opposed to subjective, or self-focused, opinion, is that it can lead to decisions that benefit a collectivity. The first part of the chapter describes the cognitive skills related to critical thinking and follows with a review of the thought processes that lead to faulty reasoning in all forms of communication and decision making. The second part focuses on a major area of manipulative persuasion, statistical data.

● Principles of critical thinking

Critical thinking is not an innate gift or talent: it develops with perseverance and dedication. To sharpen your critical thinking skills, try these strategies:

1. Think independently

Listen to other points of view, but do not follow any particular viewpoint without examining it first from different angles. Especially, be cautious not to blindly accept claims and statements just because they are issued by an authority, who 'should know.' Develop your own informed opinion.

2. Exercise impartiality

Try to see from another person's point of view, beyond your own personal concerns. When considering an issue, look beyond the interests of yourself, your family and friends, and your immediate community. Do not become too attached to a theory or hypothesis because it is yours, or because you have believed it to be correct up to now. Ask yourself whether you believe this theory or hypothesis to be accurate, and compare it fairly with alternatives. Play the devil's advocate and find reasons for rejecting it. Remember that others will, if you do not.

3. Develop intellectual perseverance

Show that you have the persistence to think through all the aspects of a problem. Do not be tempted to give up because a problem is too hard or too disturbing. Spin more than one hypothesis. If there is something to be explained, think of different ways it could be explained. Then think of how you would test each of the alternatives.

4. Read and listen closely

When you read or listen critically, make sure that you clarify and understand key words, ideas and conclusions. Generate questions about what you read and remember to place the information you read and hear in context, using audience analysis skills. For example, find out about the audience that the information is directed towards, and identify how the needs of the audience influence the selection of information and the manner in which it is presented. Find out who generated the information, and by what methods. From this, ascertain how credible and reliable the information is. In many contexts, such as science, a hypothesis can be accepted only if it is falsifiable. Something that cannot be disproved can also not be proved.

Also, when reading, try to go beyond merely understanding what the writer has said, by asking yourself questions such as:

- What information is missing from the text?
- If I could meet the writer face to face, what questions would I like to ask?
- What further information do I need to know in order to accurately evaluate the information?

5. Trace analogies

How does what you learn in one context apply to other contexts? For example, if you are a computer engineer, you could notice the similarities between computer code syntax and the rules of sentence construction in English. Pay attention to similarities and differences. Many groundbreaking discoveries were made by tracing an analogy between a phenomenon and an idea, or by serendipity, that is, by recognising connections between seemingly different topics.

6. Establish precision

Precision requires you to be focused and specific in both your ideas and your expression. In your own writing, make a conscious effort to refine generalities and avoid oversimplifications. Distinguish between relevant and irrelevant facts and use technical terminology correctly. If you are considering an argument, remember that all elements must work, not just most of them. Where possible, quantify. This could prevent you from lapsing into evaluative interpretations based on bias (although not always).

● Fallacies of reasoning

One way to study the process of persuasion is to focus on what can go wrong. Many judgements and decisions are based on assumptions made from previous experience, and preconceptions that may be irrelevant to the purposes at hand. Although much innovative thinking also makes use of assumptions, guard against constructing arguments that are based totally on unacknowledged claims and weak reasoning. In the final analysis, persuasion and reasoning depend on the rhetorical conventions of particular discourse communities. What is valid evidence for one group may not be so for another, so you maximise your chances of producing a convincing case if you know what the expectations and conventions of your audience are.

In addition to audience expectations, ethics is another area that should occupy your thoughts. For example, you may have a workable idea for a new form of plastic, and you may also have convincing evidence that this development will benefit your organisation, for example, by increasing its competitive advantage, and by reducing costs of production. However, this new form of plastic may produce toxic pollution in its manufacturing, and the organisation does not yet have the facilities to recycle such toxic waste. In such a situation, you need to weigh very carefully the organisation's advantages with the negative effects on the wider community, and decide if and how the new product should be developed.

Some of the main tactics that lead to fundamentally illogical arguments are outlined below. These are extremely common in mass media documents, but also occur in professional and academic contexts.

Appeal to tradition

This occurs when the reason given for following or not following a course of action is that it has always been done this way. This tactic relies on a fundamental psychological trait – the need to trust the legitimacy of a habit. However, as with all forms of persuasion, it can be misused by concealing inherent flaws in the arguments proposed.

Appeal to authority

This occurs when a claim or statement is considered 'true' because its source is an expert in the field, or has a respectable and/or popular position in the community. For example, there is an anecdote about a textbook used in a country's universities for many years, even though teaching staff were aware it contained some serious errors. The author was a famous professor whom nobody thought they should correct. In this case, the decision to continue on an erroneous path was based on the assumption that respect for authority should override objective evaluation.

Appeal to common sense, 'everybodiness' and universals

This occurs when, instead of providing a methodical argument that develops specific issues systematically, the writer/speaker proposes a course of action because it 'is the right thing to do', or 'everybody knows that it is so'. Sometimes what appears as 'common sense' or 'universally acceptable' is nothing but an entrenched belief that has remained unquestioned for such a long time that it has become tradition. This strategy is based on the human need to belong to a group. Many people would be persuaded to follow a course of action because it appears to fall into established but unquestioned universals, such as 'justice' or 'morality'.

Appeal to opposition or ignorance

This occurs when, in order to support a point of view, the writer/speaker relies on the fact that the opposite point of view has been disproved or is unsubstantiated. For example, some claim that laws prohibiting the use of drugs should be abolished, because there is no substantial evidence to suggest that such laws actually prevent people from using drugs. Although this claim could be a step in the reasoning process, it cannot be the determining criterion for reaching a definite conclusion. A similar example is that of the existence (or not) of God: arguing that there is a God because attempts to disprove his existence have failed (or vice versa) is a claim based on an appeal to opposition. As Carl Sagan aptly puts it, 'absence of evidence is not evidence of absence' (Sagan, 1995, p. 213).

Appeal to emotion

Very common in consumer advertising, this occurs when a writer/speaker uses an emotive style when presenting an argument, adding evaluative words and phrases or metaphors that are actually irrelevant to the piece of information presented but that have a strong sensory or emotive effect. Usually done to sway opinion on a matter, or to generate a feeling of guilt in the receivers that will induce them to take some form of action, this is what happens when perpetrators of crime are described as 'hideous monsters' and their victims as 'innocent citizens'.

Because of its strong persuasive impact, this is a common device in the mass media. It is also a widespread tactic in some forms of legal reasoning, especially when a lawyer tries to sway the jury's opinion by drawing attention to the defendant's emotional state (traumatic childhood, agitated state, etc.) as a justification of his/her action. This relies on the human capacity for empathy ('what if this happened to you?'), and not on logic.

Appeal to extremes and false dichotomies

This occurs when only two options are offered for a complex issue, undermining a balance. A choice between dictatorship or anarchy would reflect this kind of fallacy. This 'either–or' device often occurs in emergencies where people need to act urgently and do not have the time to analyse an issue in depth. It tends to occur in very simplistic arguments, for example when an element of physical force or immediate urgency overrides the logical aspects of the argument ('give me your money or I'll kill you'). 'Terrorist tactics' are based on this kind of appeal, reflecting a situation where such a state of disarray has been reached that there are not many choices open for action. This is known as the fallacy of the *excluded middle* in classical argumentation.

Appeal to generalities

This occurs when a writer/speaker abstracts certain properties from some specially selected entities and applies them to a larger number of entities. A typical example is stereotyping ('politicians are liars'). Another example is when an argument is based on universal terms ('love', 'progress') that have not been defined in terms of the requirements of the project at hand. The argument is consequently hidden behind abstract notions. The major problem with this pitfall is that it disregards the specifics of particular circumstances and situations.

Appeal to personal aspects

This occurs when a writer/speaker's ideas are rejected because of this person's status, sex, profession, past record, etc., rather than because of weaknesses inherent in the ideas themselves. Very common in the mass media and in politics, this appeal disregards the issues at hand and, instead, attempts to draw attention away from a claim and onto the personal qualities of the presenter of the claim. This is what happens, for example, when a promising and reasonable idea is rejected by a committee because it was proposed by a junior or inexperienced member. In classical argument, this is known as *ad hominen* (Latin for 'to the man' – attacking the arguer, not the argument).

Appeal to the straw man

Related to the previous fallacy, this occurs when a writer/speaker caricatures a position by oversimplifying it or taking it out of context, so that it is easier to attack and demolish. A similar tactic is the use of inappropriate humour. 'Straight' humour is a positive aspect of all communication. However, it can become inappropriate, and even sarcastic, when it is used to encourage laughter or ridicule towards an issue that deserves serious attention. If directed at those holding opposing views, this type of humour may reduce their chances of being heard.

Appeal by slippery slope

This occurs when a writer/speaker jumps to a conclusion that is not justified by the premises. Associated with paranoid reasoning, this is illustrated by a statement such as, 'If the government imposes restrictions on the petrol used for cars, what stops them from preventing us from driving cars altogether?'

Appeal to special pleading

This occurs when a writer/speaker responds to an objection or observation by claiming that it overlooks some special circumstances. This is usually an evasive or defensive tactic. For example, responding to the observation, 'Despite the measures we have in place to prevent accidents, accidents have increased in the last month', by the special plead, 'You don't understand people: they don't follow rules', would be such an appeal. A more logical response would be to examine the measures and the claim that accidents have increased.

Appeal by begging the question, or assuming the answer

This occurs when the writer/speaker bases an argument on premises that should in fact be the conclusion, thus producing a circular reasoning. For example, saying that 'we must institute the death penalty to discourage violent crime' would fall in this category. This begs the question whether the death penalty does in fact discourage violent crime.

Appeal by card stacking or observational selection

This occurs when the writer/speaker omits what does not support his or her view, and concentrates on facts that enhance his or her position.

Appeal to false extrapolation

This occurs when a writer/speaker extrapolates a claim from observed facts without considering alternative possibilities. An example would be the statement: 'We will be successful because we are innovative and law-abiding.' This is known in classical argument as *non sequitur* (Latin for 'it does not follow').

Appeal to causality, or confusion between causality and correlation

This occurs when a hasty conclusion is drawn from a fact, or when a causal relation is artificially traced between two events that simply coexist or that follow one another sequentially. An example is the claim that because it is proven that male brain structure is different from female brain structure, it follows that certain professions are suited to males and others to females. This is known in classical argument as *post hoc, ergo propter hoc* (Latin for 'it happened after, so it was caused by').

A major source of misinformation in the use of statistical evidence lies in the frequent confusion between causality and correlation. Two related events that occur simultaneously are said to be in correlation. This does not mean that one event caused the other. For example, consider the high positive correlation between the sale of alcohol and the incidence of crime. This in itself cannot prove that alcohol causes crime. There could be a third factor involved that influences both alcohol sales and crime, for example population growth.

In a causal relationship, one factor (the cause or reason) produces another (the result or outcome) only if these three factors are present:

1. There is a clear chronological sequence. A must occur before B does.
2. There is a clear pattern of repetition. To establish that A causes B, there must be proof that every time A is present, B occurs – or that B never occurs unless A is present.
3. There are no multiple causes and/or effects. For example, many factors influence reported crime rates: population distribution (age,

wealth, race), crime reporting by citizens, changes to laws and regulations, and changes to police procedures for gathering and reporting statistics. A seeming drop in crime reporting, therefore, would not mean there is less crime.

This tactic is related to interpretations of quantifiable data, and leads to the next section on statistics.

● Statistics and public opinion

This section focuses on a major trouble area of reasoning: the use of statistical or quantitative information in arguing for or against a course of action, and for justifying decisions. Interestingly, in the history of science, the study of statistics is a recent phenomenon, with origins in the 'Enlightenment' era of the seventeenth century. Prior to that period, the notion that knowledge could be quantified or counted had no substantial effects. Now, however, virtually every facet of nature and society can be expressed in quantitative terms, that is, in terms of numbers, amounts and percentages.

When discussing an issue, people often give statistics to seal an argument and close off any further debate. Also, managers in business and finance, social policy and education routinely support their policies and decisions with numbers and statistics. Statistics can give the appearance of solidity and 'hard' evidence; numbers are often thought of as irrefutable or undeniable. But actually, the appeal to statistics sets off a whole new set of questions. Where did the statistics come from? What groups in society are excluded from the statistics? If the statistics are accurate, then what decision or action should follow from them? And how can statistical relations and effects be translated into plain English, so that decision makers in business and government can understand them? After all, numbers are meaningless unless they are evaluated or placed in an argument.

This section overviews and briefly describes the main areas where statistical support to reasoning is abused in order to manipulate attitudes. The guidelines given here are explained so that non-specialists can develop an informed opinion on the topic. No prior knowledge of statistics is needed. For those wanting to pursue this topic, three seminal, and very accessible, books on statistics as they relate to persuasion are: J. A. Paulos's *A mathematician reads the newspaper* (1996), D. Huff's *How to lie with statistics* (1993) and R. Sheldon's *First course in probability* (1994).

Below are some widely used tactics for spinning bad news to make it look good, and vice versa, by manipulating statistical information. They are presented in the form of questions you should ask when confronted with statistical evidence.

1. Where do the figures come from?

Statistics are undocumented if the writer does not state their source. Possibly the most common problem with statistical information in the mass media, it makes it very difficult to ascertain whether the conclusions drawn from the statistical analysis are credible, plausible, or applicable only to selected cases that cannot lead to general conclusions. Documenting statistics means stating clearly where the statistics came from, where they are published, and if they are available to the public.

2. How were the figures generated?

Even if the source of statistics is documented, we still need to investigate further to verify that the data are valid. Questions to ask in this regard include: What kind of study was done to establish the statistics? What was the size of the sample? How was the sample selected? Is the sample representative of the general population? Were statistics gathered by interview or questionnaire? If they were gathered by questionnaire, was it filled in face-to-face or by self-reporting? What was the response rate? Who commissioned the study, who financed it, and who conducted it? When polling results are compared with results from previous years, have key definitions remained the same? Has the margin of error been specified?

3. What is the rate given?

The 'absolute rate' indicates how many items are affected by the issue in question, expressed as a number. By contrast, the 'rate of incidence' shows what proportion of the population is affected, expressed as a percentage. The rate of incidence therefore gives some indication of statistical significance. On the other hand, the absolute rate sometimes may sound more impressive, but is not as statistically relevant. For example, consider the effect of the statement that 25,000 people died from a kind of cancer in a specific country last year. Scary news? What if you now learn that this number accounts for 0.05 per cent of the whole population of the country? Which of the two statements would you choose to alarm and which to reassure?

4. Are trends really justified?

Sometimes very slight correlations or changes in occurrence of an event can be blown up to misleadingly huge dimensions. This is sufficient to set off fears or hopes of a trend, particularly in emotional or volatile aspects of human behaviour. In some cases, a typical example being that of financial markets, the perceived trend can become a self-fulfilling prophecy: if small declines in the market are taken to be evidence of a larger trend, panic selling will indeed cause the market to slump or crash.

5. Are quantities given in length or in volume?

Expressing quantities in terms of length often sounds more impressive than using volume as a measure. The example given by Paulos (1996: 79) is that of a tower and a box: Which contains more five-cent coins, a tower the diameter of a coin rising from sea level to the height of Mount Everest, or a six-foot cubical box? The answer is the box.

6. What is the measure of central tendency?

When noting the average of a series of numbers, the writer must indicate whether he/she has used the mean, median, or mode. For data that falls into a normal distribution, such as human height, these three methods of averaging will produce similar results. However, for other kinds of data spread, mean, median and mode vary markedly. For example, assume a country's average income is $40,000. Does this sound like an affluent and fair-to-all society? What if you learn that the range occurs between a high of $200,000 and a low of $10,000?

7. Are the things that are compared similar enough?

Comparisons are unhelpful if the two objects or groups being compared are too diverse; there must be some similarities to make the differences significant. An example given by Huff (1993, p. 81) is of military authorities that might respond to criticisms of the army mortality rate by comparing rates of death in the army with rates of death in the general public. However, the fact that the army consists primarily of fit young people weakens this claim considerably.

● Structuring refutation in writing

Even if you disagree with your opponent's main idea, you may also concede, or accept, that your opponent makes one or two valid points. Conceding a point or two often shows your audience that you are even-handed, thoughtful and fair.

One way to compose refutation is illustrated in this model:

1. Summarise objectively the opposing argument to show that you have understood it.

2.   Acknowledge ways in which the opposing viewpoint is correct.

3.   Use a transitional word, phrase or sentence indicating contrast, such as 'but' or 'however.'

4.   State your claim as an alternative to the opponent's proposition.

5.   Give points supporting your claim.

Resist the temptation to bring in emotional appeals, personal attacks or indeed any of the fallacies listed above. It is likely that you will be taken more seriously if you show objectivity.

For example, look at this paragraph extracted from a feasibility report. The writer was asked to investigate whether it would be advisable for Australia to implement compulsory military service, because of political upheavals in its neighbouring nations. Notice how the writer uses a model of argumentation similar to the above in supporting his claim.

Example of Refutation

The main premise of the argument in the proposal for compulsory military service is that political turmoil in Australia's neighbours presents a threat to national security. East Timor is barely recovering from war, the Solomon Islands and Fiji have been shaken with military coups, and the Indonesian political scene has had massive changes in the last two years. However, there is no evidence to suggest that this fear be anything but paranoia. Australia has no history as a military instigator nor has this nation faced direct threats in the past. Additionally, Australia's diminutive position in the economic and military world suggests that there is no incentive for any neighbour to attack Australia. Australia's military position has traditionally been one of support for its allies and there are no signs to suggest that this will change in the foreseeable future.

Activities

1. Decide which types of pitfall the following statements would fall under. Some of these are borderline, and some contain more than one pitfall.

   (i)   We either convert completely and immediately to computers, or give our administrative staff typewriters.

   (ii) I suggest that we buy Adidas products, as we have been a loyal customer since they produced their first sports shoes.

   (iii) As it cannot be proven that our new work policy in X country caused the resignations, it should be implemented by other countries.

   (iv) Intelligent shareholders are against the take-over as it is obvious that such mining results in disastrous problems.

   (v)   Given that he is the President of Amnesty International, his opinions on capital punishment should not be published.

   (vi) This is the best toothpaste on the market, as it is used by the trainer of the rugby team.

   (vii) He enjoys travelling, cooking and mountain climbing. Therefore, he would be suitable for work in public relations.

   (viii) Because you expect to be looked up to by others, you are likely to be preferred in work situations.

   (ix) During the Second World War, about 375,000 civilians died in country X and about 408,000 members of the armed forces died overseas. On the basis of those figures, it can be concluded that it was not much more dangerous to be overseas in the armed forces during that time than it was to stay at home as a civilian.

2. Bring some examples of the pitfalls in critical thinking to class and be prepared to discuss them. Your examples can include newspaper clippings as well as situations used in movies, novels or television programmes.

3. Gun Control Case Study

   Background

   The current international debate over gun control laws and the plethora of articles it has generated provide a fertile ground to test your understanding of the discussion above on reasoning and statistical manipulation.

   In most Western societies, it is illegal to purchase a firearm without first obtaining a licence from the police. The police may deny a licence on certain grounds such as age, previous criminal convictions, or mental instability. 'Gun control' refers to this set of laws restricting gun ownership. The United States is an exception to this, because the Second Amendment in the US Constitution safeguards citizens' right to own firearms, making it much easier for people to purchase guns in that country.

One reason for the controversy over the effects of strict regulations on the availability of guns is that no conclusive evidence exists directly linking high crime rates with gun possession. Researchers who study the relation between gun control and homicide rates have not come up with any convincing proof that strict gun control laws actually lessen the number of firearm murders and manslaughters.

Task

The following is an article by John R. Lott Jr. He is a well-known proponent of liberal gun laws. Using the criteria for objective reasoning and statistical analysis outlined in this chapter, objectively review the statements on which this argument is based and the conclusions that the writer draws for policy implications. In particular, answer the following questions:

1. How convincing is the reasoning presented here?
2. What more information would you need to reach more conclusive results?
3. Is the information presented valid for other developed nations, or is it strictly US based?
4. What are some legal and cultural factors that need to be considered to reach a more international solution?

The Big Lie of the Assault Weapons Ban: The Death of the Law Hasn't Brought a Rise in Crime – Just the Opposite

By John R. Lott, Jr

This wasn't supposed to happen. When the federal assault weapons ban ended on Sept. 13, 2004, gun crimes and police killings were predicted to surge. Instead, they have declined.

For a decade, the ban was a cornerstone of the gun control movement. Sarah Brady, one of the nation's leading gun control advocates, warned that 'our streets are going to be filled with AK-47s and Uzis'. Life without the ban would mean rampant murder and bloodshed.

Well, more than nine months have passed and the first crime numbers are in. Last week, the FBI announced that the number of murders nationwide fell by 3.6% last year, the first drop since 1999. The trend was consistent, murders kept on declining after the assault weapons ban ended.

Even more interesting, the seven states that have their own assault weapons bans saw a smaller drop in murders than the 43 states without such laws, suggesting that doing away with the ban actually reduced crime. (States with bans averaged a 2.4% decline in murders; in three states with bans, the number of murders rose. States without bans saw murders fall by more than 4%.)

And the drop was not just limited to murder. Overall, violent crime also declined last year, according to the FBI, and the complete statistics carry another surprise for gun control advocates. Guns are used in murder and robbery more frequently than in rapes and aggravated assaults, but after the assault weapons ban ended, the number of murders and robberies fell more than the number of rapes and aggravated assaults.

It's instructive to remember just how passionately the media hyped the dangers of 'sunsetting' the ban. Associated Press headlines warned 'Gun shops and police officers brace for end of assault weapons ban.' It was even part of the presidential campaign: 'Kerry blasts lapse of assault weapons ban.' An Internet search turned up more than 560 news stories in the first two weeks of September that expressed fear about ending the ban. Yet the news that murder and other violent crime declined last year produced just one very brief paragraph in an insider political newsletter, the Hotline.

The fact that the end of the assault weapons ban didn't create a crime wave should not have surprised anyone. After all, there is not a single published academic study showing that these bans have reduced any type of violent crime

Research funded by the Justice Department under the Clinton administration concluded only that the effect of the assault weapons ban on gun violence 'has been uncertain.' The authors of that report released their updated findings last August, looking at crime data from 1982 through 2000 (which covered the first six years of the federal law. The latest version stated: 'We cannot clearly credit the ban with any of the nation's recent drop in gun violence.'

Such a finding was only logical. Though the words 'assault weapons' conjure up rapid-fire military machine guns, in fact the weapons outlawed by the ban function the same as any semi-automatic – and legal – hunting rifle. They fire the same bullets at the same speed and produce the same damage. They are simply regular deer rifles that look on the outside like AK47s.

For gun control advocates, even a meaningless ban counts. These are the same folks who have never been bashful about scare tactics, predicting doom and gloom when they don't get what they want. They hysterically claimed that blood would flow in the streets after states passed right-to-carry laws letting citizens carry concealed handguns, but that never occurred. Thirty-seven states now have right-to-carry laws – and no one is seriously talking about rescinding them or citing statistics about the laws causing crime.

Gun controllers' fears that the end of the assault weapons ban would mean the sky would fall were simply not true. How much longer can the media take such hysteria seriously when it is so at odds with the facts?

Source: Published 28 June, 2005, in *Los Angeles Times*; Reprinted with permission by the author.

4. Epidemiology case study

Background

Epidemiology is the scientific study of the spread and control of disease. Research in this area tries to establish likely causes of disease by testing sample population groups for risk factors associated with the development of the disease. Scientists working in this field trace patterns between the occurrence of a disease and ecological, biological, behavioural and genetic patterns of particular groups. Statistical probability is, therefore, a major part of their projects.

The ethical implications of this kind of research are great. Unless great care is taken to be objective in assessing results, there is a big chance of misinterpreting the data and producing dangerously distorted images in the public mind. A case in point is the controversy surrounding AIDS in the 1980s, when little was known about the cause and nature of the disease. Because it was detected primarily in a specific social group, gay males, there was a tendency on the part of popular and scientific media to blame the sexual habits of this group for the development and spread of the disease. AIDS was, in fact, turned into a shameful or immoral disease because of this treatment, and remains so to this day in some quarters (for more on AIDS in relation to writing, see Reeves, 1990; Shilts, 1987).

Task

Give a critical evaluation of the following article on lentils and bowel cancer, by answering the following questions (the article is fictional, so no need to stop eating lentils!):

1. What do you think of the amount and type of information selected in this article? Does the article leave out important data? Does it mislead through its style? Does it 'dumb down' or over-simplify scientific research? If so, how does it do this, and how could it avoid doing so?
2. This study is an example of epidemiological research. Do you think such a study could ever prove a conclusive causal link between the consumption of lentils and the onset of bowel cancer? If yes, how could it do so?
3. Design an experiment, or a set of experiments, to find out with more certainty whether there is a link between lentils and bowel cancer. What factors would need to be taken into account?

Lentils seen as factor in bowel cancer

Lentils, celebrated as the 'meat substitute' for vegetarians and the health conscious, could do you more long-term harm than good, says a French study.

The National Institute on Cancer Research in Paris has warned people in middle age to stay off the pulse product or increase their risk of contracting cancer of the bowel.

Vegetarians cherish lentils as a non-animal source of protein and iron, and it is sometimes recommended as a health food because it is rich in healthful plant oestrogens. But phytoestrogens do not act like natural oestrogens, especially in our digestive system, nor are they good for us as once believed, say the French researchers into cancer.

Scientists followed the fortunes of 3,500 French men since 1965 to see who developed the disease. They found no positive connection between the disease and alcohol intake, smoking, education, or professional status.

Instead, they found that those men who reported eating lentils at least twice weekly when first interviewed 25 years earlier were 28 times more likely to have developed cancer of the bowel in old age than those that never ate lentils. That could be because phytoestrogens are blocking the effect of natural oestrogens in the digestive system, and preventing normal digestive processes, say the scientists.

8 Business Document Formats

This chapter outlines the standard layouts of descriptive reports, everyday communication documents, and product-based instructions and specifications. The formats discussed are **agendas**, **minutes of meetings**, **progress reports**, **letters**, **memos**, and **user documentation**. The chapter ends with an overview of different types of **visuals**, their functions and uses.

Descriptive reports

As noted in Chapter 6, descriptive reports state and describe facts, without analysis or interpretation. Objectivity and good summarising skills are necessary to produce clear and useful descriptive reports. Here are some types of descriptive reports and their functions.

Agendas

Agendas for committee meetings list the topics for discussion at a meeting. An agenda is circulated prior to the meeting to people who are scheduled to attend. Included items are the date, time and venue of the meeting, and the topics to be discussed. The second topic, after apologies of absentees, is a discussion of whether the tasks allocated at the previous meeting have been actioned – this way facilitating continuity in meetings and, therefore, in the progress of a project or the management of a section.

The following is an example of an agenda for a meeting:

AGENDA

Date: 23 October 2007
Time: 11:00–12:00
Venue: Board Room B

Items:

1. Apologies

2. Matters arising from minutes of last meeting

3. Brief discussion of project progress

4. Product specifications

5. Product architecture

6. Any Other Business (AOB)

Minutes

Minutes contain a summary of discussions held at meetings. The committee secretary is responsible for taking notes at the meeting, revising them into a minutes document, and circulating the document to committee members. Minutes should include information on tasks allocated to project or section members, and ask as a reminder to relevant parties of what needs to be done before specific dates. Here are the minutes of the meeting following the above agenda:

Minutes of Meeting, 23 October 2007

Present: John Amos, Grace Chung, Mary Ho, Steve Johnson, Adam Reeves

Apologies: George Craig, Petar Sladic

1. Progress:

   - Contacted South American representative
   - Agreed on collaboration plan with Dan Jones, local hobbyist
   - Have not yet contacted Mario Gracci
   - Have not contacted colleagues at UC Davis, and have not identified specific contact target yet
   - Finalised major decision: we will obtain all raw materials from Venezuela.

2. Product specifications:

- Discussed marketing, engineering, and manufacturing specs of final product – brandy (tentative plan attached)
- Discussed estimated engineering specs of crusher (specs attached).

3. Product architecture:

- Identified and defined major functional elements in project
- Identified sub-elements in each major block
- Identified physical components associated with each block
- Discussed crusher in detail – decided on a screw-type system

4. By next meeting, 10 December 2007:

- Adam Reeves to contact Mario Gracci
- Mary Ho to initiate contact with UC Davis and gauge interest in collaborating
- Team members to bring prototype of crusher for analysis and discussion.

Progress reports

Progress reports state tasks completed to date within a project. Progress reports compare actual progress against planned progress in terms of cost, resource use, and level of performance. Writing progress reports is an essential part of project management. With regular and timely progress reports, problems can be addressed and corrected before they damage the outcome of the project. Ideally, progress reports are written into project design as a formal requirement. For example, a systems analyst might be required to report to the project team or project manager every three weeks. This procedure reduces the risk of confusion, misunderstandings and delays.

When writing a progress report, consider:

Who to report to. Progress reports are typically addressed to both sectors of the project team: the project steering committee, who oversee the project, and the project implementation group, who put the project design into operation.

When to communicate. Project reports are generally required regularly.

What to communicate. Headings for the report may include the following:

- Major issues
- Key achievements

- Targets
- Progress against schedule (indicate whether the project is progressing according to plan)
- Resource summary against plan (compare the utilisation of resources against planned use at this stage)
- Major tasks remaining
- Forecast
- Additional comments/notation (for example, explain any deviations from the project plan).

How to communicate: As with all professional communication, expression in the report should be accurate, concise and unambiguous. It should be formatted using the standard layout of the company.

Contracts and licence agreements

Contracts and licence agreements list obligations and privileges that bind two or more parties, and describe the conditions and rules that base the transactions of the signing parties. The legal and non-negotiative nature of such documents gives them a high degree of formality.

Here is an extract from a licence agreement:

> Disk Manager/Disk Manager Diagnostics (the 'software') is copyright 1990-2000 by ONTRACK COMPUTER SYSTEMS, Inc, and is protected by International Copyright Law and International Treaty provisions. All rights are reserved. The original Purchaser ('You') is granted a licence to use the Software only, subject to the following restrictions and limitations:
>
> 1. The licence is to the original purchaser only, and is not transferable without the written permission of Ontrack Computer Systems, Inc.
>
> 2. You may make back-up copies of the Software for your own use only, subject to the limitations of this licence.

● Everyday communication documents

Business letters

In addition to reports, much professional communication takes place through shorter documents, such as letters and memos. These two documents are very similar in many respects. Their main difference lies in their recipients: letters tend to be addressed to readers outside the writer's organisation, while memos are written for colleagues and employees within the organisation.

Business letters generally serve these functions:

- They accompany a report (as in a letter of transmittal), a packaged product or advertising material (such as a brochure)

- They confirm a previous communication between writer and reader by stating the decisions or agreements that were made

- They introduce a candidate's application for a professional position (as in a cover letter to a job application)

- They notify the recipient of the outcome of his/her application

- They notify the recipient of changes or developments made in an established relationship (such as writing to shareholders to inform them of a new method of accessing financial data, or notifying employers of resignation)

- They carry a formal complaint or warning

- They congratulate the recipient on a success, or offer sympathy on a loss

- They thank the recipient for his/her support, or continued support.

Letters also used to be written to request information, and this could well still be the case in more traditional contexts. However, in most modern-day situations, this function of letter writing has been replaced with phone communication and email. Letters generally draw attention to something, whether that is an agreement, product or longer document, and should do this succinctly and directly.

The standard length of a business letter is one page. Only under special circumstances should you go to one and a half or two pages. For any situation requiring a longer document, write a short report. The standard order of items in a business letter is as follows:

1. Use letterhead for the sender company's name and address. If you are writing as an individual and have no letterhead, include your name and address as the first item on the top left of the page.

2. Follow by the date and then by the recipient's name, position and address. Always try to address readers personally. Avoid addressing them by their title and the impersonal Dear Sir or Madam. If need be, phone the company to find out the person's name. Use a title (Mr, Ms) and then the recipient's surname. Use a first name only if

you know the recipient well. Polite forms of address differ world-wide, but you cannot go wrong if you use title + surname.

3. The first sentence should state the nature of the letter. The best way is to write a short sentence beginning with 'Here is . . .' or 'This is to . . .'. The word 'Re' (short for regarding) followed by a title summarising the purpose of the letter is also often used.

4. Follow with two or three paragraphs of two to four sentences each, with the main content. Be as concise as possible, and avoid repetition and elaborate descriptions or justifications. End with a sentence indicating further action that you or the reader should carry out.

5. The most widespread courteous close is 'yours sincerely'. Although 'yours truly' and 'yours faithfully', and the less formal 'Cordially', are also used extensively, 'yours sincerely' is an internationally accepted standard. If the recipient is a close associate, you could go for the friendlier, 'Regards' or 'Best wishes'.

6. Type your name after your signature and follow by your position title.

As regards spacing, leave double space between each section. You can leave more space if the letter is short and there is a lot of white space on the page, but make sure you do not leave too many gaps between sections as this gives a fragmented appearance.

The letter on the opposite page is a letter of transmittal of a report investigating career opportunities for law graduates. The report was commissioned by a career consulting company and written by the President of the Law Students' Society.

Memoranda (memos)

Memos are internal documents, written to colleagues, superiors or subordinates within a company. Memos are rapidly being replaced with emails. Note, however, that an email message is largely a memo, as suggested by the email header, which is the same as that of a memo: To, From, Date, Subject. A formal email would, in fact, be equivalent to a memo. Print memos would still be used when the sender's signature adds value to the message.

Memos generally serve these functions:

● They confirm in writing the results of an oral communication, often also providing some more detail on the issues discussed.

Law Students' Society
4 Gladstone Terrace
X City, Y Country

Catherine Hayes ◄——————————————— Recipient's name.
Manager
Bellevue Career Counsellors
Street Address
City

24 October 2007

Dear Ms Hayes,

Please find attached the report regarding the occupational possibilities | First sentence states
of Law Majors that you requested on the 1st of October 2007. In accor- | directly the purpose of the
dance with your specifications, the report includes information on | letter.
employment opportunities, pay rates and trends – areas interesting to
graduates. Also, the report incorporates information for prospective | This being a letter of trans-
students, such as advice on appropriate choice of courses and study | mittal, it summarises the
planning. ◄ | main contents of the report,
| and connects them with the
| client's specifications.

The report outlines possible career options for law graduates and examines advantages of the profession such as the wide range of work avail-
able, the flexibility within the occupation and the high levels of | The second paragraph goes
remuneration. Disadvantages such as high stress levels and competition | into more detail on report
are also considered. ◄ | contents.

Recommendations include advice concerning appropriate professional | The body of the letter ends
development training, membership in professional associations, and | with a note on recommen-
publicity. ◄ | dations. In other types of
| letters, this would be
| replced with action to be
| taken by either the recipient
| and/or the writer.

I hope this report will be useful for Bellevue's further work on career
advice to students and graduates. Please feel free to contact me if you
have questions about the report or require additional information. ◄ |

| The letter ends with an offer
Yours sincerely, | to assist futher should it be
| required.

Franziska Federle
President, Law Students' Society

- They inform the recipient of the stage reached in a developmental procedure. In this case, they function as informal progress reports.

- They carry a formal request, reminder ('memorandum' is actually a Latin word for reminder) or suggestion.

- They notify employees of a change or development in an established course of action (for example, if set hours for coffee and lunch breaks are implemented or changed).

- They accompany and introduce documentation, such as internal reports.

Companies often have templates for internal memos. If not, follow these guidelines:

- Always use a 'memo header': To, From, Date, Subject.

- As with letters, aim for one page and do not exceed two pages.

- Begin with a personal address, especially if you are writing to one person or to group members with whom you work closely. A memo is still a relatively formal piece of communication, so beginning with 'Dear X', or 'Dear colleagues' is more palatable than an abrupt beginning. However, if you are writing to many readers who do not fall into one particular category, leave the personal address out.

- Tie your topic to a concern you expect your reader to share or to a subject you have previously discussed. For example, you could start by writing 'As you know . . .' or 'Following our meeting . . .' Do not begin abruptly with a new piece of information stated out of context.

- If appropriate, include a closing remark indicating further action, such as 'Please get back to me on this question as soon as possible'. However, a closing tie is not necessary in a memo and you can, in fact, end with your last paragraph.

- A memo is a short text that states facts, so use bullet points and lists to summarise and classify information. Avoid wordiness and detailed specifications and justifications (but you can write a memo to point the reader to a document that gives these detailed specifications and justifications). Optionally use headings, if they assist communication by signposting information.

Here is a memo written by the Staff Welfare Officer to the Human Resources Manager of the Ministry of the Interior. The memo informs the Manager of the results reached in a feasibility analysis carried out by the Staff Welfare Officer regarding coffee breaks. Note how it also acts as an informal progress report.

TO: Greg Taylor, Human Resources Manager
FROM: John Masters, Staff Welfare Coordinator
DATE: 25 November 2007
SUBJECT: Coffee breaks

Greg,

As you requested in our phone conversation last Friday, here is a summary of the issue and recommendations developed in relation to the current problem of coffee breaks. These issues and recommendations will be part of the formal report that I will submit to the Human Resources Committee on 15 January.

The Issue

Currently there is no provision of morning or afternoon coffee breaks for staff at the Ministry of the Interior. However, recent surveys and monitoring have indicated that approximately 70% of staff take unofficial breaks of between 20 and 40 minutes' duration each day. Other than causing work disruption, this also leaves staff that do not take breaks feeling disgruntled.

The issue for the Ministry of the Interior is whether it should implement an official morning and afternoon break policy, and, if so, on what conditions.

Recommendations

Studies have shown that 20-minute morning and afternoon breaks have a measurable positive effect on labour efficiency. This is reflected in the fact that three-quarters of businesses nationwide have daily break policies.

The formal report in response to this issue will contain these recommendations, briefly outlined here:

1. The Ministry of the Interior should implement an official morning and afternoon break policy. This recommendation is legal and within the powers of the commissioners to authorise.

2. The breaks should be 20 minutes long and staff should be deducted one hour's pay if their break period is longer than this (except in special circumstances).

3. No more than half the employees in any department should be on a break at one time.

4. The breaks cannot be exchanged for time off at either end of the working day.

5. The Ministry should establish a canteen on the premises to provide a facility where staff can purchase food and beverages. There is currently no such facility close to the Ministry. I have obtained the relevant costs and am currently conducting negotiations for final pricing.

Please contact me if you have any other questions at this stage.

John

The first sentence links this communication with a previous one that initiated it. The recipient is, therfore, given context for the memo.

The second sentence gives more context by stating the overall purpose of the document.

The headings signal the organisation of content.

The beginning of this section summarises the findings that justify the recommendations

The last sentence avoids an abrupt ending by offering further communication.

Although letters and memos are short documents, it is still important to take care in organising and prioritising information for maximum effect. For example, management communication researchers John Fielden and Ronald Dulek (1998) analysed over 2,000 documents in a corporate context and found that most were confusing and ineffective because they buried their main message and purpose by placing it in an inconspicuous position. This forced the reader to reread sections and to attempt to interpret the writer's intention. To remedy this, Fielden and Dulek propose a 'bottom-line' approach to business writing, by organising information so that the main message and purpose of the document are stated first, before any justifications, explanations or reasoning. All the information that follows becomes meaningful, because it is framed by the main point.

Accordingly, these writers formulated six principles, which, although relevant for all kinds of professional communication, are especially useful for letters, memos and email:

1. State your purpose first unless there are overriding reasons for not doing so.

2. State your purpose first, even if you believe your readers need a briefing before they can fully understand the purpose of your communication.

3. Present information in order of its importance to the readers.

4. Put information of dubious utility or questionable importance to the readers into an attachment.

5. In persuasive situations, where you do not know how your reader will react to what you ask for, state your request at the start in all cases except:

    ● when you do not know the reader well, and to ask something immediately would probably be perceived as being 'pushy';
    ● when the relationship between you and your reader is not close or friendly.

6. Avoid being direct straight up in negative messages. You should still be clear and unambiguous, but with more tact.   (Adapted from Fielden and Dulek, 1998, p. 185)

● Technical documentation

This section overviews the main techniques for producing documentation that instructs users how to deploy equipment and tools of different kinds. As a specialist writing to broad publics, situations abound where you need to describe procedures. In addition to the obvious examples of software development and engineering projects of all kinds, other professional situations include inducting new personnel as part of human resources programmes, maintaining safety and protocol in laboratory operations, and ensuring that relevant parties are instructed on appropriate behaviour during emergencies.

When designing technical documentation for end users, whatever its type and length, follow these steps:

1. **Plan**. Define the project, objectives, audience and project requirements. Make sure you understand what is expected from the documentation.
2. **Design**. Define the conceptual design requirements, select an organisational pattern, and page formats.
3. **Gather information**. Get information about the product from product experts and developers; outline the documentation.
4. **Write**. Draft and revise the manual using your planning and design decisions
5. **Evaluate**. Check for accuracy, consistency, accessibility and appeal: try it out and get feedback.

After you have established a design style, document it, describing typeface and size used for each element, spacing requirements, etc. Documenting your style helps others follow your design. Also, this information will assist you in revising the document in the future when you may have forgotten the design choices for the document. A simple way to document your design is to use a style sheet indicating the design choices for each element.

An effective way to think of your documentation is in terms of two factors: the way that you will lay out and sequence the sections, and the way that you will organize information in each section.

Layout patterns

When laying out the sections or chapters of a manual, use a combination of these patterns: **spatial**, **temporal**, **cause/effect**, **hierarchical**. Table 7 explains the different functions of each layout pattern.

Spatial: explains the parts of a product; is organised by physical and logical location; is the characteristic layout of reference manuals.

Temporal: shows sequence or order of occurrence of instructions, steps, processes, development or progression; is organised by occurrence in a time-line; is the characteristic layout of instructional manuals.

Cause/effect: shows which agent/problem (cause) produces what result (effect); is organised by a cause–effect or effect–cause structure.

Hierarchical: ranks quantifiable criteria, such as size, importance and ease/difficulty of performing tasks; is organised by ascending or descending order.

Table 7 Layout patterns of technical manuals

A possible plan for a manual could run this way: Organise the outline in a temporal pattern to indicate a series of lessons or tasks that must be sequentially learned. Within each lesson, select a temporal pattern for steps or directions. Where appropriate, use a cause/effect pattern to help users solve problems and correct their errors. At the end of each lesson or task use a hierarchical pattern to summarise, in order of descending importance, what the user should have learned in the lesson.

Organisational patterns

Having decided on the layout of your manual, you should think about how you will organise each section. Again, the determining criterion for your choice has to be the type of manual you are writing and its intended audience and purpose. Three commonly used organisational patterns are:

- Cookbook
- Narrative
- Action/result.

Cookbook: This pattern gives a clear sequence of temporal steps, showing users how to do something, a bit like the instructions in a recipe book. For example:

> To install the program, follow these steps:
> 1. Insert Disk 1 into Drive A.
> 2. Type [CD/], then press <Enter> to move to the Root Directory (Main Directory) on the hard disk.

3. Type [a:install], then press <Enter> to run the installation program.

Narrative: This pattern presents and develops a concept, by describing it and by changing focus from one point to another, usually in a general-to-specific sequence. A narrative pattern can prepare the users for instructions or procedures. For example:

> This chapter presents the FILE MENU and its options. Use this menu to manage text and graphic data. The FILE MENU is shown below. We will discuss how to save, copy, delete and rename files.

Action/result: This pattern states the action the user is to perform and describes the result. It often appears in user manuals for highly interactive products. For example:

Moving around the Text Editor

Action	Result
Press <ALT>	Move right one field
Press <CRL+Shift>	Change characters
Press <CRL+ALT>	Change behaviours

Writing technical documentation

Regardless of layout and organisational patterns, a set of instructions should state:

- **Purpose**: Why do it
- **Action**: What to do; what not to do
- **Safeguards**: How to protect the user and the equipment
- **Tools**: What equipment or tools to use
- **Location**: Where to do it
- **Time**: When to do it and for how long
- **Process**: How to do it
- **Agents**: Who is involved
- **Troubleshooting**: What to do if something goes wrong.

Effective technical communication needs a balance between the big picture (the main purpose and value of the activity described) and the details (the sequential tasks that must be performed to achieve this purpose). As anyone who has struggled to understand how to use a piece of equipment knows, this balance is not achieved without effort. Much technical documentation is too technical, unnecessarily detailed and lengthy and therefore discouraging for the user, or fails to set the scene properly and indicate to the users what the final result of their actions will be.

Keeping in mind the need for this balance, follow these steps:

- Analyse the procedure that you will describe. Try to remember what it felt like to perform it for the first time, as your reader will be doing.
- Distinguish between the goal to be reached and the actions needed to take you there.
- Divide the procedure into actions subdivided into tasks. Make sure that you do not fragment each action into too many steps, otherwise, you will flood the reader with disconnected details, and produce a wordy document.
- Choose verbs carefully. You may need to differentiate between similar actions. For example, when using a mouse to manipulate text on the screen, what is the difference between 'clicking', 'selecting', 'highlighting', 'choosing', 'dragging'?

The preferred sentence construction for giving instructions is to start most sentences with an action verb (imperative mood):

<u>Turn</u> the screw clockwise
<u>Press</u> the POWER button once

If time or location are important, you may begin with a prepositional phrase 'In . . .', 'When . . .':

When the green light appears, turn the knob to the left.

From this position, pull the lever slightly forward.

Writing instructions

When writing a set of instructions follow this sequence:

1. *Title*: Describe the topic of the instructions.

2. *Introduction*: Give a general, scene-setting description of the procedure and the result before going on to give any details. Include a section on definitions, if the terminology is technical or subject

specific. Think of this as introducing your characters in a script. The clearer the description the easier it is for the reader to visualise the agents and the actions.

3. *Equipment/Materials/Tools/Ingredients*: List all equipment used in the procedure. Visuals are effective in this section.

4. *General Warnings*: State any warnings that are relevant to all stages in the procedure. Put specific warnings before the piece of information to which they relate. Do not list all warnings in one section as the user may fail to remember them when their time comes.

5. *Procedure*: List and possibly briefly describe the stages, or tasks, of the procedure. Remember to list both tasks and sub-tasks.

6. *Steps*: For each stage or task, list the steps that compose it. For clearly written steps, follow these guidelines:

   - Put any requirements or restrictions at the beginning – before the steps.
   - Distinguish between steps and other clarifications or results. For example the following steps are misleading:

     1. Press the button.
     2. A red light appears.

     The appearance of the red light is the result of the action and should not be listed as a step. Instead, this should be:

     1. Press the button – a red light appears.

   - Where possible, begin all steps with an action verb that indicates the main action to be performed; avoid weak or unnecessary verbs. For example, the following step is too wordy:

     Take the plug and insert it in the socket

     The verb 'take' includes an extra step, which, in fact, is superfluous to the sequence intended. Instead, this should be:

     Insert the plug in the socket

   - Begin with a propositional phrase stating the result of a step, if that is appropriate:

     To open the case, turn the handle to the left.

   - Make sure all steps have parallel structure.

- List tasks and their steps in appropriate chronological sequence, and number them
- Integrate visuals where appropriate
- Indicate what happens when a task is completed, for example, lights, beeps, etc.
- Put warnings and cautions before the task where needed
- Avoid brackets. Brackets may confuse the user, as it is not clear whether the bracketed information should lead to action or should be ignored
- Where possible, leave white space. Instructions are clearer when they are not cluttered.

7.   *Tips/notes*: Give any tips that may facilitate the use or maintenance of the equipment, but are not necessary, like warnings.
8.   *Troubleshooting*: Explain what to do if something goes wrong.

From a technical manual:

Since the user interface for analyzer calibration refers to calibration as 'calibration', this chapter will refer to the process of calibration as calibration.

From a manual for a database package:

An action is to be taken on the third non-consecutive day that an event occurs.

From a technical manual for the British military concerning the storage of nuclear weapons:

It is necessary for technical reasons that these warheads should be stored with the top at the bottom and the bottom at the top. In order that there may be no doubt as to which is the top and which is the bottom, for storage purposes it will be seen that the bottom of each warhead has been labelled with the word 'TOP.'   (cited in a book on computer science, published by the Computer Science Department of the University of Virginia (www.cs.virginia.edu/cs/50/book/ch-programming.pdf)

From a software user manual:

When you first start the application, the options bar appears on the top left of your screen, and is where option settings are set for the options used with the currently selected tool.

WARNING: The options bar may not be located on the top left of your screen.

Table 8 'Nightmare' instructions

Very detailed instructions concentrate on actions and specify tasks; less detailed instructions focus on actions that are directly relevant to the result. Be guided by the needs and existing knowledge of your audience. Sometimes, if you make the instructions too explicit – that is, too detailed in description – you may make them unnecessarily complicated, confusing and maybe even condescending. For example, see Table 8 for some real-life 'nightmare' instructions and try to avoid falling into the same traps.

Below is an example to illustrate the above explanations. It is an extract from the operating manual of a land hovercraft. It is unclear and confusing.

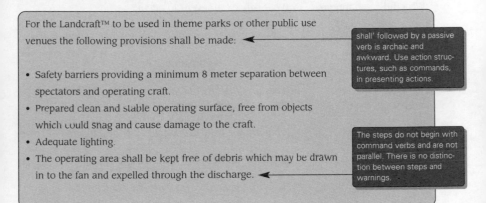

For the Landcraft™ to be used in theme parks or other public use venues the following provisions shall be made: ◄——— shall' followed by a passive verb is archaic and awkward. Use action structures, such as commands, in presenting actions.

• Safety barriers providing a minimum 8 meter separation between spectators and operating craft.
• Prepared clean and stable operating surface, free from objects which could snag and cause damage to the craft.
• Adequate lighting.
• The operating area shall be kept free of debris which may be drawn in to the fan and expelled through the discharge. ◄———

The steps do not begin with command verbs and are not parallel. There is no distinction between steps and warnings.

Here is how this extract could be rewritten with consistency and a more graceful style.

> When using the Landcraft™ in public venues, follow these measures:
>
> ● Prepare a clean and stable operating surface, free from debris and objects.
>
> Warning: Debris may cause injury if drawn into the fan and expelled through the discharge. Objects can snag and damage the craft.
>
> ● Install safety barriers with a minimum 8 meter separation between spectators and operating craft.
> ● Provide adequate lighting to see clearly all craft components.

Table 9 lists some of the most common questions of users of equipment. Keep these in mind when designing your documentation.

How do I . . . ?	*How do I perform an action, accomplish a goal or achieve a result?*
When do I . . . ?	*Under what circumstances do I perform a task or take an action?*
What is . . . ?	*What does X mean? What does it look like? Sound like?*
What's wrong?	*Why won't X work? How do I fix it?*
Why did . . . happen?	*What caused an event to occur?*
How does . . . work?	*What processes take place when I take action X?*
Which is better?	*How do I decide between X or Y?*
Why do . . . ?	*What are the advantages or benefits of X? What are the reasons for doing Y?*
Why not do . . . ?	*What are the disadvantages, costs or dangers of X?*
How else can I . . . ?	*How can I do X better, faster, more reliably?*
How are . . . and . . . related?	*How are they alike? How are they different?*
Why is . . . ?	*What is the purpose or goal of X?*
Where is . . . ?	*Where is component X? How does it relate to other components?*
What does . . . contain?	*What are the parts of X?*
How is . . . organised?	*How do the parts of X fit together?*
What can I do with . . . ?	*What problems does X solve? What can it do?*
What do I do next?	*What is the next step in the procedure?*
What must I do first?	*How do I begin? What are the prerequisites of X?*
How do I recognise?	*What does X look like? What does it sound like? What are its special features?*
What happens if . . . ?	*What will be the consequences of X? What are the dangers?*

Table 9 Common user questions

Here is a checklist for writing instructions.

User Documentation Chart

Introduction
☐ Have you told users what they need to know about:

- Aim, purpose or desired outcome of the procedure?
- Scope of the instructions?
- Assumptions about technical level of users?
- Necessary background information on the procedure?
- Definitions of terms?

Equipment
☐ Have you listed and described all equipment?
☐ Have you used visuals where useful?

Procedure and steps
☐ Have you grouped steps under appropriate tasks in the procedure?
☐ Have you given headings or other visual guidance that enables users to see the major tasks?
☐ Have you presented one action per step?
☐ Have you phrased steps as commands?
☐ Have you used parallel structure for all steps in one task?
☐ Have you described actions <u>before</u> giving explanations?
☐ Have you presented results <u>after</u> actions?
☐ Have you provided all warnings needed to protect users from harm?
☐ Have you provided all warnings to prevent users from encountering problems or damaging the equipment?

Troubleshooting
☐ Have you told users how to overcome any problems they are likely to encounter?

Visuals
☐ Have you included all visuals that users may find helpful or persuasive?
☐ Are your visuals neat, simple and easy to understand?

□ Are your visuals located in appropriate positions?
□ Have you labelled all your visuals?

Page design
□ Do the pages look neat and attractive?
□ Do they provide easy access for users to find specific information?
□ Have you used at least one level of heading?

Proofreading
□ Have you employed correct grammar, punctuation and spelling?

● Visuals

Visuals include diagrams, charts, tables, figures, graphs, photographs, drawings, clip art, and other pictorial or schematic representations. Visuals are alternative methods of presenting information and form a useful non-linear complement to the written word. Information presented diagrammatically or in pictorial form is memorable and can simplify, and thereby make clearer, complicated data. When including a visual in a document, assess it in relation to two factors: **content**, that is how it communicates meaning that is complementary to the meaning presented linguistically; and **design**, that is in terms of its size and positioning on the page.

As regards content, these points are important:

● The visual should be necessary to clarify a point in the document. Do not include a visual just for decoration. The visual must be the best way to present the particular information you wish to express. It should convey a message more emphatically, more clearly, or more concisely than written sentences, or it should clarify the meaning of the sentences.

● The kind of visual you have chosen (pie chart, image, table, etc.) should be the best for your purpose. For example, a line diagram may be inappropriate for discrete data.

● The visual must be introduced, discussed, interpreted and integrated in the text of the document. Remember that raw data is useless unless its relevance to the issue at hand is made clear. The reader should not have to work to figure out why the visual is included in the document, or what the significance of the data may be.

- The visual must stand alone in meaning. While it should be interpreted in the text of the document, it should also be self-explanatory and complete, and not obscure or confusing.

- All visuals must be numbered consecutively and given a specific, meaningful title. Include the title of a table above the table, and the title of all other visuals below the visual.

- As with all writing choices, visuals must be designed and formatted in a manner appropriate for the likely audience of the document. Will the visual be clear and appealing from the intended reader's perspective?

- If you have copied the visual from another document or website, remember to write 'Source' under the visual, followed by the name of the source.

- If using a table, make all like elements (the factors to be compared) read down, not across.

As regards arrangement and design these points are important:

- Make the visual easy for your reader to find; the visual should closely follow the reference to it in the text. Format the document so that visuals do not appear on different pages from where they are mentioned in the text.

- Surround the visual with white space and do not clutter it. This makes it easier for the reader to absorb the information presented.

- Consider whether the visual would be better located in an appendix rather than in the body of the report. If the body of your report is becoming too cluttered, some visuals may be moved to an appendix.

- As a convention, the visual should take up no less than one third of a page, again, for reasons of clarity and visibility.

- Position the visual in alignment with the text, for balance.

- If using colours, note that by ordering colours from light to dark vertically or horizontally, elements will appear to be next to each other. This is because lighter colours tend to stand out and darker colours to recede.

Charts and graphs

Here is a list of different kinds of charts and graphs with guidelines on their uses in documents.

Line graph

Useful for showing trends and fluctuations over time.

Column graph

Shows clearly comparisons of amounts. It is presented in vertical form.

Bar chart

Indicates proportions as they are related to each other. It is presented in horizontal form.

Pie chart

Indicates proportion of parts to the whole.

Scattergram

Shows correlations between different items.

Flow chart

Specifies the relationship between processes.

Gannt chart

Combines a process with the amount of time it takes to complete it.

Organisational chart

Shows relationships between things and creates a directory.

Map

Distributes events or influences over different locations.

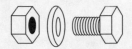

Exploded diagram

Shows components in a structure.

Schematic

Shows relationships between theoretical concepts.

1950   2000

Timeline

Indicates simple time sequences.

Activities

1. Here is a memo written by a software developer to the Public Relations Manager of a corporation. The memo concerns a new networking system, called Wizz, currently on trial at the corporation. The writer of the memo has made the common error of 'writing as he thinks', which means the memo lacks organisation and focus. Read the memo and make a list of the problems it has in communicating a clear message. Especially, answer these questions:

- Does the memo have a main message? If yes, summarise it.
- What is the implied event that triggered the writing of the memo? What problem is the memo concerned with?
- What action does the writer expect the reader to take after reading the memo? Is this action clearly delineated?
- What problems are there with content organisation and cohesion?
- What are some problems with style and sentence structure that contribute to the lack of clarity?

After answering these questions, write a revised version of the memo.

To:	Michelle Lanier
From:	David Atkinson
Date:	10 November 2007
Subject:	Wizz

The Wizz system is designed to help with the job of managing a large number of company stakeholders' access to the computer resources of the corporation. This includes configuring the network accounts up in the first place and removing the accounts at appropriate times. As it is currently implemented the system is very incomplete and is useful only as a way for any network administration staff to track how they have set up the computers.

We've had great input into developing what Wizz should be, but much less input at how Wizz should do this. Unless we have specific regulation on how to use to use it, unless we give users specific instructions, unless we get specific feedback on what problems there are, we won't know if Wizz is the best solution to the problem. Using someone who is not the designer of a component to implement it, is a test on the correctness of the design as it is likely to show up any shortfalls in it. For this reason the different approaches of a whole team of developers is valuable, based on their different interpretations or scepticism as well as their ability at solving a particular problem.

In general the Wizz software developed may be the highest quality system we have ever used. The process would work better if we had ways to get specific feedback. For this reason I don't regard the system as a total success, but feel it is a valuable experiment.

2. Below are guidelines on how to set up your work space and computer position for comfort and efficiency. Rewrite these guidelines in manual style. Rearrange information by editing the text and creating point lists for conciseness and clarity. Divide the text into sections and title the sections. Give a title to the whole document.

This will give you some useful ideas about how to sit in front of your computer and how to position your computer so as to be more comfortable and avoid stress and strain to your hands, wrists, joints and eyes. Establishing a comfortable work site is important for you and your computer. A poor work environment or stressful work habits can result in discomfort or serious injury from repetitive strain to your hands, wrists and other joints. A number of books are available on ergonomics and repetitive strain injury or repetitive stress syndrome. For more information on these topics or for tips on exercises for such stress points as hands and wrists, please check with your library or book seller. Proper ambient conditions should also be maintained for the computer's operation. In general, if you are comfortable, so is your computer, but read the following to make sure your work site provides a proper environment. Make sure there is adequate space around the computer for proper ventilation. Make sure the AC power cord connects to an outlet that is close to the computer and easily accessible. Changes in temperature and humidity are harmful to computers, so put your computer in a room where such changes can be avoided. The same goes for dust, moisture and exposure to direct sunlight. Heat sources, such as electric heaters, can also be very harmful to your computer. Do not use the computer near liquids or corrosive chemicals. Magnetic sources, such as stereo systems, cause magnetic waves that interfere with the computer's functions, so keep these away from your computer. Do not operate the computer in close proximity to a mobile phone. Leave ventilation room for the fan. Your computer display should be no higher than eye level to avoid eye strain, so the computer must be placed at a comfortable height and distance, on a flat surface. Allow adequate space behind the computer to let you freely adjust the display. The display should be angled to reduce glare and maximise visibility. Avoid placing the computer in front of bright light that could shine directly in your eyes. If possible, use soft, indirect lighting in your computer work area. Use a lamp to illuminate your documents or desk, but you should make sure that the lamp is positioned so that it does not reflect off the display or shine in your eyes. Your chair should be placed so that the keyboard is at or slightly below the level of your elbow. You should be able to type comfortably with your shoulders relaxed. Sit straight so that your knees, hips and elbows form approximately 90 degree angles when you work. Do not slump forward or lean back too far. A key to avoiding discomfort or injury from repetitive strain is to vary your activities. If you must spend long hours at the computer, finding ways to break up the routine can reduce stress and improve your efficiency. Occasionally stand up and stretch or exercise briefly. Frequently, you should look away from the screen and focus your eyes on a distant object for several seconds. Take frequent short breaks instead of one or two long breaks. The height of your chair in relation to the computer and keyboard as well as the support it gives your body are primary factors if you want to reduce work strain.

3. Below are some verbal descriptions of actions, relationships, steps and trends. Read the description and decide what kind of visual would present this information graphically. Draw the visual to illustrate. There could be more than one option for each description.

Verbal description	Visual
The budget was divided as follows: supplies 20%, salaries 40%, advertising 25%, shipping, 15%, and reserve 5%.	
The fuel-mixture container is located on the right top corner of the engine, and the main valve is located below the injector plug.	
Measured values for the X, Y and Z plants were 41.2, 50.8 and 20.5 respectively.	

First, check...Then, open...Next, move...	
The engine is composed of A, B, C and D components.	
The error rate for online help menus was about half of the rate for printed instructions	
Profits rose continuously in the last five years, even though the number of investors remained constant	
If X happens, we should do Y; on the other hand, if B happens we should do A.	

9 Working in Teams

Focus on:

- ▶ Team roles
- ▶ Project managemen
- ▶ Cooperation and conflict

Many projects in business and industry require collaboration for their completion. In fact, teamwork is rapidly becoming the norm in many business projects, especially those that entail the cooperation of specialists in different fields. Therefore, a discussion of the concepts and terms that underlie teamwork and collaboration has an important role in a guide to business communication.

As regards the writing component of team projects, two trends are common. One trend, generally the most successful one, is for the team to have a writer, usually the team member with the best communication skills. This person gathers information from other team members and produces the documents that record and report on the project. The other trend, a more problematic option, is for all team members to contribute to the writing component of projects. This tends to be effective if all team members have equal communication skills. Even in those cases, however, it is difficult to build coherence in a document that is made up of styles of different writers. Where possible, select a writer in a team project to avoid a 'cut and paste' appearance. To share accountability, however, ensure that all team members read the document and agree on its content and organisation, before submission.

This chapter overviews major elements of teamwork, especially **team dynamics**, the **allocation of team tasks**, **project management** and **conflict management**. The chapter ends with some real-life testimonials of members of team projects, evaluating their strengths and weakness of their teamwork.

● Team dynamics

At their best, teams can produce excellent results by combining the specialised skills that individual team members bring. At their worst, teams produce delays, misunderstandings, and conflicts. For this reason, the ability to deal productively with other people – peers, juniors and superiors – is a highly valued skill that contributes greatly to the smooth and successful management of an organisation. The success of a team project is largely due to such skilled procedures as effective negotiation, duty allocation and conflict management.

Teams can be effective problem solvers for many reasons, including:

- More extensive information is available in a team than an individual may have alone.

- Individuals bring different approaches to a problem within the team. This allows for a wide range of options to be considered.

- Improved understanding of the problem and possible solutions is possible, because team members are aware of the reasoning used in problem analysis.

- It is more likely that consensus will be achieved if a decision was made in consultation with members of the team, so that no one feels 'left out', and therefore is not likely to oppose a decision.

- Risks can often be managed more effectively in teams. What can be a high-risk decision for an individual could actually be a moderate-risk decision for a team, because different team members bring new knowledge to the issue, and because risk is often a function of knowledge.

- Motivation and confidence are likely to increase in decisions made in team situations because individual team members feel supported by others.

Major disadvantages of reaching important decisions as part of a team include:

- Decisions can be made too soon: teams that feel uncomfortable with conflict may decide on the first option which meets with some support from the team members, regardless of whether this would be the best option.

- On the other hand, decisions can take too long, if the team cannot agree on a topic.

- If the team structure is too democratic, there may be a lack of initiative and responsibility.

- Teams may be influenced by one person, whose charismatic or persuasive strengths may induce members to overlook pertinent factors in the problem involved.

- If there is too much conflict in a team, the team may become inoperable or ineffective.

● Teams may displace responsibility so that it may be difficult to hold a team or an individual member accountable for a negative outcome.

Generally, good team dynamics are generally achieved in three main ways:

1. members are attracted to the team's purpose.
2. members share similar values, needs and interests.
3. members fulfil for each other important interpersonal needs, such as *affection* (acknowledging each other's point of view), *inclusion* (allowing each member to play a role in activities) and *control* (allowing each member to determine certain actions pertinent to that member's role).

● Task allocation

In order for teamwork to be productive, more is needed than just faith in the goodwill and competence of individual members. What is more essential is a formally implemented system for duty allocation, negotiation, delegation of duties, monitoring of progress and feedback. Ensure that you divide the project into tasks, and allocate a task to each team member. Also, ensure that everyone knows and agrees to his/her allocated tasks at the beginning of the project – to avoid heartache and confusion later. Three common and effective models for organising team projects are the 'sequential', the 'functional' and the 'mix-and-match'.

The sequential model

In this type, each department/section in a company, or person in a group for smaller projects, is assigned a specific, non-overlapping, responsibility in the project. For example, in a software company, three departments are sometimes involved in producing the user documentation:

● software specialists assemble the material

● communication specialists are in charge of word processing and designing

● the art and printing department is responsible for publishing the documentation.

In this case, each department must finish its job before passing the material to another department for the next stage.

The sequential type of collaboration can be effective at times, especially when the work of each segment is specialised and each stage is self-sufficient. However, projects completed sequentially take longer than when other methods are employed, and a project manager is often necessary to coordinate the project and to ensure that deadlines are kept, that all parties understand requirements, and that transitions from one stage to the next are smooth.

The functional model

This type is organised according to the skills or job function of the members. All stages of a project are undertaken concurrently, and all parties can monitor procedures at each stage. For example, a four-person team carrying out a user documentation project for software might be organised as follows:

- A manager schedules and conducts meetings, assists team members, issues progress reports to management, solves problems by proposing alternatives, and generally coordinates efforts to keep the project on schedule.

- A researcher collects data, conducts interviews, searches the literature, administers tests, gathers and classifies information, and then prepares notes on the work.

- A writer/editor receives the researcher's notes, prepares outlines and drafts, and circulates them for corrections and revisions.

- A graphics expert obtains and prepares all visuals, specifying why, how and where visuals should be placed and designing the document layout. He or she might even suggest that visuals replace certain sections of text.

All parties work on the project at the same time, and interact regularly through meetings and email communication.

The mix-and-match model

In this type of collaboration, team members agree on shared objectives, and then work independently on separate sections of the project by undertaking all tasks. The team members meet at specified times to compare their work and choose the best samples from each other's work. This approach is constructive in smaller-scale projects, when team members have similar skills but cannot meet regularly.

A different version of this approach occurs when all members share the same interactive software and can work on the same project concurrently, each contributing according to their own skills which may or may not overlap. Continuing our software documentation example, a mix-and-match type of collaboration could mean that members from the engineering, communication and art departments have the same software installed in their computers and work on the same documentation project at the same time, without waiting for one department to finish their tasks before passing the project to another department. This would most likely cut costs and reduce time, compared with the sequential model, but it would necessitate that all members work cooperatively, and that project milestones and outcomes are very clearly set out and agreed by all in advance (to reduce the risk of 'you're treading on my toes' symptom).

The leader

In any kind of collaboration model, the role of a leader is vital. Even in cases where, seemingly, the team works on egalitarian principles, and all team members know their duties, liberties and constraints, the presence of a leader can act as a unifying force that helps to maintain cohesion and stability. It is a good idea to select a team leader to avoid the situation where the most dominant personality takes over unofficially. Regardless of whether their focus is to maintain cohesion or to initiate tasks, effective team leaders share certain characteristics. According to Qubein (1986, p. 96), these common characteristics are:

- They value people: they acknowledge the importance and contribution of others.

- They listen actively: they make an effort to understand the needs and desires of others.

- They are tactful: they criticise sparingly, constructively and diplomatically.

- They give credit: they praise others and their contributions publicly.

- They are consistent: they control their personal moods, and are fair in their exchanges with others.

- They admit mistakes: they take the blame for errors they committed.

- They have a sense of humour: they maintain a pleasant disposition and pleasant manner.

- They set a good example: they follow their own regulations.

Effective leaders are not only personally ambitious and well-organised, but should also be people-oriented, willing to assist and direct subordinates, and able to improvise and innovate in their field within ethical parameters.

● Project management

A project in business and industry consists of a series of activities leading to one major goal or purpose. 'Project management' refers to the planning necessary to complete a major project on time, within budget, according to specifications, and with the consultation and consent of all relevant parties. Projects tend to be undertaken by a project team, a group of people responsible for managing a project. Projects usually begin with a proposal and end with a completed outcome, and a final report showing how the initial goals were reached or not. During the progress of a project, the team is generally required to submit progress reports at specified times (such as monthly or bi-monthly), in order to keep management informed of what has been achieved and what still remains to be done.

The components of effective project management are **definition**, **planning** and **direction**. Briefly, project definition involves describing the envisioned final product and its place in the market; planning involves identifying and prioritising the tasks necessary for the completion of the product; and direction involves allocating roles to team members and setting a timeline for the execution of tasks. Consider each component more carefully.

Definition

As the first step, a project is carefully defined. Aspects of project definition include:

- *Project overview*. Is the project attempting to solve a problem? If so, for whom is this a problem? How is the problem defined? Is the project creating a new product? What are the characteristics of this product? What types of markets will it target?

- *Scope*. What issues, topics or features will the project cover? How much detail will it provide? What are the parameters that project team members have to work within?

- *Outcome*. What will the result of the project be? For example, if a computer system is being developed, what functions should it perform and to what standard?

Planning

Each step in the process is planned before further action is taken. Tasks undertaken in the planning stage include:

1. Identifying the steps required to complete the project

2. Listing the priorities: What should be done first, second, third?

3. Identifying dependent and independent tasks: Which tasks need to be put aside while other tasks are being completed? Which tasks are urgent, and which may be delayed without damaging the project?

4. Creating a timeline for task completion and allocating roles to project team members.

Project Managers usually divide tasks into three categories:

1. **A critical task** must be completed on time for the entire project to be completed on time.

2. **A milestone** is an event that signifies the accomplishment of a series of tasks during a project. A milestone often signals the ending of a stage or section in the development of the project.

3. **A deliverable** is a concrete object produced at specific stages in the project (and usually delivered to a manager or client). Deliverables are used in some types of project management, like, for instance, software design and engineering. For example, the systems requirements report, produced near the beginning of the project and describing what the projected software will achieve, is a deliverable.

Direction

Each project is directed according to a line of responsibility. Project managers are responsible for monitoring and controlling progress and activities. Members of the project team report to managers, who in turn report to upper-level management and clients. Team members who are able to meet all the requirements of the project at a minimum cost and on time are highly valued.

The direction of a project also involves issues of resources, constraints and risks, which may propel the project forward or inhibit its development:

- *Resources.* What advantages do the team have in undertaking the project? Are they highly skilled? Do they have a large budget? Do they have adequate time to complete all the tasks? Is up-to-date technology available to them?

- *Constraints.* Is the budget modest? Is the staff limited, in numbers or in knowledge? Are there tight deadlines? Is there a lack of appropriate technology?

- *Risks.* What are the possible dangers of the project and what can be done to minimise them?

Two particular dangers that often arise in project management are known as **scope creep** and **feature creep**. Both of these can lead to delays, incomplete projects and conflicts within the project team.

Scope creep is exemplified by the tendency of stakeholders and project participants to expect more and more from the outcome of the project as it progresses. For example, businesses and users might expect increasing functionality and performance from a computer system as the process of developing the system unfolds.

Feature creep refers to the tendency to add more and more features and details to the expected product of the project without bearing in mind that the incorporation of these features will take extra time and money. The type of project determines what kind of feature creep may exist. In software design, for example, feature creep leads to the uncontrolled addition of technical features to the software under development.

One way to keep the project under control and monitor progress is to have a clear plan at the beginning, agreed upon by all members, to implement a feedback process where any conflicts or miscommunication can be aired and resolved, and to discuss progress at regularly organised meetings.

● Conflict management

Conflict is embedded in human relations. It arises when there is incompatibility of orientation between individuals or groups, and it can occur in such situations as when people form incompatible goals and behaviours, when resources have to be allocated, and when decisions have to be made. Conflict is associated with:

- *Value*: underlying values are different. This is arguably the most important and serious type of conflict because values are entrenched in social interaction and behaviour, and are very difficult to change.

- *Interests*: what promotes one's self-interest opposes another's. For example, when two colleagues compete for the same promotion inevitably some degree of conflict will arise.

- *Policy*: existing regulations do not reflect current needs. This often manifests in cases where conflict leads to employees' strikes or group protests. This is what happens, for example, when prices increase but salaries remain static, leading to a strike, or when women have achieved breakthroughs in social equality but legislation regulating gender issues remains at a primitive level, leading to demonstrations, or ground breaking legal proceedings. Policy is very closely aligned with value.

- *Goals*: there is controversy or disagreement about where a project is going. In a project, for example, some members may think the goal is to produce routine results, whereas others may want to produce a radical breakthrough.

- *Method*: there is controversy or disagreement about how to arrive at the desired outcome. Such conflict may arise when one side is more optimistic about the future, while the other side wants more control over a situation, leading them to choose high-risk methods (such as war over negotiation, for instance).

Managed properly, conflict can result in growth because it allows for different points of view to be aired and considered. Managed badly, it can be destructive and costly – in resources and relationships. Groups can suffer from two opposite evils: too little conflict, and too much conflict. A little conflict can be a good thing for change and rejuvenation of outmoded structures and beliefs. A lot of conflict, however, can destroy a project and in serious cases even lead to costly lawsuits and official investigations.

When teams are not working well, it can be a very serious matter, costing the organisation money and time. While the reasons that make a team unproductive are not fixed or universal, there are some guidelines regarding what might not be working right that can be used to clarify the situation:

- The team may lack a leader, or be burdened by an incompetent leader, making it disorganised and dysfunctional as a result.

- The team may be lacking the required specialist skills to tackle a project expertly and confidently.

- Members may feel their personal skills are not appreciated and they may lose motivation (often the result of weak leadership or bad management).

- The team may feel their efforts will not be supported by authorities and funding agencies, especially if they are working under budget constraints and/or on obscure or unpopular projects.

- A conflict of values or expectations may exist where some team members may expect different results from the project or the team may be expecting different results from the management.

- The objectives and scope of a project may be unclear, leading to confusion.

- Personal conflicts may hinder the achievement of goals. This is especially true of competitive environments where people are not accustomed to working cooperatively.

Managing conflict

As it probably has become clear from the preceding discussion, managing conflict is no easy matter. In most aspects of interpersonal communication, contextual factors, such as the setting of the interaction, the background of the participants and the nature of the interaction, are important in pointing to the most appropriate reactions, and conflict management is no exception to this. However, as regards teamwork, a general process for managing conflict could take this form:

1. *Define the problem.* The definition of the problem is the most important step in finding a solution. In many cases there is low morale and a lack of commitment by team members because there is a problem that has not been voiced or made conscious within the group dynamics. An effective method of discussing the problem that caused this conflict is to describe it in writing. Each conflicting side should describe their perspective on the matter as clearly and as objectively as possible, avoiding the 'I said / he said' type of criticism. It is also important to avoid generalisations, such as 'they', 'always', 'never', etc., and to determine if the reaction is proportional to the situation. In describing the issue, consider if it had

  objective grounds to escalate into conflict, or if it is likely to have been caused by misunderstanding.

2. *Analyse the problem.* Once the group agrees on the nature of the problem, the next step is to analyse it in terms of size, causes and criteria of evaluation. At this stage, it is important not to succumb to the temptation of listing possible solutions before having analysed the problem thoroughly. Before answering the question, 'what can be done to solve the conflict?', team members should answer, 'why is this a conflict?' and 'for whom is it a conflict?'.

3. *Generate possible solutions.* Brainstorming is usually an effective way to generate ideas that could lead to the resolution of the conflict. At this stage, evaluation or nitpicking criticism of ideas should be avoided, and team members should produce as many possible solutions as they can.

4. *Evaluate and test the various solutions.* After the brainstorming stage, each possible resolution should be examined to ascertain its merits and drawbacks. Factors to consider carefully include if the solutions are likely to work, if they are fair to all, and if they can be implemented easily. This should eliminate the solutions that are not worthwhile and leave a reduced number of options.

5. *Choose a mutually acceptable solution.* From the reduced number of possible solutions the one that seems to be the most effective can be chosen for a trial period. The best way to articulate this would be, once again, in writing. At times, choosing an option is risky, with no guarantees that the selected solution will work. However, if the decision was reached by (relative) consensus, all the parties involved will be responsible for testing it and providing feedback.

One way to maximise your chances for keeping conflict under control is to institute a feedback process, through which all members air complaints, express satisfaction and propose changes to the team structure at specified intervals. During such feedback sessions, consider evaluating your own and others' contributions and participation with the following criteria.

Criteria for Evaluating Member Contribution

                  Insert 1, 2, 3, or 4*

- Is available when needed and is punctual ☐

- Communicates clearly and constructively ☐

- Does fair share of work ☐

- Contributes quality work ☐

- Helps to manage conflict ☐

- Completes tasks effectively and punctually. ☐

* 1, poor; 2, satisfactory; 3, good; 4, excellent.

Effective listening

Effective listening contributes enormously to group dynamics and conflict resolution. In interpersonal communication, poor listening skills are at fault in many, if not most, cases of misunderstanding.

When working with others, much of the communication that takes place when suggesting, instructing, requesting, criticising, praising and negotiating is non-verbal. Listening actively by making a physical and mental effort to understand what someone else is saying engages the whole body, not just ears. It is a way of communicating that signifies:

- I hear what you are feeling
- I understand how you see things now
- I am interested and concerned
- I understand where you are
- I do not wish to judge you or change you.

Here are six tips for active listening:

1. *Stop talking*. Many people talk too much because they feel uncomfortable with silence. However, you cannot listen if you are talking.
2. *Remove noise as much possible*. 'Noise' is used in the communications sense of distractions to the unhindered transmission of the message. Therefore, it refers not only to external factors such as street noise, but also to other factors, such as excessive heat or cold, and distracting mannerisms. Common distracting mannerisms include clicking pens, shuffling papers, checking clothing or fingernails, and gazing around the room. If you need to talk to a team member or colleague about something serious, it is advisable to arrange a meeting in pleasant and relaxed surroundings.

3. *Ask open questions* which begin with the 5Ws and 1H: what, when, why, where, who and how. This helps to keep the conversation on the topic and to obtain as much information as possible on it. When people answer W and H questions they have to reply in full sentences, and so their replies are more factual than they would be if the questions were of the 'Do you . . . ' type, which elicits, simpler 'yes/no' answers.

4. *Be supportive*. Let the other person know that you *want* to know what s/he is talking about. It is well attested that most people will talk if they get attention and interest from the listener. Sensing indifference or impatience discourages a constructive response.

5. *Respond to feelings*. If the situation at hand has an emotional investment by one or all the participants, it is best to acknowledge this. Hidden or 'bottled' feelings may cloud or sabotage the information you require.

6. *Summarise to check mutual understanding*. A summary ensures that both parties have the same understanding of what has been said, and helps to create closure to an issue or topic of discussion. In business, for example, a summary is formalised in a Statement of Understanding, listing the points that have been agreed upon in a previous discussion.

● Testimonials on teamwork

Below are extracts from the recommendations sections of reports on engineering team projects. These extracts describe problems in:

- unclear task allocation, leading to delays
- inadequate structure of meetings, leading to confusion on what needed to be done and who was to do it
- lack of leadership, leading to lack of disciplined progress toward goals, and, often, low morale
- inadequate planning, leading to time wasting and miscommunication.

Read what team members have to say about their experiences, and learn from their problems.

Skills, tasks and roles

One good rule in forming a team is to pick members who have a nice distribution of skills. A group whose members all specialise in the same field may be very strong in that one area but lacking in many others.

Considering the allocation of roles, it took us some time to organise ourselves. Our roles were overlapping and after some time we decided to attribute ourselves some more precise functions. We realise that a better way to do this would have been to have a clear definition of our roles from the start, which would have optimised the time spent during meetings by preventing significant overlap. For future teams, we would recommend that the attribution of roles be done with common accord and discussion between team members as early as possible.

Defining roles and responsibilities at the beginning of the project would have led to better divisions of labour. More clear responsibilities would also have been a good motivation for team members to contribute to the project.

Agendas and structure of meetings

Agendas and schedules are helpful. Project groups cover many issues in a meeting, and it is difficult to keep track of them all. Making a list ensures that all points will be addressed and not forgotten. Schedules help in time management. The large task of tackling a big design project is much more manageable when broken down into smaller tasks that can be knocked off one by one.

Our meetings were first planned electronically through email and initiated by any member. During this preliminary organisation stage, an agenda could have been delivered, which would have added structure and routine to our meetings.

Another way to enhance team efficiency is better routine. If we always had the same meeting time on the same day, it would prevent confusion and wasted time. The meetings would have more value since people would always be conveniently prepared.

The lack of agendas and minutes also led to inefficiencies during team meetings. This problem, combined with the lack of clearly defined roles, led to uncertainties during meetings as to what work needs to be done. Without the project brief, which set milestones and deliverable dates, little progress would have been made during meetings.

Intra-group communication

A group should be flexible. It should be able to account for mistakes and accidents, and be able to change plans in case of emergencies or failures. A team should not be so set on one solution that the whole group dissolves when something goes wrong.

Problems that one member encounters should be brought to the entire team, to make everyone aware of the issues that need resolution and possibly to allow the team to resolve the problem during a meeting.

Leadership

Having a leader is recommended. Leaders help organise a group which could otherwise be chaotic from miscommunication or personal conflict. It is good to have someone who can mediate when there is a problem or make executive decisions when the group cannot decide together. The leader can also impose schedules to continue pushing the project towards its goal in a timely manner.

Planning

Planning ahead and not procrastinating is key. Although teams can complete a divided workload more quickly than an individual, gathering and organising the completed work takes extra time. Procrastination is always bad, but with a group it can be even worse. It is more difficult to gather a group, and not everyone may be available at the same time. Planning ahead allows more flexibility in schedules and allows for unexpected conflicts. It also prevents the whole burden of the project from being dumped on one responsible individual at the last minute.

● Teamwork guide

Below is a template you can use or adapt to help you organise team projects in their initial stage.

1. Project name and main objective (mission)

2. Team member tasks

List the main responsibilities assigned to each team member:

Name:

1.

2.

3.

4.

3. Planning and coordinating issues

1. Decide how you will communicate (email, meetings, etc), and arrange regular times for this.
2. Write agendas for meetings, and keep a written record of important

decisions. In your record, remember to include action items, *who does what and when*. Assign roles to team members for each meeting. These should include: a *leader*, a *scribe* and a *process monitor*.

3. Decide how you will resolve conflict, before it arises. The best way to do this is to formalise a procedure for feedback. For example, allocate some time at the end of each meeting to discuss collaboration issues. Ask: 'Is everyone carrying out their assigned tasks effectively?' and 'How could we have improved this meeting?'

Below is a completed template as an example:

1. Project name and mission:

> Single Biological and Chemical Species Detector
>
> We want to investigate potential markets, devise a business plan and propose a strategy to create a product using ultra-high-Q resonators that has increased functionality over existing products at a viable cost. We would also like to find a market where we would be the first company to resolve problems with our product that cannot be resolved with existing technology.

2. Team member tasks

List the main responsibilities assigned to each team member:

> **Name**:   *Jens Larsen, Team Leader*
>
> 1. Find potential markets and estimate size.
> 2. Find all competitors in our market and see how much market share each has and why.
> 3. Analyse competitors' costs.
> 4. Identify which market would be most benefited by new technology.

> **Name**:   *Ryan Sing*
>
> 1. Contact patent holder and read papers.
> 2. Explore alternative markets and applications.
> 3. Look at prices/advantages of similar products/technology.
> 4. Analyse product lifetime.
> 5. Analyse costs of new technology over previously existing technology.

Name: *Adam Bedford*

1. Financial planning – business plan and finding potential investors.

2. Analyse feasibility of bringing product to market from concept through production to finished product.

3. Find potential customers in the early phase.

4. Patent rights and intellectual property. How solid is the patent?

5. Find empirical data and/or prototypes.

10 Job Applications

Focus on:

▶ Career values
▶ CV formats
▶ Cover letters

The shape of the work force and the idea of a 'career' have changed dramatically over the last three decades worldwide. University graduates of the 1950s and 1960s looked forward to long periods of work with the same employer. Since the 1990s, by contrast, rapid changes in technology, the globalisation of the workforce, competitive international markets, and the growth of short-term contract work have made the contemporary workplace anxious and fast-paced.

People setting out in the workforce today are likely to change careers several times over the span of their working life. Accordingly, employers now look for graduates who can demonstrate transferable skills, particularly in communication, leadership and teamwork. Such skills are transferred from one job to another, indicating a willingness and ability to adapt to new business procedures and new technology.

To survive in this quickly changing environment, you must be flexible and ready. This chapter will prepare you to 'market yourself' in the workforce by illustrating successful methods of compiling a job application consisting of a resumé and a cover letter.

● Knowing your values

Your chances of being good at what you do increase if you actually enjoy what you do. If your job is just a set of gruelling tasks, it is highly unlikely you will excel or stand out in any way. And you can only really be successful in what you value. This is why before setting out on a new career, or before changing your current career, you should assess your values. Here is a list of questions to guide you on your career quest:

Career Values

What do you want to achieve in your life?

Determine your goals and ambitions. Do you value wealth? Fame?

Spirituality? Independence? Do you want a centre-stage position in life or would you prefer to work behind the scenes?

What are your skills and talents, and can you make best use of them in your career?

Think of all your talents, interests and abilities. How can you adapt them so that they will be functional in your work? Break down all the work you have done into constituent skills and reshuffle them. For example, if you have been successful in sports, this could indicate endurance, high energy, collaborative skill, fast thinking, etc. There are plenty of other contexts where these skills would be useful.

How good a communicator are you?

Are you good at writing? Speaking in public? Explaining? Have you ever taught? Do you prefer one-to-one communication or would you rather address a large number of people?

Are you project or process oriented?

Do you like doing short-term projects that you can finalise quickly and then move on to something else, or do you prefer being part of a chain, contributing to an on-going process?

Do you prefer to lead or to follow?

Do you prefer following others' instructions, or would you rather instruct others? Do you work best in a corporate, hierarchical environment, or does self-employment appeal to you more?

What sort of culture would you prefer to work in?

Do you like strict guidelines or a more liberal way of achieving goals? Do you want to be given specific goals or would you rather work with broad parameters? How closely do you want to be managed? Would you rather be left alone to find solutions your own way? Do you want strict hours of work or more autonomy to choose your timetable?

What drives you?

Do you want status? Recognition? Money? Independence? A combination?

What location suits you?

Are you happy in a high-rise building in the centre of town, or would you prefer a suburb, or a specialised location like Silicon Valley? Do you want to have the option of working at home? Travelling? Working in two or more different places?

(Adapted from Morgan and Banks, 1999, pp. 28–30)

● CVs and cover letters

A **curriculum vitae** (CV – also known as a resumé) lists your education, work skills and work experience. A CV is often glanced at or skimmed rather than carefully read. In many cases, potential employers spend about 30 seconds on a first viewing of a CV, before deciding whether the candidate is worthy of further consideration. Thus, you should structure your CV in such a way that the potential employer can tell at a glance if you are suitable for a job.

A **cover letter** addressed to the prospective employer accompanies the CV. In the letter, introduce yourself and draw attention to your achievements relevant to the position. The cover letter gives you the opportunity to 'show-case' your talents, including your ability to write convincingly and correctly. A cover letter is also called a 'letter of application'.

● Job searching

When looking for a job, make an action plan using this four-step framework to guide you.

1. Assess yourself
Examine your goals, and make sure you understand what motivates you, what your values are, what your strengths and what your priorities. Ask yourself the questions listed earlier in the 'Knowing your values' section. Think about where you would like to be in ten years, and what you would like to have achieved. What are your lifestyle preferences and what role does work and professionalism play in these preferences?

2. Research your career goals
After the first, introspective, stage, open up to the world and see what is available to assist you in reaching your goals and achieving your desired lifestyle. The obvious way to look for a job is to peruse the classifieds in

major newspapers and visit employment websites. In addition, major recruitment consultants have their own databases where you can access information on professional job vacancies.

Another major way to find out what your options are and what opportunities are available is through **networking**. Tips for networking are:

- Get to know people at courses and through business, trade and professional associations.
- Subscribe to a business, trade or professional magazine or newsletter, or join online discussion groups and forums.
- Establish mentors. A mentor is a senior colleague whose work and personal character you respect. A mentor takes an interest in your career and is willing to advise you. If you leave a company or a programme, keep in touch with your mentor. For example, if you know your mentor is working on a particular project or has a special interest, send clippings or other relevant information.
- Contact career professionals, such as recruitment consultants and 'headhunters', and discuss your options with them.
- Do volunteer work in a related field. This can help you to meet people in the field and achievements performed as a volunteer can go in your CV.

When networking, take care to:

- Send a thank you note to people who give you helpful leads, and stay in touch.
- Never ask directly for a job! Asking directly puts people on the spot and can make you seem desperate or pushy.

3. Develop a self-marketing strategy

Market yourself as if you were a product (which, in fact, you are, in relation to the employment market). Use the '5-Ps' of marketing:

- **Product**: what do you have to offer? What key skills and qualities can you offer to potential employers?
- **Price**: what is your value in the marketplace? What value do your educational background, experience and professional strengths qualify give you?
- **Promotion**: what themes, signs, phrases or messages can you use to communicate what you have to offer?

- **Place** (distribution): How will you 'circulate' yourself? For example, will you focus on advertised positions, rely on your networking, send your CV to a senior member of a targeted company (known as cold contact or speculative job searching), post your CV online?
- **Positioning**: what distinguishes you from other candidates? Do you have a Unique Selling Proposition (USP)?

4. Prepare some versions of your CV for different purposes

Have two or three versions of your CV ready. Each version should highlight different qualities, but they should also be relevant to the job profile that you will have created using the previous three steps.

● Finding information about a company

Before applying to a company – and particularly before attending an interview – find out details such as share price, company structure, annual turnover, and product lines. Take advantage of the following resources and:

- Visit the company website. Some companies recruit through their websites.
- Browse through magazines relevant to the industry in which you hope to work and to which the company belongs.
- Browse through company literature, such as brochures, newsletters annual reports.
- If possible, visit the company itself and get a feel for its culture and atmosphere.

Find out as much as possible about the industry of a company, by asking these questions:

- What products or services does this industry offer?
- Who are the major players and up-and-comers?
- What are the critical success factors for a company in this industry?
- What is the outlook and hiring potential for this industry?
- What type of talent does this industry attract, hire and need?

Find out as much as possible about the particular company you are interested in applying to, by asking these questions:

- What distinguishes this company from others in the industry?
- What are the company's culture, values and priorities?
- Who are its leaders and what do they stand for?
- How does this company treat its employees?
- What is the company's reputation?
- What would it be like to work there?

● CV formats

CVs tend to be classified into three main categories: *chronological*, *functional* and targeted. All types of CVs should satisfy certain general standards. They should:

- Provide information that is relevant, clear and concise
- Highlight and provide evidence for your strengths and achievements
- Inspire confidence
- Form an agenda for the interview.

Chronological CVs

The chronological format lists education and work experience in reverse chronological order (most recent items listed first). Chronological CVs are useful if:

- you have a steady work history
- all or most of your recent work experience is relevant to the position

Do not use a chronological CV if:

- only one or two jobs in your work history are relevant to the position sought
- you have a complicated or diverse work history that may raise doubts as to your reliability
- you have many gaps in your work history that are difficult to explain
- you are pursuing a career change and wish to highlight transferable knowledge and skills.

Functional CVs

Functional CVs focus on knowledge and skills, rather than on dates or places of employment. They are useful if you:

- are changing careers and some of your previous experience is not relevant to your target job
- want to highlight specific skills rather than list your employment history.

In a functional CV, the most marketable information is presented at the front of the document. The functional format allows for selective organisation of information and enhances your ability to customise the CV for the particular position.

To become aware of all the knowledge you have gained in your experience, list all the responsibilities you had for each job. Think of everything that you did each day at work, including all the small tasks or the tasks that were so routine that you hardly noticed them. If your list gets too long, edit it by deleting activities that may not be directly relevant to the job you are applying for. The following verbs may help you compile your list:

Action Words to Describe Skills

accomplish	build	demonstrate
act	calculate	design
adapt	catalogue	detail
adjust	chair	determine
administer	clarify	develop
advertise	collaborate	devise
advise	communicate	direct
affect	conceive	distribute
analyze	conceptualise	draft
anticipate	conciliate	edit
approach	consult	educate
approve	contract	enlarge
arrange	control	establish
assemble	cooperate	evaluate
assess	coordinate	examine
assign	counsel	exchange
assist	define	execute
budget	delegate	expand

facilitate	mediate	report
formulate	moderate	represent
fund-raise	modify	research
generate	monitor	resolve
govern	motivate	review
guide	negotiate	revise
handle	obtain	scan
hire	operate	schedule
identify	order	select
implement	organise	serve
improve	originate	speak
increase	participate	standardise
index	perform	staff
influence	persuade	stimulate
inform	plan	summarise
initiate	present	supervise
innovate	preside	survey
inspect	produce	synthesise
install	promote	systemise
institute	propose	teach
integrate	provide	team-build
interview	publicise	train
investigate	publish	transmit
invent	recommend	utilise
lead	record	write
maintain	rectify	
manipulate	relate	

Always use verbs in the active voice to describe the activities you perform or performed in your work experience. Use the present tense for positions currently held, and the past tense for positions previously held. Omit 'I'.

Where possible, use the **STAR (Situation, Task, Achievement, Result)** method to highlight your successes, either in the CV itself, or in the cover letter. First, state the situation where you had to perform a task; second, describe the task; third, go to the outcome of your effort; and fourth, state how your employer, or profession as a whole, benefited from the way you carried out the task.

Targeted CVs

Targeted CVs follow the specifications or templates given in an application package or job advertisement. They are often similar to functional CVs, but concentrate on skills that are directly relevant to the requirements listed in the position description. When writing a targeted CV, answer the question or follow the formatting directions given by the recruiting company.

Optional features

These features are not necessary. Analyse your audience, context and professional culture and decide whether or not you wish to include them. If in doubt, leave them out.

- **Personal information** In most Western societies, gender, religious beliefs, age, ethnicity and marital status are irrelevant to many kinds of employment, and, in fact, are considered confidential by law. You are not obliged to state any of these in your CV, if applying for a job. In practice, however, job seekers include personal details in their CVs if they feel that their personal circumstances are advantageous. Examples would be: if you are a Catholic and you are applying for a position in a Catholic organisation it would be wise to mention your religion; and if you are young but have achieved a remarkable amount it would be wise to mention your age.
- **Photograph** Employers in certain countries and in certain sectors of the economy, such as public relations, may favour photographs on CVs. Others find them irrelevant or even misleading, because they de-focus objective skills and capabilities. For example, in the information technology sector or in education, a photograph is generally not necessary.
- **Hobbies/interests** Include a brief list of hobbies and interests if they indicate knowledge or skills relevant to the job, such as leadership, teamwork, resilience or determination. You can also set your CV apart from others if you specify unusual hobbies, or if you demonstrate excellence in a particular pursuit. If your hobbies are humdrum or irrelevant leave this section out altogether.
- **Career objective** A career objective states the applicant's goals and ambition within a specific industry. If you are unsure or undecided about your long-term goals, or if you want to project versatil-

ity and resilience, leave this section out (unless, of course, it is specifically requested in a targeted CV). If you do decide to include an objective, make it short but focused. It should inform the employer that you are moving in a certain direction, specify your work preferences and serve as a focal point from which to review your CV.

- **Referees**   You do not need to include names of referees or references unless they are specifically requested. However, since referees will play a role if you are shortlisted, it is wise to include a statement such as 'Referees are available on request', either at the end of the CV or in the cover letter.

- **Nationality or residential status**   This is only relevant if it affects your availability for employment – for example, if you are on a Working Visa. Include this if you have an international background, and the potential employer may wonder whether you are eligible to work in the particular country.

Presentation of CV

How the CV is set out depends on the medium of communication. For example, if posting the CV on a website, where it might be read off a screen, use more highlighting, such as bullet points and headings, and minimise the information on each page. If sending out a hard copy, where you were specified to limit the CV to one page, obviously you need to set it out differently to maximise the limited space. Adapt the following guidelines in relation to the specific circumstances of each application:

- Ensure readability by leaving as much white space as specifications allow, and by using a clear font, size 11–12.
- Align points down the page and preferably indent them.
- Do not use more than two fonts, perhaps one type for the main text and another for headings. Consider using only one font unless creativity is required by the job and you have flair for design.
- Do not use more than one highlighting technique: **bold** or <u>under-line</u> or *italics* – not all three.
- Use a clip to attach all pages rather than staples: this makes it easier for the CV to be photocopied.
- Do not use coloured paper that will hinder photocopying.
- As with other business documents, include a header or footer on each page, and page numbers, in case pages get mixed up.

● CV templates

It is not wise to copy a standard CV format from a book to which also countless others have access. Instead, by making your CV as individual as a signature, you increase your chances of attracting the attention of those that can further your career. So use these templates of a full CV as a guide or inspiration, but tailor them to suit your individual aspirations and strengths.

Template for chronological CV

Name	Your full name.
Address	Your current residential or business address (where you want your correspondence sent).
Phone numbers	Home and/or business numbers (you may include a cell-phone number, but not just that).
Email address	Your business or personal email address (if you are applying for many jobs while still working, it's best to get a Yahoo or Hotmail address to avoid too much traffic in your business address).
Education	List your educational qualifications with most recent first.
Employment history	Name of employer, Position (job title), Period of employment, Duties, Achievements. Begin with current or most recent position and work backwards.
Professional memberships	Briefly list them, if relevant.
Computer skills	List your skills of operating systems (e.g. PC, Mac), and software packages (e.g. Microsoft Word, Adobe PageMaker.)
Languages	State the languages that you know and degree of fluency.
Interests	List, only if relevant.

Template for functional CV

Name	Your full name.

Address   Your current residential or business address (where you want your correspondence sent).

Phone numbers   Home and or business numbers (you may include a cell-phone number, but not just that).

Email address   Your business or personal email address (if you are applying for many jobs while still working, it's best to get a Yahoo or Hotmail address to avoid too much traffic in your business address).

Skills and abilities   List the major skills you have acquired from your experience. List only those skills that you can demonstrate but be creative in highlighting their relevance for the job you seek.

Education   List your educational qualifications with most relevant first. Include all professional development and short courses that you attended.

Computer skills   Depending on the kind of job you seek and the kinds of skills you have, you could list your computer skills separately to highlight them. Include operating systems (e.g. PC, Mac), and software packages (e.g. Microsoft Word®, Adobe PageMaker®).

Languages   State the languages you know and degree of fluency.

Professional memberships   Again, briefly list them, if relevant.

Awards and achievements   List, only if relevant to the new job.

Employment history   Name of employer, Position (job title), Period of employment.

Interests   List, only if relevant.

Here are some commonly used phrases to summarise and highlight skills.

Skill Phrases

General skills
Work well under pressure
Able to adapt to new situations
Ability to learn quickly
Capable of accepting responsibility
Works well without supervision

People skills
Able to work as a team member
Good sense of humour
Able to deal effectively with clients
Handles people with patience and understanding
Works well with people from different cultures

Communication skills
Able to communicate effectively with clients
Capable of initiating and completing projects
Trains and supervises new staff
Able to communicate effectively with others
Excellent communicator

Organisation skills
Excellent organisation skills
Able to plan, organise and supervise projects
Capable of working on different projects
Completes projects accurately and on schedule
Punctual
Dependable in all situations

Leadership skills
Excellent leadership skills
Accepts responsibility
Deals efficiently with emergencies
Comfortable with taking the initiative
Supervises activities of team members
Successful project manager
Successfully organises staff/team members to attain goals

Look at the following chronological CV, and notice how the writer summarises his skills at the beginning and then demonstrates how he used these skills in particular work situations.

Firstname B. Surname

Address, Phone number, Email address

Summary

Accounting Professional/Payroll Administrator combining cross-functional competencies in all phases of accounting, information systems, and staff supervision and management. Proficient in managing and developing financial reports and controls using staffing and technology efficiencies. Ability to contribute as a team player and interface with professionals on all levels. Expertise includes:

- Payroll administration
- Quarterly and Year-End Reporting
- Automated Accounting Information Systems
- Inventory Control and Purchasing
- Financial Reporting
- Corporate Tax Compliance
- Corporate Accounting
- Job Costing

Education

1997: Masters in Business Administration, Y University.

1995: Bachelor in Business Management, X University.

Professional Experience

2002–present: **Controller**, Platinum Choice Corporation, City, Country

Plan, manage and provide leadership for accounting department including payroll, budgeting, cost accounting, managerial accounting, financial reporting, financial analysis and purchasing. Scope of responsibility spans both the corporate and divisional level. Provide financial expertise to outside firms, including banks, auditors and government authorities.

- Managed $4 million in annual operating budgets allocated for personnel, facilities and administrative expenses.
- Established improved accounts receivable that reduced outstanding receivables by 25% during the first quarter.
- Implemented automated cost accounting systems to analyse profit improvement opportunities.
- Worked in cooperation with management teams to restructure corporate pricing on all major product lines, resulting in a 14% profit improvement.
- Successfully guided the company through annual outside audits.

1998–2002: **Accounting Consultant**, Merrill Lynch Consultants, City, Country

Recruited to provide diverse finance, accounting, payroll and tax preparation functions for one of the largest international consulting firms.

- Responsible for preparation of financial statements, payroll, sales and property tax returns, and income tax returns.
- Streamlined accounting processes to reduce workpaper and document requirements.
- Worked closely with clients in structuring general ledgers and evaluating their software needs.

Computer Skills

- Experienced with the following software for payroll preparation: QuickBooks/QuickBooks Pro, Peachtree, PenSoft Payroll.
- Skilled in most accounting software programs including Impact Encore, Peachtree, Preform Plus, ProSystems and Quicken.
- Proficient in Excel, Word, Access and Lotus.

● The cover letter

A cover letter must be professionally presented in format, grammar, and spelling. It generally is one to two pages long, and should have a 'bottom line' organization – i.e. it should go straight to the point. Remember, employers may be reviewing hundreds of applications and may spend as little as 30 seconds reviewing each one. You cover letter should have something that stands out.

There are three main kinds of cover letter:

- A letter written in response to a job advertisement.
- A 'cold contact' letter, written unsolicited (without being requested in advance) to a senior member of a targeted company. This should not be more than one page, so as not to take the recipient's time. Always follow up a cold contact letter with a phone call after a week to ten days.
- A referral letter, mentioning a contact within the company or a previous conversation held with a staff member. A referral letter may open with a line such as, 'I am attaching my CV, as you requested during our recent conversation regarding the Human Resources counselling position opening up at your firm.'

The cover letter generally has four paragraphs, covering the following material:

Opening paragraph	Indicate the purpose of writing
Second paragraph	State relevant skills and experience
Third paragraph	Demonstrate your knowledge of the company or organisation.
Fourth paragraph	Close with confidence and request an interview

When sending a 'cold contact' letter, it is best to address it to the manager of the section you want to work in (rather than to the Personnel Department). The advantages of this are that, even if you are not employed, the manager will at least know your name and may remember you if you apply for an advertised position within the company later. People who are eager and take the initiative make a good impression professionally. Also, if the manager is dedicated to his/her area of specialty, chances are that he or she would be willing to help newcomers to join the industry, and therefore, may refer you to someone or give you some very useful advice, if you approach him/her directly. It is unlikely that the Personnel Officer would have the same commitment.

Cover letter tips

Here are some general tips for writing an effective cover letter.

- Always type your cover letter, unless the job advertisement specifically asks for a handwritten one. A CV should always be typed.
- Keep paragraphs short (two to four sentences).
- Adapt the content to the particular organisation and job position for which you are applying. That is, show that you are an insider to the industry.
- Include contact details (name, address, phone number, fax, email), either in a letterhead or in the concluding paragraph.
- Do not point to any of your weaknesses. Instead, match your skills and experience to the requirements of the position.
- Do not refer to personal interests or hobbies unless they are directly relevant to the position, or you share an interest with the recipient of the letter.
- Do not use sarcasm or irony.
- Do not criticise a former employer.
- Do not send a photocopy of a cover letter. Your signature must be original.

Bad writing in CVs

How bad a mistake can you make on your CV? We end the chapter with some real-life examples of CV 'howlers'.

> *Education*: Curses in liberal arts, curses in computer science, curses in accounting.

> I am a rabid thinker.

Proven ability to hunt down and correct erors.

My intensity is at supremely high levels, and my ability to meet deadlines is unspeakable.

Personal details: Married, 1992 Chevrolet.

Personal interests: Donating blood. 15 gallons so far.

Cover letter: Thank you for your consideration. Hope to hear from you shorty!

Appendix Writer's Reference

This chapter gives guidelines on some very common language troublespots. These guidelines answer many writers' frequently asked questions, and should prove valuable when revising, editing and proofreading your work. The chapter concentrates on selecting between active and passive voice, using participial phrases, identifying subject–verb–pronoun agreement problems, making correct punctuation choices, using relative clauses (which/that) correctly, and dealing with spelling issues. Use this chapter in combination with Chapter 3, on style, which provides some basic grammatical terminology, such as the difference between a sentence and a phrase, the definition of a clause, and different sentence types. This terminology will help you to put into context the explanations provided here.

The guidelines presented here should help you to produce grammatically correct prose, whatever the context and purpose of the document. Knowing rules and conventions of writing confers confidence and credibility, even in cases where a writer decides to deliberately ignore these rules and conventions. In the famous wise words of T. S. Eliot, 'it is not wise to violate the rules until you know how to observe them'.

● Active and passive voice

The active and passive voices are a major concern for writers, as they can colour a text profoundly by disclosing or concealing information and by highlighting different elements of the sentence. The active voice emphasises the agent and the action of a sentence. The passive voice, on the other hand, emphasises the object, person or thing acted upon. Therefore, using one or the other is a strategic choice. For example:

Active: The manager signed the contract.
Passive: The contract was signed by the manager.

Word order of active voice: subject + verb + object.
Word order of passive voice: object + be + past participle [optionally + by + subject].

Using active or passive voice is not just a matter of variety. As happens also with other forms of sentence manipulation, it orders and prioritises information and, therefore, has an evaluative function. Some people (and grammar checkers) harbour deep suspicions about the passive voice. They will tell you to use the active where possible. There are three reasons for this:

1. The passive emphasises the object, which does not carry out any action (it is acted upon). Therefore, the verb of the sentence becomes weaker. The information content of the sentence appears to be static rather than dynamic. This may be required in some cases (as discussed below). However, if it is not a deliberate choice, the passive may better be avoided to avoid weakening the sentence.

2. Often, the passive conceals the agent of the action, or at least subordinates it. This may be unacceptable in certain cases where stated responsibility for an action is required for clarity or ethics. The active voice creates a sentence with a 'who does what' content, which, in most cases is a straightforward presentation.

3. As has been emphasised throughout the book, conciseness is valued in many contexts, especially in business and public writing, and the passive adds words to sentences.

However, the passive voice has a definite role for these purposes:

1. The agent is unimportant (and, in fact, mentioning the agent may make the sentence awkward):

Awkward active: I/we use the passive voice to move components around in a sentence

Preferred passive: The passive voice is used to move components around in a sentence

Awkward active: Trucks take the logs to the factory for processing

Preferred passive: The logs are taken to the factory for processing.

This purpose of the passive is most evident in scientific writing, where processes and procedures are important because of the results and observations they lead to, rather than because of the personal role of the scientist him/herself in carrying out the process. Notice also that, in this case, the agent is not mentioned at all in the sentence.

2. The agent is unknown:

Awkward active: Someone stole the computer from the lab.

Preferred passive: The computer was stolen from the lab.

In this case, the agent is unknown and emphasis falls on the event. In fact, in some cases, such as in police reports, it would be misleading to include an agent as perpetrator of a deed, if the identity of this agent is unknown or uncertain.

3. The agent is collective:

Awkward active: People/Farmers grow tea in India.

Preferred passive: Tea is grown in India

In this case, the subject is not individual, and the result or process is more important.

However, there are occasions where using **the active voice** is a far more advisable choice. As noted above, one occasion is when you want to produce a sharp, energetic and concise piece: the active voice is certainly more direct, succinct and snappy. Another occasion is when your writing involves assuming or attributing responsibility for decisions, and making these decisions more personal. In many instances the passive voice is used to conceal the agents responsible for certain actions, and this can give a harsh and impersonal impression. For example, the impersonal nature of the following sentence gives it bad audience dynamics:

Awkward passive: Your proposal has been considered and it has been decided to reject it.

Preferred active: The Housing Board considered your proposal and the executive committee decided to reject it.

In important writing, such as proposals, formal business reports and official documents, the readers want to know who they are dealing with in order to ascertain who is responsible for different actions. In such cases, use the passive voice with the utmost care to avoid misunderstandings and conflict. The same situation occurs when you write about plans, decisions and reactions to events. Using the passive in such cases mystifies the topic, since the agents remain unknown, and produces a generalised and vague effect unsuited to professional writing.

Consider this extract. The first sentence is acceptable because it sets the scene and focuses on a process. Notice, however, how the use of the passive in the other two sentences puts the writer in a distant and detached position that leaves the reader with a general impression of the situation but with no specific, factual, information. Who raised questions? Who questioned the ethical viability of GMF procedures?

> Genetically Modified Foods (GMF) have been used commercially in food products available to the general public since 1996. This was met with general outcry and many questions were raised about the safety of the products. The ethical viability of such procedures and the impact that GMF would have on the environment were also questioned.

● Participial phrases

Participial phrases contain the past participle of a verb (verbs ending in -ing, -en and -ed), and no subject. Participials reduce clauses that show a temporal (before, after), or a causal (because, so) relationship. They add variety and, often, formality to your writing, and are useful stylistic choices. Study these sentences and their participial alternatives, and notice how using this construction can introduce variety in your writing:

Compound sentence: The CEO agreed to support the proposal, so she attended this month's meeting.

Sentence beginning with participial phrase: Having agreed to support the proposal, the CEO attended this month's meeting.

Sentence with subordinate clause: Many investors are turning to mutual funds this year, because they think that interest rates will fall even further.

Sentence beginning with a participial: Thinking interest rates will fall even further, many investors are turning to mutual funds this year.

Participial constructions generally serve the following functions:

- ● They help keep your writing concise by reducing words

- They provide you with a tool to give your writing more variety

- They make your writing more formal.

Frequent errors with participials

Using participial phrases incorrectly may lead to the common error known as 'misrelation' or 'dangling modifier'. This occurs when the verb of the participial does not agree with the noun it is identified with, which would be the noun immediately following the participial phrase:

Misrelation: While inspecting the nuclear reactor, a loud crash alarmed the supervision team.
– So was the loud crash inspecting the nuclear reactor?

Corrected: While inspecting the nuclear reactor, the supervision team was alarmed by a loud crash.
  Note that to correct the relation while keeping the participial, the sentence has to change active to passive voice.

Corrected: The loud crash alarmed the supervision team, while they were inspecting the nuclear reactor
– This removes the participial and adds a full subordinate clause.

Misrelation: Having solved the problem, it was easy for him to get any job he wanted.

Corrected: Having solved the problem, he could get any job he wanted.

Words ending in –ing

Misrelations sometimes occur because of confusion among the different functions of –ing words. A word form ending in –ing can be:

1.   **A participial form of a verb**: *Having agreed to collaborate on the project, the engineers formed their teams.* This is actually a reduced subordinate clause: *After they had agreed to collaborate on the project, the engineers formed their teams.*

2.   **A verb in a continuous tense**: *The excavation continued while it was raining.* In this case, the –ing word is preceded by the verb *be* (was, were, am, will be, etc.).

3.   **A gerund**: *Walking is good exercise.* A gerund can be the subject of a sentence, and functions as a noun.

4.   **An adjective**: *It is tedious to attend boring meetings.* In this case, the

–ing word qualifies a noun by describing its attributes (interesting, exciting, frustrating, amusing, etc.).

● Subject–verb–pronoun agreement

A common trouble spot in writing is misusing a singular verb with a plural subject and vice versa, or a plural verb with a singular pronoun and vice versa. This sentence, for example, comes from a professional document:

Incorrect: The facts in the case and all the evidence provided has been considered in the final decision.

Correct: The facts in the case and all the evidence provided have been considered in the final decision.

In the incorrect version of the sentence, the verb 'has been' does not agree with the subject, which is 'the facts in the case and all the evidence provided'. The writer wrongly assumed that the word closest to the verb, 'evidence', is the subject.

Some general guidelines for correct subject-verb-pronoun agreement are:

1. **Collective nouns** (such as 'police', 'family', 'government', 'team', 'audience', etc.) can take a singular or a plural verb. Your choice depends on whether you want to emphasise their collective nature or the fact that they are composed of individuals. However, ensure that if you use a pronoun to refer to a collective noun, it has the same number as the verb:

Incorrect: The audience showed its appreciation. They gave the speaker a standing ovation.

Correct: The audience showed their appreciation. They gave the speaker a standing ovation.

2. **Correlatives** (*'either–or'*, *'neither–nor'*, *'not only–but also'*) have two subjects. In this case, the verb must agree with the subject closest to it:

Incorrect: Not only the workers but also the supervisor were affected by the fumes.

Correct: Not only the workers but also the supervisor was affected by the fumes.

Incorrect: Not only the supervisor but also the workers was affected by the fumes

Correct: Not only the supervisor but also the workers were affected by the fumes.

3. **Phrases separating the subject and the verb** do not affect the number of the verb or pronoun:

Incorrect: The scientist, together with his troupe of devoted followers and supporters, have occupied the second floor of the building.

Correct: The scientist, together with his troupe of devoted followers and supporters, has occupied the second floor of the building.

However, subjects joined by 'and' or 'both-and' are plural and take a plural verb and pronoun:

Incorrect: The scientist and his troupe of devoted followers has occupied the second floor of the building.

Correct: The scientist and his troupe of devoted followers have occupied the second floor of the building.

4. **The pronouns 'each', 'every', 'anyone', 'everyone', 'no one'** are singular and should take singular verbs and pronouns.

Incorrect: He stated that anybody is welcome to apply for membership; as for applications, each is to be assessed according to their own merit.

Correct: He stated that anybody is welcome to apply for membership; as for applications, each is to be assessed according to its own merit.

In informal writing, as in speaking, this rule is by-passed to avoid cumbersome sentences.

Informal: Everyone brought their books.

Formal: Everyone brought his/her books.

● Punctuation

Punctuation marks are a device that introduces rhythm and pace to the written text. Although they do serve to reflect in written form the dynamic aspects of speech, it would be misleading to equate them with the breathing patterns evident in speaking because punctuation follows syntactic (i.e. grammatical), and not phonetic or physical, aspects of language. Therefore, reading a text aloud is not an accurate means of deciding where to insert a punctuation mark and what this mark should be. There are some grammatical rules that writers should know. This section overviews these rules.

A comma is the weakest pause mark. Others, in order of increasing duration or suddenness of the pause, include:

semicolon (;)
colon (:)
ellipsis (...)
dash (-)
quotation marks ('...')
full stop (period) (.)
exclamation mark (!)
question mark (?)

Correct use of punctuation has changed over the years. Older texts often use punctuation quite differently from modern texts. The following guide gives you an overview of punctuation usage that is the current international standard.

Comma

Three main categories cover most of the cases when a comma is required:

1. Inserting words, phrases, or clauses into a sentence

We often add extra information to the basic core of sentences by adding phrases that give more detail, help to keep the reader on track, or just generally add more variety to sentence structure. When adding phrases to a sentence, or moving phrases out of place to add variety, set off these additions and interjections with commas. These changes are made in three places:

(a) Sentence openers

Transition signposts: However, I . . .

Interjections: Well, I . . .
Adverbs: Often, I . . .
Prepositional phrases: In board meetings, I . . .
Participial phrases: Having completed the project, I . . .
Adverbial clauses: Whenever I try to think, I . . .
Appositives: A great actor, Lawrence Olivier . . .

(b) Sentence insertions

These have the same function as the openers, but produce a less emphatic effect. For example:

Inserted participial phrase: The executive, having completed the project, decided to take a break.

Note: If you use insertions, remember to use commas at both ends.

(c) Sentence enders

Inserting a phrase or clause at the end of a sentence gives the least emphasis to the information contained in that phrase or clause. For example:

Participial ending the sentence: Give this to the presiding officer, the woman sitting next to the door.

2. Joining two clauses with 'and', 'or', 'but', 'nor', 'yet', 'so', 'for' (coordinating conjunctions).

Two sentences can be joined with a comma and a coordinating conjunction (or, in case of a short sentence, with a conjunction alone):

Simple sentences: I took part in the competition. I came first.

Compound sentence: I took part in the competition, and I came first.

3. Listing items in a series

A comma is used to list items in the same category in one sentence.

Listing items: The position requires writing annual reports, internal memoranda, newsletters, and online documentation.

Frequent questions on the comma

A frequent question is if a comma is always needed before a coordinating conjunction. Opinions vary on this: some insist that a comma is necessary, while others suggest it is optional. Although it will never be considered wrong to include a comma in this case, it is acceptable to omit it in shorter sentences. This is especially justified when space limitations count, as in magazine and web publishing. The space taken by the comma is typographically significant, and this should be considered.

A similar question is if a comma is always needed after a prepositional phrase that begins the sentence. Again, the ideal answer is yes: you cannot go wrong by including a comma after a phrase, to set it off from the sentence that it modifes. However, if the sentence is easily read and understood without the comma, and there are typographical space limitations, omit it. This occurs more often with prepositional phrases than participial ones.

Easily understood sentence: At present (,) the company does not have a financial manager.

Confusing sentence: After moving the tenants, who inherited one million dollars, bought their own mansion.

Corrected: After moving, the tenants, who inherited one million dollars, bought their own mansion.

Frequent errors with the comma

- *Comma splice*: This occurs when you join two full sentences with a comma. This is corrected by inserting a period, a semicolon or a coordinating conjunction in the place of the comma:

  Comma splice: The committee contributed to the project by sending delegates to the meeting, however, these delegates were not adequately informed of recent developments in software design.

  Corrected using period: The committee contributed to the project by sending delegates to the meeting. However, these delegates were not adequately informed of recent developments in software design.

  Corrected using semicolon: The committee contributed to the project by sending delegates to the meeting; however, these delegates were not adequately informed of recent developments in software design.

Corrected using coordinating conjunction: The committee contributed to the project by sending delegates to the meeting, but these delegates were not adequately informed of recent developments in software design.

● Subject–verb disjunction. This occurs when the subject is separated from its verb with a comma. Subjects may be separated from verbs with prepositional and participial phrases as well as with subordinate clauses. In these cases, commas are inserted at either end of the phrase or clause. This way, the phrase or clause is set off from the rest of the sentence:

Incorrect: Authorised to seal the agreement, the company representatives, will meet with each board member individually during their visit.

Correct: The company representatives, who are authorised to seal the agreement, will meet with each board member individually during their visit.

Incorrect: Designers, play a pivotal role in the success of marketing products, through their skills in attractive presentation.

Correct: Designers play a pivotal role in the success of marketing products, through their skills in attractive presentation.

Correct: Designers, through their skills in attractive presentation, play a pivotal role in the success of marketing products.

Semicolon

The semicolon is used in the following cases:

1. It joins together two independent sentences. It indicates a stronger pause than a comma, but a shorter one than the period, and shows that there is a close relationship between the two joined sentences. For instance, the first example below consists of two sentences that distribute information equally. The second example below consists of one sentence with two clauses joined with a semicolon. This suggests that the second clause is directly related to the first as an explanation or result.

Two sentences: Branding is a major stage in the marketing process. It determines how consumers will visualise and relate to the product through its name.

Two clauses joined with semicolon: Branding is a major stage in the marketing process; it determines how consumers will visualise and relate to the product through its name.

2. It separates items in a list, when one item or more in the list already contains a comma. The sentence below illustrates this.

Listing with semicolons: Attendees from overseas should submit a copy of their passport, showing the photo page; a certified check or money order, payable in local currency; and a stamped, self-addressed envelope.

Frequent errors with the semicolon

Connecting a phrase to a sentence. This occurs when a semicolon is used to connect a participial or prepositional phrase to a clause. The correct punctuation mark for this case is the comma.

Incorrect: The project team could not continue with the intended plan; having encountered unexpected opposition from major stockholders.

Correct: Having encountered unexpected opposition from major stockholders, the project team could not continue with the intended plan.

Correct: The project team could not continue with the intended plan, having encountered unexpected opposition from major stockholders.

Correct: The project team, having encountered unexpected opposition from major stockholders, could not continue with the intended plan.

- *Introducing a list*: This occurs when a semicolon is used to introduce a list of items or bullet points. The correct punctuation mark for this case is the colon.

   Incorrect: With your application include the following;
   - A complete CV with contact details of three referees
   - Transcripts of academic qualifications
   - A completed application cover form

   Correct: With your application, include the following:
   - A complete CV with contact details of three referees
   - Transcripts of academic qualifications
   - A completed application cover form

Colon

The colon has the following uses:

1. It introduces quotations that are a sentence or longer in length. If the quotation consists of a few words, a comma will suffice. Each case is illustrated by the example below.

   No use of colon before quotation: The CEO made it clear that 'only under exceptional circumstances' will the plan change.

   Use of colon before quotation: The CEO made it clear that 'only under exceptional circumstances' will the plan change. He said: 'The situation is pretty clear-cut. The majority of stockholders have voted for the new system to be implemented on an experimental basis for three months. Until this trial period passes, there is nothing more to be done.'

2. It introduces a list of things, whether the list is written in-line or vertically. The example below illustrates this.

   Three groups may attend the meeting:
   - Members of the executive committee
   - Press representatives
   - Stockholders

3. It shows the outcome or effect of an action. In this case, the colon plays a similar role to a semicolon. However, it has a more visual and, therefore, more dramatic effect than a semicolon. The sentence below illustrates this.

   He looked at an amazing sight: the house had totally collapsed.

Ellipsis

Ellipsis marks are much rarer in business writing than in creative or informal writing, because they reflect an incompleteness that is inconsistent with the purposes of professional documents. Ellipsis marks are mainly used for the following purposes:

1. To show hesitation or interruption. This is the most conversational use of the ellipsis, very rare in business writing. The extract below, from one of

Ian Rankin's 'Inspector Rebus' novels exemplifies this in the representation of Rebus's meandering train of thought:

> Rebus commiserated for a couple of minutes, thinking of his own doctor's appointment, the one he was missing yet again by making this call. When he put the phone down, he scribbled the name Marr on to his pad and circled it. Ranald Marr, with his Maserati and toy soldiers. You'd almost have thought he'd lost a daughter...Rebus was beginning to revise that opinion. He wondered if Marr knew how precarious his job was, knew that the mere thought of their savings catching a cold might spur the small investors on, demanding a sacrifice...   (Rankin, 2001, p. 352)

2. In quotations, to show that a part of the speaker's statement has been omitted, usually because it was irrelevant to the writer's main concern. This is the most common use of ellipsis in business and academic writing. To show that the ellipsis is not part of the quotation, enclose it in square brackets. For example, in the quotation below I have included the introductory sentence to a section, then omitted the remainder of that paragraph going straight on the next paragraph, from where I have also omitted a few words that refer to a diagram that is irrelevant to my discussion:

> All researchers must support contestable claims with evidence, but they must then explain that evidence, treating each major bit of evidence as a claim in a secondary argument that needs its own evidence. [. . .] If you like doing things visually, put this on a wall-sized chart. Pin-up index cards [. . .], then try different combinations of secondary arguments.

Dash

The dash has the following uses:

1. They enclose information that is secondary to the main point of the sentence and that can be omitted or skipped – similar to brackets (parentheses). In this case, a dash goes at each end of the additional information. Avoid this in sentences that contain important information or when you want the reader's undivided attention, because, like brackets, dashes show a divergence from the main issue and can be distracting. Also, keep in mind that they can make a sentence unnecessarily long, so, where conciseness or directness is your aim, avoid them. The following examples illustrate this.

She would have liked to see those letters. Chances were, they couldn't be recovered, either because they'd perished – been disposed of with Lovell's effects when he'd died – or had gone overseas. An awful lot of historical documentation had found its way into collections overseas – mostly Canada and the US – and many of these collections were private, which meant few details of their contents were available. (Rankin, 2001, p. 228)

Both developers were away from the meeting – one at home sick, the other attending a trade fair – so no major decisions were made that would affect the outcome of the project.

2. They have a similar function to the colon in introducing a set of things, and to the comma in setting off a comment on the information presented in the main clause. As opposed to the colon or comma, however, the dash makes the information it sets off more emphatic.

In this case, the dash can actually make the sentence more concise by enabling the omission of introductory phrases or subordinate clauses. Place the dash before the additional information at the end of the sentence. The examples below illustrate this:

The CEO's decision to support the proposal was welcomed by stockholders – an unusual reception given the specialised nature of the proposal.

An unprecedented number of professionals attended the meeting – most of them engineers.

Apostrophe

Apostrophes are used for two purposes:

1. They show possession or ownership. In this case, they come before the possessive s. The traditionally correct usage of a possessive s after a noun that ends in s is to add the possessive s after an end-of-word apostrophe (e.g. boss's). However, where the space occupied by the extra s is a layout concern (such as in business document templates and magazine article formats), the s after the apostrophe is increasingly being dropped, making this a viable option for such documents. For example:

the dog's tail (one dog)
the dogs' tails (more than one dog)
the student's grade (one student)
the students' grades (more than one student)
the boss' plan (one boss)
the bosses' plans (more than one boss)

2. They make contractions (combine two words into one). In this case, the apostrophe shows that there is a word, like *is, has* or *not*, missing. This is not a frequent use of apostrophes in professional writing, because contractions are avoided in formal documents. For example:

> isn't it a nice day!
> don't say it!
> it's important
> they've arrived

Frequent errors with the apostrophe

- **Apostrophe in plurals**: This occurs when an apostrophe is inserted before a plural *s*, like it would be before a possessive *s*. Distinguish between the possessive *s* (which requires an apostrophe) and the plural *s* (which does not).

  Incorrect: The information is in two video's.

  Correct: The information is in two videos.

  Incorrect: The presidents move was foreseen by many.

  Correct: The president's move was foreseen by many.

Quotation marks

Quotation marks are used when reporting the exact words of a speaker or writer. If the quotation takes up more than three lines, indent it in a block paragraph and set it off the rest of the text. In this case, do not use quotation marks – the indentation signals that the text is a quotation.

Other guidelines for quotation marks are:

1. Use single quotation marks for the beginning and ending of quotations, and double quotation marks for words or phrases that are quoted within a quotation.
2. Use double quotation marks when you want to show that a word or phrase should be taken figuratively or is out of context.
3. Place periods, commas, semicolons, colons, exclamation marks and question marks outside quotation marks, unless the quotation itself contains them. This, however, is a controversial point. In American publications, for example, periods and commas are placed inside quotation marks, whereas colons and semicolons are placed outside. Question

marks and exclamation points are placed, according to American convention, inside quotation marks unless they apply to the whole sentence.

With spelling, quotation marks are one of the contestable points in stylistic convention. Now, there are no international standards in quotation mark usage. The best advice is to select a method and be consistent, and, if your organisation has a style guide, to adhere to it.

● Relative clauses: *which* and *that*

Grammatically, both 'which' and 'that' are subordinating conjunctions, signalling a subordinate clause. However, as grammar checkers often indicate, they are not used interchangeably.

The clause that begins with 'which' gives information about the noun that directly precedes it. If the 'which' clause in a sentence is necessary to define the identity of the noun that precedes it, do not separate the noun from the 'which' clause by putting a comma. In such cases, the 'which' clause is called a **defining** or **restrictive** clause. The sentences below illustrate this.

The committee accepted the proposal which the project team had been working on for months.

The committee accepted the proposal, which the project team had been working on for months.

In the first sentence, the word *proposal* is relative. That is, the sentence literally means that the project team submitted several proposals and the committee accepted the one that the team had been working on for months. In this case, the *which* clause is *defining* and does not require a comma preceding it. It defines which of the proposals was accepted. In a defining clause, *which* could be replaced with *that*.

In the second sentence, on the other hand, the word *proposal* is absolute. That is, the sentence literally means that there is just one proposal in question here. In this case, the *which* clause is *non-defining*, meaning that it is not necessary in order to determine the identity of the noun that precedes it. In a non-defining clause, it could not be replaced with *that*, and always requires a comma to set it off from the main clause.

Because of this double use of *which*, it has become common practice in professional contexts to avoid it in defining clauses. Use *that* in defining clauses, and *which* in non-defining clauses.

Brown hens, which lay yellow eggs, have a modified genetic structure
– all brown hens lay yellow eggs

Brown hens that lay yellow eggs have a modified genetic structure
– brown hens may lay eggs of different colours; however, only the ones
   that lay yellow eggs have the modified genetic structure

Global *which*

You can also use a *which* clause to refer to the whole statement that
precedes it. In such cases, do not use *that*. Always put a comma before the
clause that begins with *which*. The sentences below illustrate this function of
which.

The troops surrendered their weapons, which surprised the army
command.

The candidate did not get the position, which was a mistake.

However, because a global *which* is often ambiguous, it is best to avoid it
where possible in formal writing. For example, the above sentences would
be more precise as below.

The army command was surprised that the troops surrendered their
weapons.

Not giving the candidate the position was a mistake.

● Spelling

Unfortunately, English has no specific rules that you can learn to improve
your spelling. The best way to improve your spelling is to read, read, read. A
more systematic method is to focus on words that you repeatedly misspell,
memorise their spelling and practise writing sentences with these words. For
example, set yourself a weekly limit of about 30 words and give yourself 15
minutes a day every day for a specific period (from three to six months, or
even a year depending on how bad your spelling is). Every couple of weeks
or so test your learning to see if your programme is working. There are no
quick-fix schemes for spelling.

As a writer, it is important not to underestimate spelling. Bad spelling is
not a minor problem for writers. It shows that you are, at best, sloppy, at
worst, illiterate. Also, relying on computer spellcheckers is not a good idea,

as they do not identify the context a word is used in. For example, they do not distinguish between **homophones** (words that sound the same but are spelled differently and have a different meaning). *Sun* and *son*, *I* and *eye*, *there* and *their*, *so* and *sew*, *weather* and *whether* are all pairs containing homophones with radically different meanings – indistinguishable by spellcheckers.

The following is a list of commonly confused words to practise.

Commonly confused words

accept	receive (verb)
except	with the exclusion of (preposition)
absent	not present (adjective)
absence	being away (noun)
advice	recommendation (noun)
advise	to recommend (verb)
affect	to produce an influence on (verb)
effect	consequence of an action (noun)
already	by this time
all ready	fully prepared
altogether	thoroughly
all together	everyone or everything in one place
brake	device for stopping
break	destroy, make into pieces
canvas	material (noun)
canvass	solicit, ascertain, survey (verb)
choose	to pick
chose	past tense of choose
complement	round out, add to, complete
compliment	praise, flatter
council	administrative body (noun)
counsel	advise, consult (verb)
device	a plan, an implement
devise	to create
eminent	distinguished, notable
imminent	impending, about to happen

ensure	make certain of
insure	take out an insurance policy
envelop	to surround (verb)
envelope	container for a letter (noun)
formally	conventionally, with ceremony
formerly	previously
lead	heavy metal; to guide
led	past tense of lead
loose	unbound, not tightly fastened (adjective)
lose	to misplace (verb)
passed	past tense of pass
past	at a previous time
personal	intimate
personnel	employees
precede	to come before
proceed	to continue
principal	foremost; chief, leader
principle	moral conviction, basic truth
quiet	silent, calm
quite	very
stationary	standing still
stationery	writing paper
wave	surf
waive	to relinquish, give up
weather	climatic condition
whether	if
which	one of a group
witch	female sorcerer

The following is a list of commonly misspelt words for your reference.

Commonly misspelt words

absence
academic
accidentally
accommodate
achievement
acknowledge
acquaintance
acquire
address
aesthetics
amateur
answer
apparently
appearance
arctic
argument
arithmetic
ascend
athlete
attendance
basically
beautiful
beginning
believe
benefited
bureau
business
cemetery
changeable
column
commitment
committed
committee
competitive
completely
conceivable
conscience
conscientious
conscious

criticism
criticise
decision
definitely
eighth
eligible
embarrass
emphasise
entirely
environment
exaggerated
exercise
exhaust
existence
extraordinary
extremely
fascinate
foreign
forty
fourth
government
grammar
guard
harass
height
humorous
incidentally
incredible
independence
indispensable
inevitable
intelligence
irrelevant
irresistible
knowledge
license (noun) (American);
licence (British)
license (verb) (American
and British)

lightning
loneliness
maintenance
maneuver
(American);
manoeuvre
(British)
marriage
mischievous
necessary
noticeable
occasion
occurrence
pastime
permanent
perseverance
phenomenon
playwright
preference
preferred
pronunciation
publicly
receive
referred
rhythm
schedule
seize
sergeant
strictly
succeed
surgeon
thorough
tomorrow
transferred
unnecessarily
vacuum
vengeance
villain
weird

● **Style guides**

Many corporations, large organisations and government agencies have style guides or manuals that describe the stylistic and formatting conventions followed. This is a very useful item, since it directs writers on how to structure their documents. If your company does not follow the conventions set out in a style manual, consider creating such a manual, proposing that one be created, or suggesting that an available manual be adopted. Existing manuals include the APA (American Psychological Association), MLA (Modern Languages Association), and Chicago Style Manuals.

Even in cases where you only need to produce one document, it is useful to create a style sheet documenting the spelling, formatting and other choices that you made. This not only helps you when revising the document, it also helps others who may take over writing the document, or who may wish to write a parallel document.

Style guides and style sheets help to maintain consistency within a document and in a set of documents produced by the same source. They also answer writers' questions about how they should present their writing. When designing a style guide, include information on the following aspects and make sure that your choices are justified in relation to the communication situation and the mission of the organisation:

Spelling: Do you use American or British spelling? Or are both acceptable as long as consistency is maintained?

Fonts: What regulations will you create about size and type of font?

Formatting: How much space will you allow between lines? How much margin? How will you section and how will you number sections?

Numbers: When do you use figures and when words? The standard convention is to use words up to ten and figures after that, returning to words when you reach thousands, millions and billions. Will you keep this standard or use another?

Abbreviations: What will you abbreviate and how? For example, will you write St or Street? Dr or Doctor?

Punctuation: How will you punctuate? Will you use any punctuation at the end of bullet points? Will you include punctuation marks inside quotation marks or outside?

Visuals: What rules will you have for visuals? Will you have any restrictions on size of visuals in a document? How will you title visuals?

Activities

Active and passive voice

1. Convert these sentences into the passive, if possible, and discuss their effects.

   - He returned from the trip, reassured and in high spirits.
   - The experts that the CEO invited confirmed the gravity of the situation.
   - The terrorist squad disarmed the bomb that threatened to destroy the building.
   - The project team leader could not organise the meeting because he broke his leg.
   - The manager decided to extend the deadline by a week to allow the team to finish the first part of the project.

   Now convert these sentences into the active and discuss their effects.

   - The chemicals are sealed in containers and taken to the laboratory for tests.
   - The city was destroyed by an earthquake ten years ago and has since been rebuilt.
   - The analyst felt sure that the files had been tampered with.
   - The plan was approved and permission has been granted to begin implementing it.
   - Your report should be revised carefully before it is submitted for consideration.

2. This extract is written mostly in the passive. Rewrite it using active structures, and making any other necessary changes. Then observe and discuss the effect of the two versions.

   The Employment Contracts Act 1991 has been controversial since it came into force. Generally, it has been opposed by trade unions and supported by employers' organisations, although different views might have been held by individual unions and employers. In this Act, the machinery of Industrial Conciliation as the primary means of wage fixing was abolished. Also, state sponsorship of the trade union was ended, and protected status taken away from employees. Trade Unionism has been affected substantially by the 1991 Act, and the power in industrial relations was tilted towards employers.

   In contrast, in the Employment Relations Act 2000 unions are given the right to represent their members in bargaining for collective employment agreement with employers. This is particularly significant because only union members can be covered by collective agreement. Collective bargaining may be undertaken by non-union members, but any agreement that is reached will be individual.

3. Write six sophisticated sentences (that could appear in professional documents) in the active voice. Then exchange them with a partner's and rewrite each other's sentences using the passive voice, if possible. Discuss the effects of each sentence.

4. Examine a scholarly journal article (or chapter in a university textbook), and a business magazine article. See how the active and the voice are used in each. How much did the subject of the document influence the writer's choice of voice? Is this effectively done?

Participial phrases

1. Write three sentences using participial phrases and then rewrite them without the participial. Discuss the different effects in your group.

2. Combine the following sentences by turning one of them into a participial.

- The managing director allocated an extra $2 million to our department. He was pleasantly disposed towards our supervisor's project.
- The General Manager was faced with numerous accusations of misconduct. He was forced to resign in June.
- Small business owners can give too little attention to choosing a good location for their business. This results in lower profits or even bankruptcy.
- She attained a good reputation and the admiration of her colleagues in the corporation. Because of this status, she had no problem finding a new job.
- The Employment Relations Act is based largely on the presumption that the employment relationship is a human relationship. With this attitude, it has been possible to solve successfully many disputes.
- The unexpected settlement money that the company won in the court case gave them the opportunity to expand their business internationally. This resulted in a surge in confidence and increased optimism among all company members.

Subject–verb–pronoun agreement

Select the correct verbs in the following sentences:

- The mob (was, were) mindless of the consequences of their actions.

- Neither the general nor his men (was, were) prepared for the sudden attack; not only the men but also their leader (were, was) ready to retreat.
- Assessments of essays and the exam (is, are) expected to be completed tomorrow.
- An estimation of profits and losses (are, is) advisable before deciding.
- The lecturer, together with her tutors, (are, is) going to attend the meeting.
- Confidence and initiative and courage to take risks (lead, leads) to promotion in that field.
- The issue most on his mind (are, is) efforts to negotiate a settlement.
- The audience (were, was) conscious of its power to influence the course of the performance.
- The decision to install the new computers and to update the software programs have been finalized by the executive committee.
- Sharks, because of their secretive nature, and potentially aggressive behaviour, has always been a difficult topic of study.

Punctuation

1. Insert suitable punctuation marks in the following sentences, if necessary:

- Proposals a common business document are a major problem for writers.
- The hotel chain provides its customers with affordable reliable and comfortable service.
- Travel is educational it broadens your horizons.
- The operator ran the program the disk drive was faulty.
- The project is finished.

2. Insert apostrophes where needed in the following phrases:

- six years afterwards
- womens fashion
- the videos box
- the two familys houses
- its hers
- my coats colour
- Mars atmosphere
- a spys story
- hes somebodies friend
- Mikes grade was the best
- This is television at its best
- The cat licked its fur

3. Discuss and correct the punctuation errors in these sentences.
   - In addition to cleaning the assistant janitor must safeguard building keys.
   - At present the campus covers 40 hectares most of it is planted in lawns trees and shrubs.
   - In some cases students have doubled their reading speed; effectively halving their time spent in researching for assignments.
   - Everything seemed so different, so condensed, the buildings were all made of red brick and were all very new.
   - Pigs cannot handle bulky feeds or fibrous foods, this is because they only have a simple stomach.
   - The energy needs of the pigs are met mainly by cereals, however, pigs need 22 per cent protein, and this cannot be met by cereals.
   - The government 'red tape' has hindered business operations therefore it is important to assist these businesses in such issues.
   - The majority of young shareholders voiced opposition to the proposed plan, this shows that what older generations took for granted is unacceptable for the younger generations who are better informed on alternative options.
   - If you are tired of three-dimensional reality of the laws of physics and of cause, and effect; then virtual reality games will be congenial for you. As here you can: continually defy the odds, encounter firsts, and lasts, and perform miracles.
   - Martial arts training brings many benefits to stressed professionals; it is good for self-rehabilitation in the health of body mind and spirit. An excellent method for the ailing to energise themselves in the search for well-being, vitality is enhanced and can lead to the confidence required for professional success; in any field.

Relative clauses: *which* and *that*

1. Write three sentences with defining clauses and three with non-defining clauses, and compare your sentences with a partner's.

2. Rewrite these sentences to avoid ambiguity.

   - The interest rates fell by 5 per cent, that is interesting.
   - The equipment which we ordered arrived on time which was a great relief.
   - There is only one solution to the problem, which is the course of action, which we must take.
   - Here is a program which eliminates many of the problems which the team has had with previous models.
   - Methodologies which are a formalised approach to implementing the system vary in their approach which involves both analy-

sis and design.

- One major problem in science is that no matter how extensively a subject is researched, there will still remain the unknown variable of 'time', which often reveals something which was not considered.

Spelling

1. The following extract contains several spelling errors. See how many you can fix before consulting a dictionary.

> Most of you will create your vizuals on a computer, using softwear that gennerates charts and graphs autommatically. Beware, however: most softwear pakages create vizuals that look good but do not communicate as well as they should. Softwear developpers are more interested in glizzy pictures, the fansier the better, than in vizuals that tell there story effectivly. If you use charting softwear, resist the temtation to use all of its fetures. Expect that you will have to import the visual created by your charting softwear into a grafics pakage in order to adjust it.

General proofreading activity

These sentences contain errors in grammar, style, accuracy, clarity, spelling or punctuation. Test yourself to see how well you learned the guidelines given in the book.

1. Having approved the project, the necessary staff was recruited.

2. The basic principal of good writing is clarity.

3. Today pneumatic tyres are fitted to almost all road vehicles, originally they were developed for use on bicycles.

4. One has to be aware of all the facts before you reach an opinion.

5. The decision to introduce computers have already been made.

6. It is estimated that more than a thousand people were effected by the radiation leak.

7. In advertising the brand information includes not only information about the product but also the image related to the product.

8. Although the situation required expert advice, however they attempted to solve it on their own.

9. The refinement process has already started when the minerals will

be sealed in the special containers.

10. The report was logical, short, and reading it was easy.

11. In the last couple of years, a pattern has emerged on campus that shows an increase in student enrolments.

12. Brief summaries of the recommendations made in the formal report in response to this brief are set out below.

13. Everybody must agree for the recommendations to be implemented. This being the standard course of action for implementing recommendations.

14. Through public education, controlling manipulation techniques by making all testing of Genetically Modified Food (GMF) products compulsory, and increasing government funding, safety and acceptance of GMF can be established.

15. The objectives of this report are to establish and strengthen the relationship between small business and government organisations.

16. Judging from the growth rate in small business at 1.4 per cent, it shows that the country's economy is in good shape.

17. The government 'red tape' has hindered business operations therefore it is important to assist these businesses in such issues.

18 With the change in government policy there represents many potential problems that translate to higher costs for employers and a less flexible work force.

19. Having an information system that is not integrated and cohesive could result in X company's inability to effectively capture business information about its operations and customer base, which will in turn affect its competitiveness in the market and have a negative effect on its reputation as a company that produces cutting edge products valued by international business world-wide.

20. As pollution becomes more and more widespread today, we are more and more concerned about the problems caused by pollution.

21. This article mainly concerns on the effect of antibiotics.

22. The Museum offers people a general range of activities, whether as members of the audience, attending events, being part of a guided tour group, retail therapy, enjoying the restaurants and bars or simply taking a stroll.

23. A detailed analysis of trends and an evaluation of the relations between state and corporation is the purpose of this article.

24. The using of function keys by a user allows the user to carry out some specific functions within the program.

25. Internet companies are installing spyware to watch users every move in the name of better marketing, or to redirect them to websites that pay the spyware companies from those that do not.

Editing activity

The following is an extract from a book on relationship marketing. It has been modified to include stylistic and grammatical errors. Revise and edit the text, checking for errors in these areas:

- verbosity
- inappropriate use of the passive voice
- parallel structures
- spelling
- punctuation
- subject–verb–pronoun agreement
- misrelations
- fragments
- consistency.

Strategy formulation

When the internal analysis steps and strategic review is complete, the next step is strategy formulation. Strategy formulation is concerned with an examination of the alternative strategies availible to an organization, and involves two basic questions that must be addressed. These two basic questions that must be addressed are: in what product-market areas should the company compete, and what strategy should be adapted within these product-market areas? What should have been made is a decision on the firm's key markets in determining the mission statement. To identify the product-market area in which to compete, these options must be considered:

- Market penetration
- How to develop the market
- What products should we develop?
- Diversifying

The company should review its strengths in considering moving beyond their present markets and products. Firms that have extremely close relationships with there existing markets may wish to develop new products for them and adopt a product development strategy. This strategy is also relevent for firms with a single product or service being offered to a particular customer group. We term this product development cell that these firms may wish to adopt the 'relationship building box', where we can meet additional customer needs through the development of new products or services for existing clients.

At the start of the strategy formulation, the firm should develop objectives and the planning assumptions should be identified. Objectives need to be developed in terms of: growth; how profitable they are, and what is the acceptable risk in the chosen product-market areas. The planning assumptions will cover general aspects, such as economic, social and technological issues, as well as more specific ones, deeling specifically with the industry and competition within it.

Generic strategies

There are several basic strategies that can be adopted once a decision has been made regarding which products and which markets to be involved in. Different writers have proposed different alternative natural or generic strategies that a firm can adopt. Porter (1992) suggests that one of three generic strategies is appropriate for a given business, these include: a cost-leadership strategy, a differentiation strategy, or a focus strategy.

Cost-leadership strategy. A cost leadership strategy requires a company to set out with the objective of being the lowest cost producer in the industry. Using this strategy, companies must seek technology not available to other firms, preferential access to raw materials and cost minimization over a wide range of areas.

Differentiation. With a differentiation strategy a firm seeks to be different within the industry it is operating in by being different in some dimension or set of dimensions, and as a result hopes to earn premium price for its products or services.

Focus strategy. A focus strategy involves concentrating on a particular buyer group, geographic area or product/market segment. Thus, it is a strategy of differentiation within a particular segment. By selecting a particular segment or group of segments, a strategy can be developed that serves the needs of this segment better than the competition.

The approach favored for a focus strategy varies considerably and can take many forms. The focus strategy is concerned

> with a specific market segment and is more concentrated
> that the cost-leadership or differentiation approaches, which
> apeall to a wider market. While Japanese motor car manufac-
> turers adopt a cost-leadership approach and manufacturers
> such as Ferrari and Lamborgini focus on a tightly defined
> market segment.   (Adapted from Christopher, Payne and
> Ballantyne, 1991)

● A final note . . .

The book ends with an overview of some major reasons for difficulties or failures in communication in professional contexts. These are taken from specific cases where miscommunication led to disasters or serious damage. Having worked your way through this book, you are now equipped to handle such situations expertly.

Major reasons for faulty communication are:

Ignoring the company or project's role distribution: In many cases, time is wasted, with documents being exchanged between parties that will not be the final decision makers. When dealing with important projects, involve the right people in the chain of communication, and speak (or write) to them in ways they can understand. For example, in engineering projects, administrators, and possibly even marketing managers, are most often involved in the lifecycle of a product. They may not be engineers themselves, so they would require technical concepts to be interpreted.

Not following the rule of 'one document – one message': If you have many pieces of information to communicate, write different documents. Do not attempt to cut corners by cramming as much data as possible in one document. Documents that lack a main message, or 'bottom line', fade in significance, and the important issues they may contain are lost if they are buried in a maze of facts presented indiscriminately. For example, when delivering PowerPoint® presentations, do not clutter slides with all the information that you want the audience to know. Use the slides to complement, not contain, your oral explanations, and supplement the talk with written documents, such as technical and progress reports.

Adopting an unsuitable style: Readers are offended if their 'attitude' (the frame of mind in which they receive the document) is not respected. Do not be overly friendly and casual with readers who may expect more respect and formality, and do not adopt a lighthearted approach with topics that the reader treats with gravity. Remember that your sentence structures emphasise different elements, and construct them deliberately and with a clear intent. Remember that, after having lost a client, or alienated a manager, it will be near impossible to regain their trust.

Not being clear, accurate and concise: If you are vague, confusing and inaccurate you come across as unprofessional and untrustworthy. Plan your writing carefully so that you can collect appropriate and adequate data to make it informative for your readers. Revise well to avoid repetitions and what may come across as self-indulgent verbosity. Remember that professional contexts value bottom-line writing and that time is precious for business readers.

Not having enough signposting, highlighting and closure: Readers are not in your mind, so direct their reading by signalling changes in direction (such as contrast, exemplification, additional points, etc.), distinguishing data according to their order of importance, and indicating where one chunk of information ends and another begins. Business readers do not have the disposition to work laboriously through 'stream of consciousness'-type writing, trying to trace the important points. Preview the structure and purpose of your documents in a clear executive summary and introduction, sum up points in appropriate positions, and make sure you make clear what action you require the reader to take.

Being unconvincing or irrelevant: People respond more positively to those who communicate on their 'wavelength'. Also, they pay more attention to information that is relevant to their needs, desires and expectations. If you want your advice or warning to be heeded, make sure it is pertinent to the values and goals of your audience. To achieve this, do your 'homework' by learning as much as you can about your readers, and relate your descriptions and explanations to situations that are familiar to them.

Not acknowledging the 'big picture': Documents concerning projects with a public relevance may become public at any time. Even if you are an engineer working on technical equipment, your correspondence and notes could come under public scrutiny, if, say, the users of your equipment are harmed because of malfunctions. Therefore, always write documents about professional projects with the idea that more than just your intended readers may end up reading them. Another example is email. If a message you send to a particular person includes information that is pertinent to others, your recipient may distribute the email. Be careful how you phrase email that may be distributed. Have you insulted someone who may receive it? Have you written something that may be misunderstood by some readers? Use foresight when writing.

Not paying enough attention to deadlines: This is a very common problem in all types of writing tasks. The best advice is not to be over-optimistic about how much time you have to complete a task. Plan your time carefully and at different times during the task. Have contingency plans: if you get stuck when doing the task move to something else that you can do more easily. Train yourself to multi-task. And always remember to leave some time for revision.

References

Ball, P. (2006). Walk this way. *New Scientist*, 4 February pp. 40–3.

Barnett, L. (1948). *The Universe and Dr Einstein*. London: Dover.

Barry, P (2006). What's done is done . . . *New Scientist*, 30 September, pp. 36–9.

Bazerman, C. & Paradis, J. (Eds). (1991). *Textual dynamics of the professions*. Madison: University of Wisconsin Press.

Bohm, D. (1998.) *On creativity*, ed. L. Nichol. London: Routledge.

Branscum, D. (1991, March). Ethics, e-mail, and the law: When legal ain't necessarily right. *Macworld*, 63, 66–67, 70, 72, 83.

Christopher, M., Payne, A. & Ballantyne, D. (1991). *Relationship marketing*. Oxford: Butterworth Heinemann.

Csikszentmihalyi, M. (2003). *Good business: Leadership, flow and the making of meaning*. London: Hodder & Stoughton.

Davidson, C. (1998). Agents from Albia. *New Scientist*, 9 May.

Economist, The (2004). Love is all about chemistry, 12 February, pp. 10–11.

Eliashberg, J., Elberse, A. & Leenders, M. A. A. M. (2005). *The motion picture industry: critical issues in practice, current research and new research directions*. Harvard Business School: Working Knowledge.

Fahnestock, J. (1986). Accommodating science: The rhetorical life of scientific facts. *Written Communication*, 3, pp. 275–96.

Fahnestock, J. (2004). Preserving the figure: Consistency in the presentation of scientific arguments. *Written Communication* 21, 1, pp. 6–31.

Fielden, J. S. & Dulek, R. E. (1998). How to use bottom-line writing in corporate communications. In K. J. Harty (Ed.) *Strategies for business and technical writing*. New York: Allyn & Bacon, pp. 179–88.

Fox, B. (2001). Raising the dead – can Russia bring its space shuttle back from the grave? *New Scientist*, 30 June.

Gates, B. (2002). *Think it, build it, bit by bit*. Accessed 2 April 2003 from: www.microsoft/t.com/issues/essays/2002.

Gurak, L. J. & Lannon, J. M. (2007). *A concise guide to technical communication*, 3rd ed. New York: Longman.

Hamer, M. (1998). Roadblocks ahead. *New Scientist*, 24 January.

Hauser, G. (1986). *Introduction to rhetorical theory*. New York: Harper.

Hawkins, D. (1995). The future of fun. In F. Biocca & M. R. Levy (Eds), *Communication in the age of virtual reality*. Hillsdale, NJ: Lawrence Erlbaum Associates.

Herndl, C. G., Fennell, B. A. & Miller, C. R. (1991). Understanding failures in organizational discourse. In C. Bazerman & J. Paradis (Eds), *Textual dynamics of the professions*. Madison: University of Wisconsin Press.

Hill, S. (2001). Get tough! *New Scientist*, 30 June.

Howard, T. (2003). Who 'owns' electronic texts? In T. Peeples (Ed.), *Professional writing and rhetoric*. New York: Longman, pp. 250–63.

Huff, D. (1993). *How to lie with statistics*, 2nd ed. New York: Norton and Company.

Kane, T. (1984). *The new Oxford guide to writing*. Oxford: Oxford University Press.

Katjala, D. (1999). *What are the issues in copyright-term extension – and what happened?* Accessed 20 November 2006 from www.public.asu.edu/~dkarjala/what.html

Kawasaki, G. (2004). *The art of the start: The time-tested, battle-hardened guide for anyone starting anything*. New York: Penguin Portfolio.

King, S. (2000). *On writing*. London: Hodder and Stoughton.

Lewin, R. (1998). Family feuds. *New Scientist*, 24 January.

Lott, J. R. (2005). Hype and reality. *Washington Times*, Friday, 28 October.

Marsen, S. (2006). *Communication studies*. Basingstoke: Palgrave Macmillan.

Matthews, R. (1998). Don't get even, get mad. *New Scientist*, 10 October.

Morgan, G. & Banks, A. (1999). *Getting that job: How to establish and manage your career into the new millennium*. Sydney: HarperCollins.

Newitz, A. (2006). The boss is watching your every click . . . *New Scientist*, 30 September, p. 31.

Nielsen, J. (2000). *Designing web usability: The practice of simplicity*. New York: New Riders Press.

Nielsen, J. & Tahir, M. (2001). *Homepage usability: 50 websites deconstructed*. New York: New Riders Press.

Pagels, H. R. (1983). *The cosmic code: quantum physics as the language of nature*. Harmondswoth: Penguin.

Paulos, J. A. (1996). *A mathematician reads the newspaper*. New York: Anchor.

Peeples, T. (2003). *Professional writing and rhetoric: Readings from the field*. New York: Longman.

Qubein, N. R. (1986). *Get the best from yourself*. New York: Berkley.

Rankin, I. (2001). *The falls*. London: Orion.

Reeves, C. (19990). Establishing a phenomenon: The rhetoric of early medical reports on AIDS. *Written Communication*, 7, 3, pp. 393–416.

Rosenblatt, R. (1999). The whole world is jumpable. *Time*, 19 July.

Sagan, C. (1995*). The demon-haunted world*. Chicago: Chicago University Press.

Samuel, E. (2001). Paint the town red. *New Scientist*, 30 June.

Schaub, B. (2006). My android twin. *New Scientist*, 14 October, pp. 42–6.

Sheldon, R. (1994). *First course in probability*. New York: Macmillan.

Shilts, R. (1987). *And the band played on: Politics, people and the AIDS epidemic*. New York: St Martin's.

Sokal, A. D. (1996). Transgressing the boundaries: Toward a transformative hermeneutics of quantum gravity. *Social Text*, 46–47, 217–28.

Srinivasan, M. & Ruina, A. (2006). Computer optimisation of a minimal biped model discovers walking and running. *Nature* 439, 5, pp. 72–75.

Steuer, J. (1995). Defining virtual reality: Dimensions determining telepresence. In F. Biocca & M. R. Levy (Eds). *Communication in the age of virtual reality*. Hillsdale, NJ: Lawrence Erlbaum.

Stewart, I. (1998). Rules of engagement. *New Scientist,* 29 August.

Thwaites,T. (2006). Hello solar. *New Scientist*, 14 October, pp. 52–5.

Toulmin. S. (2003). *The uses of argument*, 2nd ed. Cambridge: Cambridge University Press.

Ward, M. (1998). There's an ant in my phone. *New Scientist*, 24 January.

Bibliography

Aitchison, J. (1999). *Cutting edge advertising.* Sydney: Prentice-Hall.

Alexander, J. E. & Tate, M. A. (1999). *Web wisdom: How to evaluate and create information quality on the web.* New Jersey: Lawrence Erlbaum.

Alred, G. J., Brusaw, C. T. & Oliu, W. E. (2000). *The business writer's handbook,* 6th ed. New York: St Martin's Press.

Ballenger, B. (2007). *The curious researcher: A guide to writing research papers,* 5th ed. New York: Longman.

Bargiela-Chiappini, F. and Nickerson, C. (eds). (1999). *Writing business: Genres, media and discourses.* London: Longman.

Barker, T. T. (2003). *Writing software documentation: A task-oriented approach,* 2nd ed. New York: Allyn & Bacon.

Bivins, T. H. (1999). *Public relations writing,* 4th ed. Lincolnwood, Ill.: NTC/Contemporary Publishing Group.

Booth, W., Colomb, G. & Williams, J. (1995). *The craft of research.* Chicago: The University of Chicago Press.

Bunnin, B. (1990, April). Copyrights and wrongs: How to keep your work on the right side of copyright law. *Publish,* 76–82.

Candlin, C. N. & Hyland, K. (1999). *Writing: Texts, processes and practices.* London: Longman.

Cottrell, S. (2003). *Skills for success: The personal development planning handbook.* Basingstoke: Palgrave Macmillan.

Cottrell, S. (2005). *Critical thinking skills.* Basingstoke: Palgrave Macmillan.

Davis, A. (2004). *Mastering public relations.* Basingstoke: Palgrave Macmillan.

DeWitt, S. L. (2001). *Writing inventions: Identities, technologies, pedagogies.* Albany, NY: State University of New York.

Dias, P. et al. (1999). *Worlds apart: Acting and writing in academic and workplace contexts.* Mahwah, NJ: Lawrence Erlbaum.

Dwyer, J. (1997). *The business communication handbook,* 4th ed. Sydney: Prentice- Hall.

Finkelstein, L. Jr. (2000). *Pocket book of technical writing for engineers and scientists.* New York: McGraw-Hill.

Fiske, J. (1990). *Introduction to communication studies,* 2nd ed. London: Routledge.

Flower, L. & Ackerman, J. (1994). *Writers at work: Strategies for communicating in business and professional settings.* Fort Worth, TX: Harcourt Brace.

Freund, J. E., & Simon, G. A. (1992). *Modern elementary statistics,* 8th ed. Englewood Cliffs, N.J: Prentice-Hall.

Gardner, H. (2004). *Changing minds.* Boston: Harvard Business School.

Garrison, B. (2004). *Professional feature writing,* 4th ed. Mahwah: Lawrence Erlbaum.

Greenbaum, S. & Quirk, R. (1990). *A student's grammar of the English language.* Harlow: Longman.

Hacker, D. (2007). *The Bedford handbook,* 7th ed. New York: Bedford St. Martin's.

Harty, K. J. (ed.) (1999). *Strategies for business and technical writing,* 4th ed. New York: Allyn & Bacon.

Hay, V. (1990). *The essential feature: Writing for magazines and newspapers.* New York: Columbia University Press.

Heskett, J. (2005). *A very short introduction to design.* Oxford: Oxford University Press.

Hirschberg, S. (1996). *Essential strategies of argument.* New York, NY: Allyn & Bacon.

Horton, W. (ed.) (1995). *The web page design cookbook: All the ingredients you need to create 5-star web pages.* New York: John Wiley and Sons.

Hyland, K. (2002). *Teaching and researching writing.* London: Longman.

Johnson-Sheenan, R. (2002). *Writing proposals: Rhetoric for managing change.* New York: Longman.

Jones, D. (1999). *The technical communicator's handbook.* New York: Allyn & Bacon.

Kirkman, J. (1992). *Good style: writing for science and technology.* London: Spon.

Kolin, P. C. (1998). *Successful writing at work,* 5th ed. Boston, MA: Houghton Mifflin.

Kostelnick, C. & Roberts, D. D. (1998). *Designing visual language: Strategies for professional communicators.* New York: Allyn and Bacon.

Lannon, J. (2006). *Technical Communication.* 10th ed. Boston, MA: Addison-Wesley.

Leval, P. (1990, March). Toward a fair use standard. *Harvard Law Review,* 1105–36.

Littleford, D., Halstead, J. & Mulraine, C. (2004). *Career skills: Opening doors into the job market.* Basingstoke: Palgrave Macmillan.

Long, K. (2003). *Writing in bullets: The new rules for maximum business communication.* Philadelphia: The Running Press.

Nesheim, J. L. (2000). *High tech start-up.* New York: The Free Press.

Niederst, J. (2001). *Web design in a nutshell*. Cambridge, MA: O'Reilly and Associates.

Peck, J. & Coyle, M. (2005). *The student's guide to writing*, 2nd ed. Basingstoke: Palgrave Macmillan.

Petelin, R. & Durham, M. (1992). *The professional writing guide: Writing well and knowing why*. London: Longman.

Rodman, L. (1996). *Technical communication*, 2nd ed. Toronto: Harcourt Brace.

Rosenfield, L. & Morville, P. (1998). *Information architecture for the World Wide Web: Designing large scale web sites*. Cambridge, MA: O'Reilly and Associates.

Roush, C. (2004). *Show me the money: Writing business and economics stories for mass communication*. Hillsdale, NJ: Lawrence Erlbaum.

Rude, C. (1998). *Technical editing*, 2nd ed. New York: Allyn and Bacon.

Shimp, T. (1997). *Advertising, promotion and supplemental aspects of integrated marketing communications*. Chicago: Dryden Press.

Sides, C. H. (1999). *How to write and present technical information*, 3rd ed. Phoenix: Oryx Press.

Siegel, D. (1997). *Secrets of successful web sites: Project management on the World Wide Web*. Indianapolis: Hayden.

Stott, R. & Avery, S. (2001). *Writing with style*. London: Longman.

Stott, R. & Chapman P. (2001). *Grammar and writing*. London: Longman.

Strunk, W. Jr. et al. (2000). *The elements of style*, 4th ed. New York: Allyn and Bacon.

Surma, A. (2005). *Public and professional writing: Ethics, imagination, rhetoric*. Basingstoke: Palgrave Macmillan.

Tway, L. (1995). *Multimedia in action*. Burlington, MA: Academic Press.

Van Alstyne, J. S. & Tritt, M. D. (2001). *Professional and technical writing strategies: Communicating in technology and science*, 5th ed. New York: Prentice-Hall.

Windschuttle, K., & Elliott, E. (1999). *Writing, researching, communicating: Communication skills for the information age,* 3rd ed. Sydney: McGraw Hill.

Woolever, K., Trzyna, T. N. & Batschiet, M. (1999). *Writing for the technical professions*. Boston, MA: Addison-Wesley.

Index